Gertrude Postl & Brigitte Buchhammer (Eds.)

Feminist Philosophy

Women* Philosophers at Work

A Series of SWIP Austria

edited by

Brigitte Buchhammer

Sonderband
Special volume

LIT

Feminist Philosophy

A Close Encounter with the Work of Herta Nagl-Docekal

edited by

Gertrude Postl & Brigitte Buchhammer

LIT

Proofreading:
Stephen O'Connor, Ph.D., B.A. (Hons)
stephen.oconnor@englischschmiede.at
www.englischschmiede.at

Formatting and copy editing:
Michael Stork, micstork@yahoo.gr
http://independent.academia.edu/MichaelStork

Bibliographic information published by the Deutsche Nationalbibliothek
The Deutsche Nationalbibliothek lists this publication in the Deutsche Nationalbibliografie; detailed bibliographic data are available on the Internet at http://dnb.dnb.de.

ISBN 978-3-643-91224-4 (pb)
ISBN 978-3-643-96224-9 (PDF)

A catalogue record for this book is available from the British Library.

Flössergasse 10
CH-8001 Zürich
Tel. +41 (0) 76-632 84 35
E-Mail: zuerich@lit-verlag.ch https://www.lit-verlag.ch
Distribution:
In the UK: Global Book Marketing, e-mail: mo@centralbooks.com
In North America: Independent Publishers Group, e-mail: orders@ipgbook.com
In Germany: LIT Verlag Fresnostr. 2, D-48159 Münster
Tel. +49 (0) 2 51-620 32 22, Fax +49 (0) 2 51-922 60 99, e-mail: vertrieb@lit-verlag.de

CONTENTS

ACKNOWLEDGEMENTS

It was a great delight when Gertrude Postl invited Waltraud Ernst, Cornelia Eşianu, Bettina Zehetner and me to participate in a Close Encounter Panel in cooperation with Herta Nagl-Docekal, on the subject of Herta Nagl-Docekal's extensive philosophical works. The panel was organized as part of the biannual conference of the *Association for Philosophy and Literature* (APL), held at the Alpen-Adria University of Klagenfurt in 2019.

I would like to take this opportunity to warmly thank Gertrude Postl for her kind invitation and her willingness to co-edit this volume on the subject of our discussions together; special thanks to the contributors for making their essays available; heartfelt thanks to Herta Nagl-Docekal for her collegial collaboration and her considered response. For the English proofreading, I would like to cordially thank Stephen O'Connor, who from the very beginning has generously supervised and supported the English proofreading of the SWIP Austria volumes in an immensely committed manner. For the copy editing and layout of the volume we owe a great debt of gratitude to Michael Stork, without his careful, patient, and dedicated work a volume like this could not be produced in the professional form it deserves. I would also like to thank the LIT Publishing House for their wonderful cooperation in producing this volume.

Now I wish our dear readers inspiration and delight in their reading of our book.

Brigitte Buchhammer

GERTRUDE POSTL

FEMINIST PHILOSOPHY AS A CALL FOR GENDER JUSTICE: THE WORK OF HERTA NAGL-DOCEKAL

When the decision was made back in 2018 to revive the International Association for Philosophy and Literature (IAPL) as the Association for Philosophy and Literature (APL) with a conference in Klagenfurt, Austria, the APL Executive Committee members agreed that the conference should – among other goals – also serve as a platform to offer some insights into the philosophical scene in Austria. In response to this decision, the first thought that came to my mind was to organize a "Close Encounter Panel" on the work of Herta Nagl-Docekal. The format of a Close Encounter has had a long and successful tradition during previous IAPL conferences, a tradition we wanted to continue; it basically means that panelists are invited to discuss the entire corpus of work by a given scholar with this scholar being present in order to respond. There was no doubt in my mind that Professor Nagl-Docekal would be the perfect candidate for this kind of endeavor. She is one of just a few contemporary Austrian philosophers with an international reputation and stature and it was thus decided that a panel on her work might be of interest for the international spectrum of APL attendees. The sheer volume of her publications, many of them translated into a variety of other languages, in particular her book *Feministische Philosophie* (2000),[1] her decades of involvement with the Fédération Internationale des Sociétés de Philosophie (FISP) and

[1] Translated into American English as *Feminist Philosophy* (NAGL-DOCEKAL 2004), and reissued in German (NAGL-DOCEKAL 2016).

the organization of the World Congress of Philosophy, her founding role and ongoing commitment to the International Association of Women Philosophers (IAPh), her status as *membre titulaire* of the Institut International de Philosophie (IIP), Paris, all these activities render her known far beyond the philosophical scene of the German language context. She is also a full member of the Austrian Academy of Sciences (ÖAW) and is involved in the Austrian branch of the Society for Women in Philosophy (SWIP Austria). Throughout her career – as author, editor, and organizer – she has worked tirelessly in fostering the international exchange of ideas and on personal encounters between philosophers across schools, disciplines, and countries. In her capacity as organizer of the annual ÖAW Leibnitz Lectures, through her involvement in the commission "The North Atlantic Triangle" at the Austrian Academy of Sciences, and her many functions during her long tenure at the University of Vienna she not only managed to bring some of the most influential contemporary thinkers to Vienna (e.g. Seyla Benhabib, Martha Nussbaum, Anthony Appiah, or Nancy Fraser), but also provided international exposure to many Austrian scholars and students.

On a personal note, organizing a panel at an APL conference on the work of Herta Nagl-Docekal ties together two separate trajectories of my own life. My intense involvement with IAPL since the late 1980s, on one hand, and my background of graduating in philosophy from the University of Vienna, which included having studied with Herta Nagl-Docekal, on the other. Providing a forum for her work within the context of an academic society so close to my heart in an Austria town so famously reminiscent of Ingeborg Bachmann (also very close to my heart) seemed like a challenge I did not want to pass up.

Facing the difficulty of how to narrow down Nagl-Docekal's breadth of philosophical research for the proposed panel, we decided to focus on Feminist Philosophy, given that gender issues run like a connecting thread throughout all of her texts. In pursuing this project, I was very fortunate to find panelists who were not only familiar with Nagl-Docekal's work but also willing to engage in a "division of labor," so as to cover the various philosophical areas she addresses from a feminist perspective. The panel included papers on the practical application of Nagl-Docekal's work for feminist counseling services (Bettina Zehetner), on the interconnection of moral philosophy and epistemology

(Waltraud Ernst), on feminist aesthetics (Cornelia Eşianu), and on Nagl-Docekal's contributions to a feminist philosophy of religion (Brigitte Buchhammer). Needless to say, many crucial aspects and insights of Nagl-Docekal's work had to be left out due to the time constraints of a standard academic conference panel.

It is close to impossible to offer an overview or summary of Nagl-Docekal's research that would do justice to the thematic range of her work which involves nearly all the major areas of philosophy: philosophy of history, ethics, and social philosophy, philosophy of religion, philosophical anthropology, and – time and again – feminist theory.[2] A connecting and recurring reference point for this range of philosophical interests is the philosophy of Immanuel Kant, in particular his insistence on the intrinsic worth of every individual human being. The second formulation of the categorical imperative, not to treat others merely as means but always as ends in themselves, could serve as a guiding principle that describes not only the main concern of Nagl-Docekal's philosophy, but her very personal actions and pursuits. However, while Kant serves as the main reference point of her thought, Nagl-Docekal worked on many other important figures in the history of philosophy, including Leibniz, Rousseau, Hegel, and others. But what really connects her broad scope of interests is not so much a specific theory or philosopher, historical or contemporary, but, rather, a view of philosophy as having practical implications. For Nagl-Docekal, philosophy should provide rational arguments against any forms of injustice, discrimination, or lack of freedom. Philosophy, for her, is not an ivory tower indulgence but a means to interfere in a very concrete sense in matters of life so as to change and improve them. The celebratory volume for her 75th birthday, edited by Brigitte Buchhammer and published in 2019, is not coincidentally entitled *Freedom – Justice – Love*.[3] This is to say, Nagl-Docekal's main philosophical concerns are not particular figures or the promotion of one school of thought over the other but, rather, the genuine belief that philosophy has something to contribute to limiting the injustices of the world and that it is the personal

---

[2] For a concise and insightful overview of Herta Nagl-Docekal's work, see BUCHHAMMER 2019a.

[3] See BUCHHAMMER 2019b.

responsibility of every philosopher to engage in this kind of activity. In short, her view of philosophy is actually inherently political. And her interest in questions of gender discrimination – socially, institutionally, and philosophically – has to be placed within this broader context of justice and freedom. It is her fundamental concern for the inherent value of human life and subsequently for issues of justice that made her turn to issues of gender. To quote from Brigitte Buchhammer's introduction to the Celebratory Volume already mentioned:

> *With untiring commitment and effort she reiterates that one of the primary, key tasks of philosophy is – in the Kantian sense – to develop an adequate notion of a human being, i.e. to consider with the best philosophical arguments and at the highest level of reflection what it means to live as a human being in our world.*[4]

There are many ways to pursue this goal and to philosophically address "what it means to live as a human being in our world," which includes issues of injustice, discrimination, and exclusion. After the publication of her landmark text *Feministische Philosophie* in 2000, Nagl-Docekal turned to the themes of morality, justice, and freedom, and, discussing the debates on post-metaphysical conceptions of morality with reference to Habermas and Honneth, to issues of religion as a foundational ground for morality.[5] Most recently, she moved more explicitly towards embedding moral issues within sociopolitical questions by discussing the meaning of community.[6] However, throughout these more recent projects, she never left the gender question behind; even those texts not explicitly labeled as "feminist" refer to issues of gender justice and discuss examples of hierarchically structured gender relations.

Given that the panel under consideration focused on Nagl-Docekal's contributions to feminist philosophy, here follows a brief attempt to locate her within this – by now – diverse and still expanding field. The most influential lines of separation within feminist philosophy are

---

[4] BUCHHAMMER 2019a, 10.
[5] See NAGL-DOCEKAL 2014.
[6] See NAGL-DOCEKAL 2018a; 2018b; 2020.

commonly characterized by using the labels of "equality feminism" versus "difference feminism." In light of Nagl-Docekal's Kantian background and her anchor in the philosophical tradition, her response to the discrimination of women (within philosophy and otherwise) is marked by an undeterred demand for equality for all human beings, regardless of their sex – what is commonly called gender justice. Whereby the task of philosophy as feminist philosophy, "focuses on what means philosophy can offer to make discrimination against women visible in its full extent, and how it can help develop alternative conceptions that provide the theoretical underpinning for the elimination of existing asymmetries."[7] This is to say, feminist philosophy's role or purpose is to provide arguments towards realizing gender justice on all levels and within all the relevant philosophical disciplines, it is a "philosophizing guided by an interest in the liberation of women."[8] And it is this broad spectrum of her outlook on philosophy that renders Nagl-Docekal's work particularly relevant. She did not limit herself to for example exploring issues of ethics or epistemology from a feminist point of view. Rather, as stated already, it is the entire field of philosophy that has to be scrutinized and rethought.

> *The central claim of feminist philosophy is aimed at confronting the entire field with the problem of the hierarchical relations of the sexes. This claim covers not only the full range of systematic subfields (e.g. epistemology, ethics, aesthetics, etc.) but also the different schools of thought by which the canon of the history of philosophy as well as the contemporary debate are determined.*[9]

Responding to the diversification of the field of feminist philosophy during the course of the 1990s and ever since, Nagl-Docekal takes an explicit stand against any form of dogmatism in favor of "argumentative reasoning"[10] as the only proper foundation for feminist philosophy. This leads her to a nuanced critique of the various manifestations of

---

[7] NAGL-DOCEKAL 2004, xix.
[8] NAGL-DOCEKAL 2004, xix.
[9] NAGL-DOCEKAL 2004, xviii.
[10] See NAGL-DOCEKAL 2004, xx–xxi.

difference feminism, such as French Feminism, post-structuralist feminism, and constructivism.[11] The relevant authors Nagl-Docekal explicitly engages with are Hélène Cixous, Luce Irigaray, Julia Kristeva, Carol Gilligan, and Judith Butler.[12] In doing so, she disagrees with key points of their version of feminist criticism, such as the alleged masculine connotation of the philosophical subject in terms of identity formation, the claim that language (including grammar) and symbolic representation are male-created systems of signification that deny women a voice of their own (which they can [re]gain via an *écriture féminine*), the attack on Western reason as "phallogocentric" and grounded in binary thinking, the assumption of a distinct feminine morality, or the blurring of the sex/gender distinction which treats the body as part of gender and thus as a signifying entity.

Contrary to these positions, which shall be discussed here in summary, Nagl-Docekal holds that the logical disjunctions that mark a binary thinking – although sometimes problematic – are indispensable for criticizing the status quo of women's ongoing discrimination. If "any distinction that uses a dichotomy, such as good/bad or responsible/ irresponsible must be discarded ... how is it then possible to denounce the abjection of the other?"[13] The danger of a feminist critique of reason, to be found, for instance, in the texts of Luce Irigaray or Hélène Cixous, is but a disguised revival of the traditional association of women with irrationality – something, that feminists should aim to overcome, rather than offering it as a path towards liberation. Not reason itself is the problem, Nagl-Docekal asserts, but an "often tacit transition from an elaboration of the general concept of reason to a theory of masculine character traits." Thus, what needs to be overcome is "the traditional masculinization of reason"[14] and not reason itself. A comparable argument is developed with respect to feminist critique of traditional theories of ethics and the claim of a distinct

---

[11] These labels partly overlap and their usefulness has been debated and challenged even by feminist theorists. They shall serve here only as crude structuring devices.

[12] See CIXOUS 1981; GILLIGAN 1982; KRISTEVA 1984; IRIGARAY 1985a; 1985b; BUTLER 1990; 1993.

[13] NAGL-DOCEKAL 2004, 18.

[14] NAGL-DOCEKAL 2004, 132.

feminine morality or "ethics of care" as formulated by Carol Gilligan.[15] While admitting a "masculine bias in the history of moral philosophy" and the legitimacy of "studying the moral experiences of women,"[16] Nagl-Docekal views the claim of an "ethics of difference" as undermining the very concept of morality. "The point is that every person – regardless of sex – has the same right to be respected independently of whether or not the individuals share certain virtues or interests."[17] Regarding the so-called constructivism debate, associated with the work of Judith Butler, Nagl-Docekal takes a clear stand in favor of a distinction between sex and gender and thus a separation between the biological sex and the cultural aspect of gender roles. Arguing against constructivism and holding on to the existence of two sexually distinct bodies, she aims to address the social-cultural side of gender. Not the body as such is at issue but the behavioral norms and expectations that have been derived from two distinct body types, leading to historically established gender asymmetries. To overcome the numerous instances of gender injustice resulting from these asymmetries, the cultural-social level has to be addressed through rational arguments and not the body as an allegedly signifying entity. In summary, according to Nagl-Docekal, it is not the concept of the subject, reason, language, or morality as such that is the problem. Rather, the inherent incoherence of these positions as well as their allegedly tacit reaffirmation of objectionable gender stereotypes makes them an easy target for attack and thus endangers the entire project of feminist criticism: "Rhetorically excessive theses have frequently been used as easy targets by those who wish to fight off the entire project of feminist philosophy." To avoid these dangers "with argumentative means," her strategy is "to carve out those elements of feminist philosophy that are so well founded that they can no longer be disregarded by philosophers who claim to reflect in their work the current state of their discipline."[18]

In spite of Nagl-Docekal's critique of some of the most influential positions of difference feminism, some of her ongoing concerns have

---

[15] See GILLIGAN 1982.
[16] NAGL-DOCEKAL 2004, 147.
[17] NAGL-DOCEKAL 2004, 147.
[18] NAGL-DOCEKAL 2004, xxi.

– in my view – a certain affinity with aspects of those positions. Her plea for a culture of listening, developed within the context of a broader critique of a morality of reciprocity presupposed in contemporary popular debates of contractualist social philosophy,[19] resonates with Cixous' and Irigaray's arguments in favor of – what they call – a feminine economy, an economy that does not count, that refuses to conceive of relations with others in terms of mutual payback or strictly reciprocal measurements but, rather, an economy of the excess and of the gift. Her extensive work on love[20] and the claim that love is not sufficiently addressed in contemporary moral or social philosophy demonstrates a concern and interest that, again, is shared by some of the so-called post-structuralist authors – Irigaray as well as Kristeva wrote extensively on love, be it the love between individuals on grounds of difference, as is the case for Irigaray, or religiously mediated forms of love, such as Kristeva's study on Teresa of Avila.[21] Furthermore, Nagl-Docekal's more recent work on questions of the community[22] could be related to a (post-structuralist) feminist critique of competition, hierarchy, and individualization typical of life in late capitalism and frequently equated with masculine gender norms.

In other words, Nagl-Docekal's work on issues of freedom, justice, religion, and love is at the forefront of contemporary philosophical debates in that it responds to urgent political and social questions of our time. Whereby she often highlights aspects of a given theme that are only insufficiently addressed by the mainstream philosophical discourse, such as the moral and social implications of love, a culture of listening, or a concept of community not based on reciprocity and individual atomization. What makes Nagl-Docekal's work unique – in my view – is that its contemporary relevance is achieved through a sophisticated reading of the philosophical tradition, in particular Kant and Hegel – often against the grain of the dominant Kant or Hegel scholarship. As previously stated, her main concern is a moral one: to ensure the fundamental value of every person by contributing, through

[19] See NAGL-DOCEKAL 2014, 92–102.
[20] See among other texts NAGL-DOCEKAL 2014, 129–147.
[21] See IRIGARAY 1985a; 1985b; 1996; KRISTEVA 2014; see also KRISTEVA 1987.
[22] NAGL-DOCEKAL 2018a; 2018b; 2020.

philosophical argumentation, to the elimination of injustice and discrimination, including any form of gender hierarchy and unjust gender relations. Thus, her extensive work on gender issues can be viewed as an ongoing undercurrent that seeps into her studies on morality, religion, and freedom, and guides her overall belief in the power of philosophy to contribute to a better world. As she states – with reference to Kant – in her critique of contemporary conceptions of morality that are too narrowly focused on reciprocity and individuation: "Ultimately, the task of humanity consists in bringing about, to the greatest extent possible, a harmony of morality and happiness."[23] Listening to others, viewing love as foundational for human communities, or reviving a possible religious source of practical reason, all this within the context of her brand of feminist criticism renders Nagl-Docekal's work as a prime example for how philosophy can contribute to more just relations between individual human beings – of either gender.

To return to our panel: Given my own research interest in French Feminism and in issues of discourse, representation, and the signifying potential of the body,[24] led at points to a philosophical parting of ways with Prof. Nagl-Docekal. However, these differences in approach to feminist philosophy never got in the way of a mutual interest in and respect for each other's work and a shared commitment to the necessity of institutional and political change, so as to improve the situation of women (including women philosophers). On these grounds of a common goal and a mutual understanding, organizing the panel on Herta Nagl-Docekal's work is also to be taken as a sign of appreciation for her contributions to the field of feminist philosophy and her ongoing support for women philosophers, on the philosophical as well as the institutional level. Nagl-Docekal's tireless work in various academic capacities on the national and international level helped to make women visible – from her discussion of women philosophers in history, her practical and theoretical support for generations of women philosophers at the institutional level (be it at the University of Vienna or through her work within the IAPh and FISP), all the way to conveying the urgency of addressing gender discrepancies within philosophy at large.

---

[23] NAGL-DOCEKAL 2014, 13 (English translation G. P.).

[24] See POSTL 2009; 2015; 2017.

REFERENCES

BUCHHAMMER Brigitte, 2019a, Introduction: The Philosophical Works of Herta Nagl-Docekal, in: Brigitte BUCHHAMMER (ed.), *Freiheit – Gerechtigkeit – Liebe, Freedom – Justice – Love. Festschrift zum 75. Geburtstag von Herta Nagl-Docekal. Celebratory Volume for Herta Nagl-Docekal's 75th Birthday*, Vienna: LIT, 9–40

BUCHHAMMER Brigitte (ed.), 2019b, *Freiheit – Gerechtigkeit – Liebe, Freedom – Justice – Love. Festschrift zum 75. Geburtstag von Herta Nagl-Docekal. Celebratory Volume for Herta Nagl-Docekal's 75th Birthday*, Vienna: LIT

BUTLER Judith, 1990, *Gender Trouble: Feminism and the Subversion of Identity*, New York, NY – London, UK: Routledge

BUTLER Judith, 1993, *Bodies That Matter: On the Discursive Limits of "Sex,"* New York, NY – London, UK: Routledge

CIXOUS Hélène, 1981, The Laugh of the Medusa, in: Elaine MARKS & Isabelle DE COURTIVRON (eds.), *New French Feminism: An Anthology*, New York, NY: Schocken Books, 245–264

GILLIGAN Carol, 1982, *In a Different Voice: Psychological Theory and Women's Development*, Cambridge, MA: Harvard University Press

IRIGARAY Luce, 1985a, *Speculum of the Other Woman*, trans. Gillian C. Gill, Ithaca, NY: Cornell University Press

IRIGARAY Luce, 1985b, *This Sex Which Is Not One*, trans. Catherine Porter, Ithaca, NY: Cornell University Press

IRIGARAY Luce, 1996, *I love to you. Sketch of a Possible Felicity in History*, trans. Alison Martin, New York, NY – London, UK: Routledge

KRISTEVA Julia, 1984, *Revolution in Poetic Language*, trans. Margaret Waller, New York, NY: Columbia University Press

KRISTEVA Julia, 1987, *Tales of Love*, trans. Leon S. Roudiez, New York, NY: Columbia University Press

KRISTEVA Julia, 2014, *Teresa, My Love: An Imagined Life of the Saint of Avila*, trans. Lorna Scott Fox, New York, NY: Columbia University Press

NAGL-DOCEKAL Herta, 2004, *Feminist Philosophy*, trans. Katharina

Vester, Boulder, CO – Oxford, UK: Westview Press

NAGL-DOCEKAL Herta, 2014, *Innere Freiheit. Grenzen der nachmetaphysischen Moralkonzeptionen*, Berlin – Boston, MA: De Gruyter (Deutsche Zeitschrift für Philosophie, Sonderband 36)

NAGL-DOCEKAL Herta, 2016, *Feministische Philosophie. Ergebnisse, Probleme, Perspektiven*, Frankfurt/M.: Fischer ([1]2000; [2]2001)

NAGL-DOCEKAL Herta, 2018a, Towards a Global Non-Exclusive Community, in: *Learning to be Human. Congress Volume of The XXIV World Congress of Philosophy*, August 12–20, 2018, Beijing, 73–83

NAGL-DOCEKAL Herta, 2018b, Why Ethics Needs Politics: A Cosmopolitan Perspective (With a Little Help from Kant), in: Kuisma KORHONEN, Arto HAAPALA, Sara HEINÄMAA, Kristian KLOCKARS & Pajari RÄSÄNEN (eds.), *Chiasmatic Encounters. Art, Ethics, Politics*, Lanham, MD: Lexington Books, 149–166

NAGL-DOCEKAL Herta, 2020, Between Berlin and Königsberg: Toward a Global Community of Well-Disposed Human Beings, in: Ruth ABBEY (ed.), *Cosmopolitan Civility. Global-Local Reflections with Fred Dallmayer*, New York, NY: SUNY Press, 83–96

POSTL Gertrude, 2009, Liebe im Kontext einer Politik der sexuellen Differenz: Zum Wandel von Irigarays Liebesbegriff, *Mitteilungen des Instituts für Wissenschaft und Kunst* 3–4 (= *Liebeskonzepte und Geschlechterdiskurs*, ed. by Susanne Hochreiter & Silvia Stoller), 9–15

POSTL Gertrude, 2015, Feminist Philosophy – A Question of Style?, in: Brigitte BUCHHAMMER (ed.), *Neuere Aspekte der Philosophie: aktuelle Projekte von Philosophinnen am Forschungsstandort Österreich*, Vienna: Axia Academic Publishers, 19–31

POSTL Gertrude, 2017, Language, Writing, and Gender Differences, in: Ann GARY, Serene J. KHADER & Alison STONE (eds.), *The Routledge Companion to Feminist Philosophy*, London, UK – New York, NY: Routledge, 292–302

BRIGITTE BUCHHAMMER

"PHILOSOPHIZING ON THE GUIDE OF FEMINIST INTEREST"[1]

CENTRAL ASPECTS OF HERTA NAGL-DOCEKAL'S FEMINIST-PHILOSOPHICAL WORK. AN INTRODUCTION

As an introduction to this encounter with Herta Nagl-Docekal's feminist philosophy it would be fruitful to first sketch the main features in a concise, but slightly more detailed overview.

In giving feminist philosophy new impetus, Herta Nagl-Docekal underscores its core features. None of her developed concepts have become obsolete. In the introduction to *Feminist Philosophy* (1990), she mentions seven elements that are crucial for the conception of feminist philosophy. Feminist philosophy is still deeply connected to the political movement for more gender justice, although a distinction must be made between the political context on the one hand and the methodological scientific work on the other. Feminist philosophy can be critical of ideology without being an ideology itself – pointedly stated: "Feminist philosophy philosophises in the interests of the liberation of women."[2] It is not a philosophical endeavor of women, for women, about women, but discusses the theoretical foundations of the practical commitment to more justice in terms of gender relations; it is not a unified movement – the demand for a unified theory strays dangerously close to dogma. The claim is rather to develop an open and carefully discursive culture of argument.

[1] NAGL-DOCEKAL 1990, 11.

[2] See NAGL-DOCEKAL 1990, 11: "Feministische Philosophie ist Philosophieren am Leitfaden des Interesses an der Befreiung der Frau." – All German citations from Herta Nagl-Docekal's and others' works in this text are translated into English by the author.

First of all, philosophizing on the guide of feminist interest requires a reconstruction and critical analysis of the view of gender relations in the history of philosophy. Secondly, it calls for a hermeneutic of suspicion to examine those statements that claim gender neutrality for misogynist and discriminatory content or to exclude gender stereotypes. Thirdly, making women's achievements in the history of philosophy visible is a major concern.

All sub-disciplines of philosophy should be subjected to a transformation on the guideline of feminist interest.[3] The perspective of gender justice should become a self-evident aspect of today's philosophical discourse, otherwise the necessary prerequisites for an adequate philosophical examination of the recent global problems are not given.[4] Nagl-Docekal underlines the critical potential of feminist-philosophical research in the following terms: "To what extent can philosophy contribute to the elimination of structures of discrimination and oppression? This question was and is decisive for my research in the field of feminist theory. Especially in my book *Feministische Philosophie: Ergebnisse, Probleme, Perspektiven* [*Feminist Philosophy*], I sought to work out the critical potential that central philosophical sub-disciplines – from philosophical anthropology through aesthetics, from the theory of reason and science to the philosophy of law – possess. Using methods of philosophical analysis, the widespread, deep-seated gender-hierarchical concepts can be precisely pinpointed and argumentatively rejected, e.g. in the form of proof that they are based on a naturalistic fallacy. Of course, this critical potential can only come fully to fruition when it is addressed that and in what way discriminatory views have also found manifold expression in the 'mainstream' of philosophical thought to date. On the contrary, I want to make it clear that the perspective of gender equality should become a self-evident element of contemporary philosophy. If this is neglected, the necessary prerequisites for an appropriate philosophical examination of current global problems would not be fulfilled."[5]

---

[3] See NAGL-DOCEKAL 1990, 15.

[4] See NAGL-DOCEKAL 2010, 113–114.

[5] NAGL-DOCEKAL 2010, 113–114: "Welchen Beitrag kann Philosophie zur Beseitigung von Strukturen der Benachteiligung und Unterdrückung leisten? Diese Frage war und

In the context of philosophical sub-disciplines such as anthropology, aesthetics, theories of reason, epistemology, political philosophy, moral, legal, and social philosophy, she sets innovative accents of a philosophical differentiation of recent feminist debates.[6]

FEMINIST PHILOSOPHICAL ANTHROPOLOGY OF THE SEXES

The aim of feminist philosophy in addressing the philosophical anthropology of the sexes is to develop categories in order to analyze and reject both naturalistic and constructivist reductionisms. The terms "women" and "men" are ambiguous, since these terms are used to describe biological bodily differences on the one hand and social or symbolic constructions of order on the other. The paired terms "sex/gender" were originally developed by feminists in order to be able to distinguish the bodily differences between men and women on the one hand (sex) and the symbolic and social constructions on the other (gender). The term "gender" is also used to address the historicity of ideas of difference. Gender stereotypes, as Nagl-Docekal elucidates, go back to the sentimental conception of femininity and the complementarily

ist für meine Forschungen im Bereich feministischer Theorie ausschlaggebend. Insbesondere in meinem Buch *Feministische Philosophie. Ergebnisse, Probleme, Perspektiven* suchte ich das kritische Potential herauszuarbeiten, über das zentrale philosophische Teildisziplinen – von der philosophischen Anthropologie über die Ästhetik, die Vernunft- und Wissenschaftstheorie bis zur Rechtsphilosophie – verfügen. Mit Methoden philosophischer Analyse können die verbreiteten, tief sitzenden geschlechterhierarchischen Vorstellungen präzise aufgezeigt und argumentativ zurückgewiesen werden z. B. in Form des Nachweises, dass sie auf einem naturalistischen Fehlschluss beruhen. Dieses kritische Potential kann freilich erst dann zur vollen Entfaltung gelangen, wenn thematisiert wird, dass und in welcher Weise diskriminierende Auffassungen auch im bisherigen 'mainstream' philosophischen Denkens vielfältigen Ausdruck gefunden haben. Im Gegensatz geht es mir darum, einsichtig zu machen, dass der Blickwinkel der Geschlechtergerechtigkeit zu einem selbstverständlichen Element der heutigen Philosophie werden sollte. Unterbleibt dies, sind für eine angemessene philosophische Auseinandersetzung mit den globalen Problemstellungen der Gegenwart die nötigen Voraussetzungen nicht gegeben."

[6] See BUCHHAMMER 2019.

constructed conception of masculinity of the late 18th century.[7] Education and socialization lead to gender norms being literally incorporated: in this respect, the human body is corporeality that is culturally interpreted and shaped from early childhood onwards.[8]

The deduction of social norms from bodily givens occurs in two ways: wanted by nature and given by nature. Both ways of derivation serve to justify the norms that should be considered immutable. But norms cannot, in principle, be justified from nature. In this context, it is important to take the perspective of action seriously: Speaking about action means speaking from the perspective of the first person singular. An ought can only be formulated if it is also possible to decide otherwise; if a norm formulates an ought, this does not yet mean that one will also make decisions and choices according to this norm. It only makes sense to call a process "natural" if it – spoken from the perspective of action – happens by itself, i.e. not on the basis of human planning. Formulating a norm only makes sense with respect to situations in which we can actually make a decision – even if it is a quandary. "The term norm only makes sense in the context of a theory of freedom – however it may be conceptualized in detail. [...] [N]orms appeal to people who face a decision."[9] The reference to the intention of nature in this context has no compelling character – because we are in the freedom of decision. Rather, those who assume the intention of nature run into a performative self-contradiction. "The fact that an ought is formulated at all suggests that the case in question is not left to the discretion of a natural course."[10]

In terms of action theory, our gender-differentiated bodies also form a situation that can be acted upon in very different ways. "Human

---

[7] See NAGL-DOCEKAL 2008, 296: "Der Begriff 'gender' bringt zudem die Historizität von Differenzvorstellungen in Sicht. [...] Die Klischeevorstellungen, von denen die Alltagswelt in den westlichen Industrieländern weithin geprägt ist, gehen auf den 'sentimentalen Weiblichkeitsentwurf' des ausgehenden 18. Jahrhunderts – und den dazu komplementären Männlichkeitsentwurf – zurück."

[8] See NAGL-DOCEKAL 2008, 296: "So werden die sozialen Konstruktionen buchstäblich *einverleibt* – [...] D. h., der menschliche Körper ist von der frühkindlichen Sozialisation an kulturell gedeutete und gestaltete Leiblichkeit [...]."

[9] NAGL-DOCEKAL 2004, 3.

[10] NAGL-DOCEKAL 2004, 8.

bodies either show predominantly female or male forms or they combine sex characteristics in such a way that a clear assignment is not possible […]. The crucial point is that these conditions constitute an issue of freedom. My physical features do not tie me down to one particular way of life."[11] It is important always, first, to assume an acting position on the bodily givens, and, second, to take an acting position on the cultural interpretations of corporeality. The dubiousness of the term "perversion" must also be analyzed in this context.

"The questionable basis of the term perversion is obvious. Insofar as this expression denounces behavior *contra naturam*, it is marked by a performative self-contradiction. The term perversion assumes that the norm condemning all sexual relations that are not heterosexual could be derived from the fact that there are bodies with female sex characters and bodies with male ones. But such a way of thinking has to be confronted with its own unreflected implications: The fact *that* a norm is formulated presupposes the insight that the sexual life of human beings is not determined by nature but is developed in social interactions. Human sexual relations can be generally called *contra naturam* since they are always (independently of whatever form they take) based on the fact that natural conditions are being dealt with in action. Only as part of the realm of freedom can sexual relations be the object of moral judgment (and legal regulations). The question is not whether a specific form of sexual relations violates the natural order, but how the individuals involved treat each other."[12]

The differentiation of sex and gender is criticized from constructivist theoretical approaches. This critique, or the claim that this differentiation is obsolete, does not do justice to the intention that led to the formation of this pair of terms. The analytical category of gender provides the crucial instrument to illustrate that designs of social order represent a specific level distinct from the conditions of nature.

Constructivist positions formulate their critique, for example, in such a way that, in order to overcome discrimination, they postulate that biological gender as a whole is an "effect" of cultural construction:

---

[11] NAGL-DOCEKAL 2004, 10.
[12] NAGL-DOCEKAL 2004, 37.

e.g. Butler speaks of "styles of the flesh."[13] In these discourses the given raw material is called flesh, but the term flesh belongs to the language game of the organic. Nagl-Docekal points out the inconsistency of such theories, all of which fail to adequately capture human generativity. In speaking of flesh (of matter), a sexually differentiated corporeality is presupposed. "Flesh exists only in dependence on the existence of animals. Without this background, the word flesh makes no sense. [...] Living animals, including human organisms, cannot be understood without sexual difference. For flesh to come into existence, there already had to be female and male individuals who ensured the preservation of their species."[14] The shortcoming of deconstructivist thinking in terms of philosophy of nature becomes fully apparent here, Nagl-Docekal argues.

Here again, the task of philosophy consists of the differentiation of the various points of view. To effectively denounce discrimination, a critique of power is needed. Power has its genuine place in the sphere of freedom, of action. However, regulating norms must not be entangled with the capacity of language in the constitution of empirically appearing objects ("body as effect of discourse"). Regulating norms – juridical, medical, disciplinary norms – for their part always presuppose natural givenness. It is only through this differentiation, of the constitution of objects on the one hand and the power of regulating norms on the other, that normative discourses can be purposefully critiqued at all. This blurring, according to Nagl-Docekal, leads to a new revival of naturalistic conceptions. This constitutional theory is ultimately also based on a naturalistic fallacy. "The current widespread haziness about this point invites a recurrence of naturalistic concepts. The constitution thesis seems based on a false naturalistic conclusion. Both versions of this thesis seem to hold that the idea of a given corporeal difference between men and women introduces inescapable norms, including the enforced heterosexuality criticized by Butler."[15]

[13] BUTLER 1999, 177: "I suggested that gendered bodies are so many 'styles of the flesh' [...]."
[14] NAGL-DOCEKAL 2004, 30.
[15] NAGL-DOCEKAL 2004, 33.

If one starts from a concept of action, and that means freedom, it should be said that the freedom of the human being consists precisely in the ability to act on natural specification. Nagl-Docekal maintains that the pair sex/gender provides an important tool for differentiation: "The sex/gender dyad offers a suitable instrument to demonstrate that social norms must be distinguished from bodily conditions, even though they may be literally incorporated. I insist on the fruitfulness of this distinction because the current debate is marked by some striking theoretical insufficiencies in this regard. Since feminist authors today are almost required to do without the differentiation proposed here, theories oscillate between two forms of reductionism. Body and discourse are alternately used as the leading categories of monocausal explanations. Another version of this problem occurs when a unity of nature and culture is assumed [...]."[16] The difference between nature and culture means that we have to deal with our corporeality in an active and formative way.

Nagl-Docekal's argument proposes the obliteration of the concept of gender roles without replacement, wherever the ideal of a free society is to be considered. "This statement implies no denial of bodily differences. This point is that we should not be coerced into a dichotomous code of behavior merely because we were born with a male or a female body. In short, seriously thinking through the differentiation of sex and gender would result in a demand to abolish man and woman as social categories."[17]

FEMINISM AND AESTHETICS

In her philosophical research on feminist aesthetics, Nagl-Docekal critically examines Sigmund Freud's central relevant theses in a first step, in order to clearly highlight the links from feminist theorists to Freud and Lacan, and to examine the shortcomings in these areas (psychoanalysis as well as the main directions of feminist theories of aesthetics).

[16] NAGL-DOCEKAL 2004, 38–39.
[17] NAGL-DOCEKAL 2004, 25.

"[W]hat should be the specific nature of a 'feminist aesthetics'?"[18] In pursuit of this question, it is essential to examine what the term "feminist aesthetics" means in general. What is the specific feminist philosophical task regarding the question of gender justice in the context of aesthetics? "All philosophical schools are confronted by feminist discourse with the problem of the hierarchy of the sexes […]. The goal of feminist criticism is an aesthetic theory freed from the burden of masculine patterns of thought."[19] She urgently warns that it leads to dangerous imbalances when works of art "must be judged according to whether or not they serve feminist aims," because in doing so, "the creative potential is subordinated to political norms," which would lead to untenable consequences.[20]

If one considers art as an independent sphere, it requires a specific kind of judgment, "that does not allow a subordination under categories alien to art."[21] From this perspective, Nagl-Docekal argues, it is "strictly inadmissible to speak of a 'feminist' aesthetic."[22] Nonetheless, this should not be misunderstood to mean that art has nothing to do with political aims.[23] On the contrary, if art educates people to a "new way of seeing," for this reason it is also to be expected, "to alter our view of political conditions. But the political impulse in this case is a result – and not the condition – of the creative activity. […] From a feminist perspective, one question arises that must be asked in each case anew: What are the implications of the altered perceptions initiated by art for the relationship of the sexes?"[24]

A common opinion in Western thinking is that women lack artistic creativity. Here, the invisible normative character of this apparent statement of fact must first be unmasked. In doing so, it is important to deconstruct the cult of the genius.[25] The focus is not merely on talent,

---

[18] NAGL-DOCEKAL 2004, 83.
[19] NAGL-DOCEKAL 2004, 83.
[20] NAGL-DOCEKAL 2004, 84. See also the debates about official art in the totalitarian regimes of the 20th century.
[21] NAGL-DOCEKAL 2004, 84.
[22] NAGL-DOCEKAL 2004, 84.
[23] See NAGL-DOCEKAL 2004, 85.
[24] NAGL-DOCEKAL 2004, 85.
[25] See NAGL-DOCEKAL 2004, 42.

but also on the question of how far it was possible or impossible for girls – at least in European history – to undertake studies at an academy of art or to be apprenticed to one of the great masters.[26] Another question of relevance is that of the reception of women's art, which is very often pejoratively labeled under the term "commercial art." In galleries and exhibitions, works by women are underrepresented and fetch lower prices.[27] The discussion of these conditions in the history of ideas and social history is multifaceted: it ranges from the historical-critical endeavor of rediscovering women artists of the past, and the rewriting of a "general history of the arts," to the investigation of the representation of women or gender relations in the arts. Examining the fact that "these representations have predominantly been shaped by masculine imagination,"[28] we find that the imaginary world, in which the artistic creativity of women has no place, is often evident in the productions themselves. Women should have the same chances as men to receive artistic education and they should have the freedom to choose their own subjects.[29]

Nagl-Docekal analyzes Kant's theory of aesthetics from a feminist-philosophical perspective. Do the categories of his aesthetic theory (e.g. the beautiful and the sublime, reflective judgment, and disinterested pleasure) have to be rejected or is it possible, that these categories can be used without reference to speculation on the character of the sexes (the category of the beautiful to the feminine, and the sublime to the masculine)? Could the framework of this aesthetic theory perhaps also be examined through a feminist lens (e.g., the theory of disinterested pleasure)? The real task of feminist critique in this case is to reject the linking of aesthetic categories with notions of gendered virtues. "But if terms like beautiful and sublime are read as insinuating a patriarchal character per se, then this combination is not seen as a problem but remains in force."[30]

[26] See NAGL-DOCEKAL 2004, 42.
[27] See NAGL-DOCEKAL 2004, 43.
[28] NAGL-DOCEKAL 2004, 44.
[29] See NAGL-DOCEKAL 2004, 45.
[30] NAGL-DOCEKAL 2004, 77.

Examining the thesis of women's lack of cultural ability, Nagl-Docekal turns in a first step to some of Sigmund Freud's key theses. With the means of psychoanalysis, according to Nagl-Docekal, "the most ambitious attempt to provide a scientific foundation" for the thesis that there are "a-historical differences between the sexes" was undertaken.[31]

Central Aspects of Freud's Theory from a Feminist-Philosophical Perspective

In Freud's theory the area of the psyche has a double distinction, on the one hand from the field of consciousness and on the other hand from the bodily. Of central importance is the conception of the unconscious: unconscious willing and thinking. How was the relation between unconscious willing and thinking to conscious willing and thinking established?[32] Freud's theory of desire should be taken into account here: that desire, i.e., sexuality in the broad sense of Freud's meaning, is involved in all human cultural, artistic, and social activities.[33] With one of the essential *termini technici*, that of sublimation, Freud explains that "energy is turned aside from its sexual goal and diverted towards other ends, no longer sexual and socially more valuable."[34] In the context of his theory of sublimation, Freud explains that women have less capacity for sublimation than men. It follows, he says, "that they are less able to participate in cultural achievements. In explicit terms, for example, Freud holds that women should be credited with 'little sense of justice', and he also largely agrees with the widespread opinion that 'they have made few contributions to the discoveries and inventions in the history of civilization'."[35] But why are women less capable of sublimation than men? Freud summarizes the results of his psychoanalytic method as experiential findings which showed that the psychosexual development of the girl is more complicated than

[31] See NAGL-DOCEKAL 2004, 45.
[32] See NAGL-DOCEKAL 2004, 46.
[33] See NAGL-DOCEKAL 2004, 47.
[34] FREUD 1935, 48.
[35] NAGL-DOCEKAL 2004, 47.

that of the boy because it involves two additional tasks. The girl, according to Freud, must exchange erogenous zone and love object, whereas the boy retains both.[36] In Freud's sketch of early childhood development, however, Nagl-Docekal sees a deviation from Freud's intended purely descriptive method at crucial points. With regard to masturbation, Freud emphasizes: "We are now obliged to recognize, that the little girl is a little man."[37] Freud's opinion is, that the clitoris is a "penis-equivalent." Nagl-Docekal analyzes this as follows: "With this view, he starts to deviate from a purely descriptive procedure. Beginning with his characterization of the girl's body, his attempt to do the empirical facts justice with a specific terminology gives way to indirect descriptions through the medium of the comparison. The body of the boy becomes the yardstick – in a rather unmetaphorical sense – to which the body of the girl is compared. The statement of equivalence quickly turns into a description of deficits."[38] Using the example of masturbation: From the child's inner perspective, it would be about the experience of creating lust for oneself. Freud leaves this point of view in favor of the external perspective, in which again the male model dominates: "the little girl appears as a little man, only under this precondition can Freud speak of phallic phase."[39] What is observable is, "that the little girl 'knows how to get pleasure by the excitation of her clitoris', but not that she thereby behaves in a 'masculine way'."[40] Nagl-Docekal's analysis at this point: "Freud's belief in the empirical validity of his conclusion has consequences that should not be underestimated: A scientific appearance is generated for a speculation in which parts of women's infantile sexual experiences are viewed as unfeminine, via a kind of retrospective expropriation."[41] She also questions Freud's central thesis that the girl must exchange her erogenous zone: why should an exchange have to be made? "Would it not also be possible to speak of an additional dimension?"[42] This switch

[36] See NAGL-DOCEKAL 2004, 48.
[37] FREUD 1933, 118.
[38] NAGL-DOCEKAL 2004, 48–49.
[39] NAGL-DOCEKAL 2004, 49.
[40] NAGL-DOCEKAL 2004, 49.
[41] NAGL-DOCEKAL 2004, 49.
[42] NAGL-DOCEKAL 2004, 49.

from clitoris to vagina might betray a narrowing of sexuality to procreation. In Nagl-Docekal's sense, it is necessary to distinguish between sexual sensations on the one hand and the generative function of certain organs on the other. "If the vagina is assigned an exclusive meaning in Freud's argument, then we may suspect that both levels remain fairly unseparated and the sexuality of the woman is investigated with a focus on procreation. Such a conception agrees with the identification of the terms woman and mother, which marks the traditional gender image that was characteristic of the social stratum to which Freud belonged."[43] The thesis of the passivity of the woman and the activity of the man also stands in this context of thought. But if the woman is conceived as passive, her sexual experience is marginalized.[44]

A further central point of Freud's theory has to be examined philosophically: the relationship between the Oedipus complex and the castration complex, which, according to Freud, are opposed to each other. The Oedipal beginning of the girl is the castration complex. "She can take refuge in it as in a haven."[45] The girl discovers "that her mother is castrated"[46] and she turns away from the mother, she "rejects her love for the mother and in the process not infrequently represses a good part of her sexual aspirations altogether."[47] The girl turns away from the mother and builds the Oedipal relationship to the father. With the removal of the fear of castration, Freud argues, the main motive for the girl to overcome the Oedipus complex no longer exists. "In these circumstances the formation of the super-ego must suffer; it cannot attain the strength and independence which give it its cultural significance."[48] However, what remains convincing, according to Nagl-Docekal, in Freud's theory is that cultural achievements demand drive sublimation and that dealing with desire must be learned in early childhood. This entails "painful experience of alienation" from primary caregivers.[49]

---

[43] NAGL-DOCEKAL 2004, 49.
[44] See NAGL-DOCEKAL 2004, 50.
[45] FREUD 1969, 559.
[46] FREUD 1969, 126.
[47] FREUD 1969, 559.
[48] FREUD 1969, 559–560.
[49] See NAGL-DOCEKAL 2004, 51.

In the context of explaining the Oedipus and castration complex, another *terminus technicus* occurs: that of penile envy. "The castration complex of girls is [...] started by the sight of the genitals of the other sex. They at once notice the difference and, it must be admitted, its significance too. They feel seriously wronged [...] and fall a victim to 'envy the penis', which will leave ineradicable traces on their development and the formation of their character."[50] Nagl-Docekal asks at this point what is the "meaning" that the little girl "immediately" ascribes to the penis and that is supposed to cause "such a strong feeling of envy?"[51] Freud elaborates on two shock reactions he describes: The girl feels severely affected, often expresses that she "would like to have something like it [penis] too,"[52] and now falls prey to penis envy, which leaves indelible traces in her development and character formation. On the one hand, the girl lets herself spoil the pleasure of her phallic sexuality. "This assessment, however, is hardly comprehensible. Since it is not stated that the girl experiences lust through the 'sight of the genitals of the other sex', it is not clear why the girl should, based on this perception, cease to satisfy herself with the help of her clitoris. Freud has changed his perspective and turned away from the girl's internal point of view."[53]

The second and more substantial shock scenario: "As soon as the little girl recognized that not only she but also her mother is castrated, she drops her as a love object."[54] But how should the little girl go from the perception of "penis-lessness" to the idea of "castration"? "These two statements are not the same. The lack of a penis describes physical difference, but the term *castration* implies an entire story."[55] How should the girl who observes that her body does not have a penis come up with a narrative that goes something like this: the mother once had a penis, the punishing father who enacts the rules that the mother did not follow cut off her penis so that the little girl now has no penis either. Nagl-Docekal sees the key in the whole concept in Freud's thesis,

[50] FREUD 1933, 125.
[51] NAGL-DOCEKAL 2004, 51.
[52] FREUD 1933, 125.
[53] NAGL-DOCEKAL 2004, 51–52.
[54] NAGL-DOCEKAL 2004, 52.
[55] NAGL-DOCEKAL 2004, 52.

"that through the 'discovery of women's lack of penis they are debased in value for girls just as they are for boys and later perhaps for men'."[56] But how should this socially observable lack of esteem derive from the anatomical fact of penislessness, Nagl-Docekal asks.[57] Wouldn't the perspective be reversed here? Children observe that women are little respected by men and also often by their children. Therefore, this observation that women are very little respected or often marginalized in society would be at the root, not the observation of biological sex differences. The root of the disrespect for women lies in political and social conditions: "Those whose bodies do not feature a penis are often relegated to an underprivileged position and subjected to lack of respect," as Nagl-Docekal pointedly summarizes.[58] She emphasizes: "This depiction is not a causal explanation but presents a historically contingent connection of penislessness and disregard whose genesis falls into the field of historical research [...]."[59] Here, too, Nagl-Docekal finds a methodological inconsistency: the socio-political structure of the lifeworld forms the guide and basis for interpreting "the child's expression of wanting to 'have something like that, too'."[60] Perhaps, Nagl-Docekal asks, this is what Freud had in mind when speaking of the "meaning" that the little girl understands?[61] This issue has been taken up by those feminist authors who see Freud as a critic of the bourgeois social order.[62]

While there is no biological determinism in Freud, he nevertheless also speaks of inescapability: the girl must go through this development. "Freud, who first declared his intention to keep psychoanalysis free from 'any prerequisite foreign to it, be it of an anatomical, chemical or physiological nature' [...] formulates in this context a strong postulate: 'The anatomical (sex) distinction must express itself in psychical consequences'."[63] What exactly is the structure of Freud's argu-

[56] NAGL-DOCEKAL 2004 52.
[57] See NAGL-DOCEKAL 2004, 53.
[58] NAGL-DOCEKAL 2004, 53.
[59] NAGL-DOCEKAL 2004, 53.
[60] NAGL-DOCEKAL 2004, 53.
[61] See NAGL-DOCEKAL 2004, 85.
[62] See NAGL-DOCEKAL 2004, 54.
[63] NAGL-DOCEKAL 2004, 54, with reference to FREUD 1933, 124.

ment? Obviously, the starting point are gender hierarchical ideas shaping his own life experience, which are projected onto the little girl (as girls realize that they have no penis); girls are now assumed to link penislessness with being devalued, which has the consequence of interpreting the subordination of women as a result of the anatomical sex difference, whereby the historically contingent background is rendered unrecognizable, which is why Freud's thesis suggests that any desire for change in the prevailing society would be pointless. The result is that this Freudian argument might have a legitimizing function.[64]

As a next step, Nagl-Docekal turns to Freud's thesis of women's lack of cultural capacity. "Freud's psychoanalytic theory cannot provide a scientific foundation of the thesis. One rather finds a *petitio principii* – the reduced cultural potential of the woman, which according to the claim is explained from the infantile development of the libido, stands de facto already at the beginning of the argumentation […]. The crucial thought is that in girls the formation of a superego and therefore the ability for drive sublimation are handicapped."[65] It is important to consider, however, that the girl lives in a social environment under conditions of bourgeois socialization, in which she can only develop a successful relationship with the father by subordinating herself. (The husband is the head of the family and guardian of the female family members.) "In the relationship to the father, the girl practices what remains determinant for the entire coming life. […] The girl is thus required to relinquish essential dimensions of her autonomy at an early age."[66] Likewise, the woman is denied intellectual and artistic competence.

Thus, Nagl-Docekal draws attention to a problem that results from the fact that, regarding the origins of these limitations on women, Freud points to the dynamics of penis envy. "In this manner the bourgeois construction of gender relations, in which there is, among other things, no place for women artists, is projected back into the libidinous logic of the little girl who judges her body to be unsatisfactory."[67] Freud

---

[64] See NAGL-DOCEKAL 2004, 55. For a recent queer examination of psychoanalysis see https://queeringpsychoanalysis.wordpress.com; see also HUTFLESS 2022; HUTFLESS & ZACH 2017.

[65] NAGL-DOCEKAL 2004, 55.

[66] NAGL-DOCEKAL 2004, 55.

[67] NAGL-DOCEKAL 2004, 56.

interprets clitoral masturbation as masculine: the girl relinquishes this source of pleasure, performing a "passivity thrust," "masculine" activity is repressed altogether.[68] As "Freud dismisses the formulation 'feminine libido' as absurd, [...] he rejects in the same breath the thought of female creativity. The projective element of his thinking remains unreflected however."[69]

Examining the connection between "genius" and "masculinity," we find that the anatomical sex difference is considered as determining psychological features: "This means that the bourgeois social construction no longer appears as historically contingent; the constellation of the sexes that is outlined in this construction is presented in such a manner that it seems to be based on empirically evident physical difference and therefore appears to be inevitable [...]."[70] For girls, there are two possibilities in Freud's sense: Either they choose the Oedipal relation to the father, as the path into the "normal" heterosexual relationship; the price is a deficient formation of the superego and cultural insignificance and meaninglessness.[71] Or they do not turn completely to the father which allows them to connect in a sublimated form to the activity of their phallic phase, with the consequence that they would be capable of intellectual and artistic achievements, but at the price of not being "real women."[72] They are, according to Freud, "rather male than female."[73]

Astonishingly, many feminist theorists take up this view in an affirmative manner. "Nothing seems more obvious than the need to problematize such a (non)placing of the woman artist or the intellectual from a feminist perspective [...]," Nagl-Docekal argues, yet, surprisingly "this aspect of Freud's theory has enjoyed broad acceptance in feminist theory."[74] In some feminist theories intellectuality is also considered a masculine characteristic.[75] She asks, why "should withdrawal from this

[68] See NAGL-DOCEKAL 2004, 56.
[69] NAGL-DOCEKAL 2004, 56.
[70] NAGL-DOCEKAL 2004, 56.
[71] See NAGL-DOCEKAL 2004, 56.
[72] NAGL-DOCEKAL 2004, 56.
[73] See FREUD 1933, 118.
[74] NAGL-DOCEKAL 2004, 57.
[75] See NAGL-DOCEKAL 2004, 57.

social construction be equated with masculinization?"[76] As Nagl-Docekal further explains, "[i]f women also claim for themselves a place hitherto occupied only by men, this need not mean that they develop a masculine identity; rather, it is primarily a matter of liberating this place as a whole from its gendered connotations."[77]

Importantly, Freud emphasizes that in his sexual theory he described the woman only from the point of view of sexual functions. Freud writes: "But do not forget that we have described the woman only insofar as her nature is determined by sexual functions. This influence is far-reaching, but we have to keep in mind that the individual woman might be beyond that also a human being."[78] Nagl-Docekal asks: "Should feminist theory not take this advice too?"[79]

Feminist Theories of Aesthetics

How do feminist theorists relate to Freud? While on the one hand, it was a concern to work out the patriarchal aspects in Freud's thinking, on the other hand, theorists pursued the question of whether the libidinous biography of women could not be thought of in a completely different way.[80] Thinkers who criticized Freud's theory of women's lack of cultural competence attempted to counter his view with a theory of female libido and thus to establish specific cultural competencies of women.[81] One direction of feminist theorizing that became established in France (French Feminism) was the philosophical project of an *écriture féminine*. Taking Hélène Cixous as an example, Nagl-Docekal highlights central elements of these theories and points out the aspects that are problematic from a feminist perspective.

First, let us briefly recall the summary provided by Nagl-Docekal. Hélène Cixous follows Lacan in basic aspects of his thinking, especially in the conception of the "symbolic order" and the combining of

[76] NAGL-DOCEKAL 2004, 57.
[77] NAGL-DOCEKAL 2004, 57.
[78] FREUD 1933, 135.
[79] NAGL-DOCEKAL 2004, 57.
[80] See NAGL-DOCEKAL 2004, 58.
[81] See NAGL-DOCEKAL 2004, 50.

psychoanalysis with language theory. Important elements of Lacan's theory that she refers to are the theory of the mirror stage, the imaginary (imaginary identity of the child with the mother), and the symbolic order as structured by the law of the father, of which the phallus (which is not the same as the penis) is the symbol. Cixous distances herself from Lacan, however, by pointing out that it is not the entirety of human culture whose libinous past Lacan has analyzed but merely the occidental one, which has developed historically and is therefore also changeable.[82] Here, the law of the father determines the social structure, in which women are put in a "position marked by subordination and speechlessness."[83] "For authors like Cixous, the task is to investigate why the girl in the course of her infantile development gets into this subordination and falls silent."[84] While acknowledging that Lacan offers the theoretical tools to expose the mechanisms by which girls are silenced in this situation,[85] Cixous criticizes Lacan for failing to decisively analyze the privilege of the man – a failure that "has contributed to the stabilization of it."[86] She demands a redefinition of the meaning of "phallus": As she emphasizes, this term signifies not only the symbolic order in general, but also the supremacy of the male. With this reading, the term "phallus," as a metaphorical concept, moves closer to the term "penis." "Phallus" becomes a cipher for feminist critique of the patriarchally structured society.[87] Moreover, authors of French feminism diagnose "phallogocentrism" in occidental thought, using a term that Derrida has introduced as he rejected elements of metaphysical thought.[88]

In her outline for an alternative interpretation of the infantile development of girls, Cixous describes the beginning of the Oedipal phase – as it usually happens in Western culture – as a time when the girl is forced to deny herself, to give up her own spontaneity and strength. The beginning of the Oedipal phase for the girl is the discovery,

[82] See NAGL-DOCEKAL 2004, 60.
[83] NAGL-DOCEKAL 2004, 60.
[84] NAGL-DOCEKAL 2004, 60.
[85] See NAGL-DOCEKAL 2004, 60.
[86] NAGL-DOCEKAL 2004, 61.
[87] See NAGL-DOCEKAL 2004, 61.
[88] See NAGL-DOCEKAL 2004, 61.

"that she sees her libidinous and creative self threatened with death."[89] However, Cixoux underscores, it is not the girl herself who represses activity, but the phallogocentrically shaped environment. Therefore, Cixous can attribute more potential for resistance to the girl.[90] In spite of threatened sanctions and internalized sensations of being frightened by their own desire, girls are usually able to resist the pressure to a certain extent. The term "castration" is now inappropriate, since it implies a denial of the girl's libidinous energy.[91] Here is where the project of an *écriture féminine* comes in, as Nagl-Docekal explains. "Cixous argues for a writing that gives expression to the buried female libido."[92] Cixous' plea is that "[w]oman must write herself." While even women's texts are commonly structured by the phallic order, there are exceptions which Cixous lists: Colette, Marguerite Duras, and Jean Genet (men are also capable of *écriture féminine*).

Nagl-Docekal reconstructs the way in which Cixous locates the source of a different form of expression in the realm of the imaginary, the pre-Oedipal unity of the child with the mother, which precedes the symbolic order.[93] "The imaginary is formed through feminine creativity into an anti-Logos weapon. While the phallus stands for the rationally shaped symbolic order, it is now confronted with the figure of the mother, as the personification of a nonverbal relationship developed in the medium of corporality and the sound of the voice. Cixous requests that an *écriture féminine* ensures with specific means that this figure is listened to. 'In women's speech, as in their writing, that element which never stops resonating … is the song: first music from the first voice of love which is alive in every woman … A woman is never far from *mother*. … There is always within her at least a little of that good mother's milk. She writes in white ink'."[94]

The goal of this writing in white ink is not, as Nagl-Docekal points out, to strengthen women's self-confidence in the struggle for gender justice, but rather to overcome the struggle of the sexes (as an always

---

89 See NAGL-DOCEKAL 2004, 61.
90 See CIXOUS 1981, 246.
91 See NAGL-DOCEKAL 2004, 62.
92 NAGL-DOCEKAL 2004, 62.
93 See NAGL-DOCEKAL 2004, 96.
94 NAGL-DOCEKAL 2004, 63, with reference to CIXOUS 1981, 251.

reciprocal castration) *toto genere*. "For Cixous, the image of the mother mediates an alternative relationship model in which giving oneself away and opening up to heterogeneity are characteristic features."[95]

Nagl-Docekal identifies several problematic points in the central theses of *écriture féminine*. Most importantly, she unconvers a shift of perspective: On the one hand, Cixous follows Lacan who seeks to explain the imaginary from the inner perspective of the child (girls and boys), referring to the imaginary unity of the child with the mother before it is able to say "I am." On this basis, however, a theory of the specifically female libido cannot be elaborated. On the other hand, Cixous speaks from the viewpoint of the mother nursing the child.[96] From this perspective, however, Lacan's theory of the imaginary does not take hold. After all, the nursing mother is not reduced in her social relations to the relationship with her baby, but also maintains other relationships with many different people, with diverse psychic dynamics. It is exclusively from the infant's experience, that the bodily and vocally mediated care is the only decisive sensitivity characteristic of the mother. "To defend a conception that reduces motherliness in such a drastic fashion approaches, even if unintentionally, a naturalistic concept of the rearing of the next generation." Analyzing this inconsistency, Nagl-Docekal notes: "In short, the problem here is that the feminine libido is determined through the perspective of the baby. In the end, this theory comes close to the reductionist perspective already observed in Freud according to which the sexuality of woman is defined through the figure of the mother."[97] As she points out, this problematic line of thought affects the concept of *écriture féminine* as a whole.

Discussing the limits of the conception of writing "with white ink," Nagl-Docekal addresses the issue of receptivity, arguing that readers must not be thought of as limited by gender. "In terms of the referentiality of artistic production to reception, literature always transcends the limits of gender-typical experiences – even if it tries to express just those experiences."[98] Furthermore, she examines what it means that Cixous

[95] NAGL-DOCEKAL 2004, 63.
[96] See NAGL-DOCEKAL 2004, 63.
[97] NAGL-DOCEKAL 2004, 64.
[98] NAGL-DOCEKAL 2004, 65.

cites the works of Jean Genet as an example of *écriture féminine*. "Here the adjective feminine has lost its original meaning and no longer refers specifically to the libidinous energy of women."[99] In other words, "the dividing line no longer separates forms of language derived from the libidinous economy of men and women. Differing styles of thought and expression are open to men as alternative options [...]."[100] Indeed, boys also experience a form of relationship in their early childhood socialization that is distinct from masculine dominance. Nagl-Docekal traces back this obvious vagueness in Cixous to a blurring of conceptuality. As she demonstrates, Cixous (like other thinkers of the *écriture féminine*) operates with five conceptual dyads that she seems to consider as equivalent, while closer scrutiny reveals that in each case different fields of reference are addressed: symbolic order vs. imaginary fusion; law of the father (phallus) vs. voice of the mother; masculine hegemony vs. feminine recognition of the heterogeneous; male libido vs. female libido; rationality vs. poetic mode of expression.[101]

Most importantly, we need to note: While both language and culture as a whole are imbued with masculine notions of order, they are not per se shaped by masculinity.[102] Therefore, two different tasks need to be taken up: On the one hand, careful historical, sociological, and literary studies are required in order to adequately analyze hegemonic structures of order.[103] On the other hand, "the capacity for language and culture as basic human capabilities has to be discussed in an examination that refrains from the dimension of content and focus on the question of preconditions."[104] These two levels have to be clearly distinguished.

A significant inconsistency results from the tracing back of the symbolic order to the law of the father, which Cixous does not question. Nagl-Docekal argues that Cixous does not go far enough in her distancing from Lacan. She suggests that the interpretation of the symbolic order with the competence of distinguishing "I-am" and "he-she-it-is"

[99] NAGL-DOCEKAL 2004, 65.
[100] NAGL-DOCEKAL 2004, 68.
[101] See NAGL-DOCEKAL 2004, 65.
[102] See NAGL-DOCEKAL 2004, 65.
[103] See NAGL-DOCEKAL 2004, 66.
[104] NAGL-DOCEKAL 2004, 66.

does not necessarily imply the notion of the father's supremacy. "On closer examination, Lacan's theory is marked by a circular structure of thought similar to that found in Freud. While the powerful father may appear to stand behind all culture and language, the symbolic order only seems to be phallic since the hierarchy of the sexes of the bourgeois family has been projected on it. But this kind of projection means that again women's competence for participation in human cultural achievements is negated. Therefore the most urgent task of a feminist criticism is to reject the joining of the symbolic order and phallus concepts."[105] Where this disconnection is not accomplished, there is nothing left but "the effort to provide women with an anti-Logos weapon."[106] This effort amounts, however, as Nagl-Docekal points out, to rejecting participation in politics and social life as well as feminist critique of distortions in the space of the political. Significantly, Cixous distances herself both from demands for equal rights and from the term "feminist" (in pursuance of Derrida, who disqualified feminism as "phallic" and therefore irrelevant).

What does all this imply for the woman artist? She is forced to produce outside the symbolic order and pressured to create the "totally Other." At this point, well-known resentment against women artists as masculinized reappears. Consequently, many feminist authors demand that "feminist aesthetics" should not be equated with a theory of "female art." With regard to the female vs. male libido distinction it is obvious that even where artists express their early childhood libido in their artworks, no evidence can be derived from this for a juxtaposition of "feminine" and "masculine" writing.[107]

In more general terms, Nagl-Docekal asks: Why should abilities and virtues that can find recognition as human competencies in men and women be apostrophized as "masculine" and "feminine" at all?[108] The feminist purpose here is once again to disconnect, i.e. to introduce distinctions. That there are different styles of expression (poetry, science, economics, etc.) is evident. But their gendered connotation should be

[105] NAGL-DOCEKAL 2004, 67.
[106] NAGL-DOCEKAL 2004, 67.
[107] See NAGL-DOCEKAL 2004, 67.
[108] See NAGL-DOCEKAL 2004, 69.

scrutinized. "Why should women and men not have or acquire abilities in both fields?"[109]

A FEMINIST-PHILOSOPHICAL INVESTIGATION OF THE CONCEPT OF REASON

In her investigation of feminist critique of reason, Nagl-Docekal starts from the feminist critique of the fact that "the concept of reason is connoted as masculine in everyday understanding," which for women means on the one hand "that their capacity for reason is in doubt," and on the other hand "that the cultivation of their rational faculties is rejected as unfeminine – a rejection in pejorative terms such as *bluestocking*."[110] As she pointedly summarizes, "[t]he ideal image of gender difference in Western culture assigns reason to men and emotion to women. […] The widely shared view […] implies a hierarchical pattern. Since reason and emotion are commonly perceived in a relation of subordination, the abilities assigned to the man are understood as superior to those of the woman. This means that the concept of reason, in its common understanding, carries with it a claim of patriarchal power."[111]

As feminist critique of reason includes very different approaches, "ranging from calls to reformulate the concept of reason to outright rejection of it,"[112] the task of feminist philosophy is to carefully examine the various discussions. While the debate "reveals a number of plausible arguments," it is also apparent that there is "a tendency toward overdrawn objections."[113] Herta Nagl-Docekal lucidly addresses the core theses of feminist critiques of reason, covering very different fields of research, including theory of science, cultural studies, the philosophical theory of the moral subject, and anthropological conceptions of gender characters that promote a division of labor between the sexes, based on the opposition of reason (man) versus emotion and

[109] NAGL-DOCEKAL 2004, 69.
[110] NAGL-DOCEKAL 2004, 87.
[111] NAGL-DOCEKAL 2004, 88.
[112] NAGL-DOCEKAL 2004, 88.
[113] NAGL-DOCEKAL 2004, 127.

diminished judgment (woman). "This kind of masculinization of reason constitutes the actual scandal for the feminist critique of reason – especially since these clichéd ways of thinking and gendered norms are still prevalent today."[114]

The starting point of feminist theory of science was the diagnosis that "the mainstream scholarship was marked by a masculine bias."[115] What are the "origins of the androcentric character of many mainstream theories"?[116] On the one hand, this androcentrism is due to the worldview of the individual scholars, on the other hand, it is due to some of the methods of research themselves. How can we work on this topic in a feminist-methodological way? What are the criteria for qualifying scientific statements as valid ones? When is a statement to be qualified as "scientific"?[117] Does androcentrism constitute an element of "normal science" because "traditional methods of research obviously lack sufficient mechanisms for warding off masculine bias"?[118]

As regards the term "feminist epistemology," it must be considered that a conception of "feminist epistemology" in the sense of a "female logic of research" leads into a problem. This term is legitimized only when it refers "to a specific mode of questioning – where it expresses the critical intention to confront the received theory of science with the facts of androcentrism that can no longer be denied."[119] Strictly positivist methods are obviously unable to avoid that, for example, prejudiced everyday ideas influence the results of the sciences. At this point, the postulate of value freedom needs to be questioned. Science based on a positivist approach, Herta Nagl-Docekal plausibly points out, may "help preserve a patriarchal order of the sexes."[120] Not only common gender biases but also "patterns of thinking such as ethnocentrism, Eurocentrism, racism, and class prejudice," often flow unreflectively into scientific work.[121]

---

[114] Nagl-Docekal 2004, 128.
[115] Nagl-Docekal 2004, 89.
[116] Nagl-Docekal 2004, 90.
[117] See Nagl-Docekal 2004, 91.
[118] Nagl-Docekal 2004, 91.
[119] Nagl-Docekal 2004, 91.
[120] Nagl-Docekal 2004, 93.
[121] Nagl-Docekal 2004, 94.

If the "mainstream" of scientific work is patriarchally shaped, what is the *modus operandi* of feminist theory building? "Should it reject the science project in its entirety, or can it define itself as a different type of scholarship – and if so, how?"[122] Nagl-Docekal examines different paths taken by diverse researchers.

Some authors have argued that science should be abandoned *toto genere*. In this position, the fact of situatedness is tendentiously (and overdrawn) interpreted in the sense (often with reference to Foucault) that all research is interested in maintaining the power of the privileged classes. Nagl-Docekal points out the performative self-contradiction of this argument: The critics exclude themselves from it, "they discuss the linkage of knowledge and power in a manner that they do not see as being itself guided by power interests."[123] Moreover: critics can only elaborate their criticism if they themselves work with scientific methods. Nagl-Docekal points out that "feminist criticism should not lose its footing by unrestrictedly questioning scientific rationality."[124]

Further the concept of "reason" itself: First, we have to distinguish between the content of thinking (that we may consider reasonable or unreasonable) and thinking itself: "our ability to make such a judgement, traditionally described with the expression reason."[125] Being able to critically reflect on the contents of our thinking presupposes that we have the competence of judgment, i.e., that we are capable of learning.[126] "If the difference between the content of thought and the capacity for thinking is not kept in mind, this leads to a sweeping suspicion of reason, which implies that feminist criticism can no longer account for its own mode of arguing."[127] Feminist critique of androcentrism requires reasoned reflection. But in precisely what does this ability to think and to judge consist? In this regard, feminist critique of reason would be well served to draw on philosophical investigations of the concept of reason, Nagl-Docekal argues.

---

[122] NAGL-DOCEKAL 2004, 95.
[123] NAGL-DOCEKAL 2004, 95.
[124] NAGL-DOCEKAL 2004, 95.
[125] NAGL-DOCEKAL 2004, 96.
[126] See NAGL-DOCEKAL 2004, 96.
[127] NAGL-DOCEKAL 2004, 97.

Secondly, the conception of "women's way of knowing"[128] needs to be examined. How is this conception formulated in feminist critique of science? On the one hand, gender-specific differences in thinking skills are assumed on the basis of biological gender differences. This argumentation is not plausible, as Nagl-Docekal convincingly explains: after all, men and women communicate with each other in an argumentative way, so there must be an understanding, whereas the assumption that there exist two completely different ways of thinking would preclude such an understanding. On the other hand, the concept of "women's way of knowing" is also derived from social gender. Nagl-Docekal agrees that, due to the division of labor between the sexes, specific experiences are formed, which have an effect on work in the sciences.[129] She contends, however, that the danger of social determinism needs to be kept in mind.

Feminist standpoint theory is not without problems either. This position assumes (with reference back to Marxist theories) that women, due to their experiences of discrimination, would rather have a clear view of reality and therefore achieve better scientific findings. But: "the underprivileged position of women" does not achieve "*eo ipso* warrant expectations of (in comparison to mainstream research) more appropriate or merely different modes of investigation."[130]

Nagl-Docekal focuses on one aspect which Sandra Harding brings into the debate, namely that "the place of women" does not exist. What matters is "that there is no need to insist on a viewpoint shared by *women as such* in order to challenge masculine thinking, but to make a *feminist* focus the basis of research."[131] Essentialism is to be found wherever "it is insinuated that women (or men) unavoidably share certain experiences due to their sex."[132] It is of equal importance, however, to be aware of the danger of an exaggerated anti-essentialism: "On the one hand, the idea of a feminine experience shared by all women has to be rejected, since women have very different opinions and aims in

[128] See NAGL-DOCEKAL 2004, 98.
[129] See NAGL-DOCEKAL 2004, 98.
[130] NAGL-DOCEKAL 2004, 99.
[131] NAGL-DOCEKAL 2004, 99.
[132] NAGL-DOCEKAL 2004, 100.

the most varied positions in society. But the consequence is not that any assumption of common experiences must be denied."[133] In short, insofar as feminist critiques of science are concerned with opening up research to other points of view, the term "*women's way of knowing* should not be employed [...], since this would suggest a homogenous feminine approach."[134] The point of scientificity is "that theories must be well founded and accessible to an intersubjective examination. A thesis can be considered valid only if it has been checked as far as possible, by the available methods and confronted with an extensive series of objections."[135]

The key issue addressed by the conception of the situatedness of knowledge, concerns "the question [...] how to define the claim of science if, on the one hand, the inevitable contextuality is taken into account and, on the other, an epistemological relativism is to be avoided."[136]

One aspect of the situated knowledge is concerned with the insight that "research starts with questions resulting from problems we encounter in everyday life."[137] The other aspect is based on the observation that the categorical framework of scientific work is never independent of history and culture.[138] Science cannot achieve truth that is valid for all times. The concept of objectivity Nagl-Docekal proposes "formulates the task of entering a process of thorough weighing, beginning from the different perspectives that can currently be brought to bear on research topics, in search of the most plausible theories (from today's perspective)."[139] A theory cannot be disproved merely by uncovering it in a particular historical, cultural, or social setting, but only on the basis of informed inquiry. "Context of discovery" and "context of justification" need to be differentiated, but this differentiation should be repositioned. Significant is not the rejection of objectivity, but rather, with co-reflection of the situatedness of thinking, an

[133] NAGL-DOCEKAL 2004, 100.
[134] NAGL-DOCEKAL 2004, 100.
[135] NAGL-DOCEKAL 2004, 101.
[136] NAGL-DOCEKAL 2004, 101.
[137] NAGL-DOCEKAL 2004, 105.
[138] See NAGL-DOCEKAL 2004, 103.
[139] NAGL-DOCEKAL 2004, 104.

increased objectivity. It is important to keep in mind that normative questions cannot be ignored, the normative implications of research must be discussed.[140]

Value-free research is "not only unredeemable but counterproductive […]; the aim of establishing value-free theories is not desirable."[141] If one considers the background of interests in the sciences, it becomes clear that research topics do not merely arise from our need for information, but also from our current problems of practical orientation. Therefore, the demand for value-free theories means ignoring a central task of research.[142] "A discussion of the normative aspect of research is of elementary significance for feminist criticism of the sciences." If it is taken seriously, "that the idea of value-free scholarship is not redeemable and that its validation is not desirable, then we see that controversies evolving around normative language concerning, for instance, the social position of women, gender relations, and so on, are a genuine element of historical research."[143]

As regards the tools of feminist scrutiny, the formality and universality of the moral principles brought to bear must not be rejected per se, because this would undermine the possibility for feminist philosophy of science to invoke universally valid principles (e.g. human rights) in its critique of patriarchal distortions. If universalist concepts of morality are rejected as "masculine," the goal of transforming the sciences must also be dropped. "[P]rocesses of research should be altered in such a way that they are no longer shaped by masculine ideas but are oriented toward equal consideration of both sexes."[144]

A central object of investigation for Nagl-Docekal is the feminist critique of the occidental concept of Logos. Here, theorists mainly refer to the thinking of Derrida and Lacan. This is examined in more detail in the presentation of Nagl-Docekal's philosophical engagement with theories of aesthetics.

---

[140] See NAGL-DOCEKAL 2004, 105; and in general NAGL-DOCEKAL 1982, 227–243.
[141] NAGL-DOCEKAL 2004, 105.
[142] See NAGL-DOCEKAL 2004, 105.
[143] NAGL-DOCEKAL 2004, 106.
[144] NAGL-DOCEKAL 2004, 109.

Using the example of Luce Irigaray, Nagl-Docekal illustrates the problems of an exaggerated logos-criticism. If Irigaray (and those thinkers who hold this logos-critical concept) narrows down the concept of reason to the rationality of the modern natural sciences, then criticism is justified; thinking that uses only quantifying methods in a very restricted way obviously has limits. Many areas of human experience (e.g. morality, aesthetics) cannot be grasped with a concept of reason restricted to rationality of purpose. But does the objection of phallogocentrism apply here? By criticizing European philosophy as masculine, as phallogocentric, while simultaneously criticizing the concept of reason, Irigaray exposes herself to a burden of proof. After all, Nagl-Docekal argues, European philosophy is not generally oriented to the narrow concept of rationality of the empirical sciences; on the contrary, one of the central tasks of philosophy is always to criticize the exclusive claim of this understanding of rationality. Irigaray operates with a juxtaposition of rationality versus irrationality – but from which viewpoint is she able to formulate her critique?[145] Another aspect of Irigaray's critique of reason consists in her critique of language: she maintains that the sentence itself has phallogocentric character and thus the syntax must be overthrown. But such an alternative language, as Irigaray strives for, represents something inconceivable, Nagl-Docekal underlines. Here, there is no clear differentiation between the content of language (which can be androcentric) and the formal instrumentality of language as such. Irigaray sees the content of the sciences as already inherent in the form of language. Criticism of the content, however, must be distinguished from the formal aspect. "The core problem with the methods of quantification in the humanities does not lie in the fact that these methods originate from a phallogocentric thrust, but that they do not offer the means to understand contexts of human action and aesthetic experience."[146] Based on her comprehensive critique of the concept of reason as masculine and phallogocentric, Irigaray's only remaining option is to relate the irrational to women. In doing so, however, she perpetuates the traditional patriarchal conception of the feminine. Injustice, discrimination, and marginalization

[145] See NAGL-DOCEKAL 2004, 163.
[146] NAGL-DOCEKAL 2004, 121.

of women cannot be denounced by referring to the alleged irrationality of women, but only by enabling women to participate equally in public discourses and deliberative processes, also in the sciences. Thus, a concept of autonomy is called for. "This means nothing less, however, than that issues which were addressed in the history of modern philosophy with the concept of practical reason need to be reconsidered."[147]

A further exploratory step focuses on the thesis that the concept of the subject is shaped by instrumental reason. What is criticized in feminist positions maintaining this thesis is a mode of action that is guided by universally valid principles. While Judith Butler's anti-essentialist motivation is convincing, "it remains to be asked how she takes up this motive in her philosophical reflections. In this regard, a number of difficulties emerge."[148] Butler defines the traditional idea of the subject through the concept of identity, claiming that identity is formed by means of a rejection of "whatever is interpreted as the other."[149] For Butler, subjectivation is a process of subjugation, and, as she elaborates, this subject is always already male. At this point, Butler's critique also challenges universalist conceptions of morality.[150] She argues that the innermost core of any universalist moral theory is cultural imperialism.[151] Here, Butler mingles different topics, however, and the task of philosophy is once again to introduce distinctions. Butler's critique is legitimate and plausible, where a group of people elevate their values to a norm that should be universally valid for all, but she fails to take into account that philosophical conceptions of universal norms, as elaborated, for instance, in discourse theory, "lie in quite the opposite direction."[152] Thus, we are dealing here with two incompatible concepts of universality.

"The procedural concept does not amount to a dogmatization of specific values. On the contrary, its character is strictly formal. The main point is that only norms which everyone – all those affected by a particular action – can consent to in an unconstrained discourse can

[147] NAGL-DOCEKAL 2004, 122.
[148] NAGL-DOCEKAL 2004, 123.
[149] See NAGL-DOCEKAL 2004, 123.
[150] For a more detailed view see below the subsection *Feminist Ethics*.
[151] See NAGL-DOCEKAL 2004, 123.
[152] NAGL-DOCEKAL 2004, 124.

claim validity."[153] In her critique, Butler fails to notice, "that the consensus framed by discourse theory is not supposed to be justified from an external perspective; whether or not a consensus has been achieved is also something everyone who is involved must agree on. Butler disregards this central point of discourse ethics since she does not go into the difference between formal and substantive universalism."[154] Butler disregards the fact that transcendental philosophy and discourse theory criticize ethnocentrism and imperialism in fundamental ways. Nagl-Docekal points out a performative self-contradiction: "Since Butler opposes the instrumental subject, the thought on which this critique is based, although not made explicit, must run as follows: 'No woman may be used as a mere instrument for the purposes of masculine self-realization, since all individuals must be recognized as persons and must also be respected in their differentness.' Without the background of this kind of norm, Butler's critique cannot be understood. This norm corresponds precisely to what Kant regards as the one formal law of practical reason, which he elaborates in his conception of the categorical imperative."[155]

Feminist critique cannot be accomplished without normative foundations. The problem with these feminist approaches is that they deny their own presuppositions of thought.

The relationship between emotion and reason is a further issue that Nagl-Docekal addresses. The task of feminist critique of reason lies in critically focusing on the fact, "that the concept of reason commonly has masculine connotations."[156] As Nagl-Docekal highlights, "the actual target of the critique is not the faculty of reason (in both its theoretical and practical use) per se; rather, it is the view that this faculty is part of the masculine character."[157]

In the case of reason versus feeling, the issue is "the well-known model of masculinity characterized by toughness and distance towards others. This model is part of the common idea of a gendered division

---

[153] NAGL-DOCEKAL 2004, 124.
[154] NAGL-DOCEKAL 2004, 124–125.
[155] NAGL-DOCEKAL 2004, 125.
[156] NAGL-DOCEKAL 2004, 127.
[157] NAGL-DOCEKAL 2004, 128.

of labor, according to which women are expected to cultivate emotional faculties, particularly empathy and care for others."[158] It is important to distinguish between two modes of opposition: "reason versus lack of judgment" and "reason versus emotion." Regarding the oppositional pair of reason versus lack of judgment, it was necessary to "reject ways of thinking that exclude women from rational discourses in science, politics, law, and so on; […]"; regarding the oppositional pair of reason versus emotion, "the problem lies in the construction of an identity that emphasizes strategic rationality at the cost of the cultivation of emotions. Addressing the second problem, the feminist critique points out that enforced toughness creates the behavioral basis of patriarchal domination."[159] If reason is connoted in this way, the meaning of the term reason is reduced to calculating rationality of purpose: rational calculation of one's own benefit and a calculating way of dealing with others – humans, living beings, or nature.

The separation of reason and emotion, as basis for the conception of gender characters, leads to a division of the human being into two parts. "The concept calling for gender-specific characters is *toto genere* outdated. A plausible alternative to the concept lies in the idea that men and women should have equal opportunities to individually unfold their emotional capacity as well as their ability to reason (which in this case is no longer restricted to instrumental rationality)."[160]

Nagl-Docekal states that many feminist works are marked by blurring and lack of differentiation on this point. In many feminist approaches to the critique of reason, the critique of rationality of purpose, of masculine toughness, is intermingled with a dismissal of the concept of reason *toto genere*. But philosophy has to examine the basis of "our capability for judgment in theoretical as well as practical matters. Moreover, it is part of such a philosophical inquiry to lay the theoretical foundations for a critique of dominant behavior." Thus, Nagl-Docekal pleads for a careful tracing of reductionism and for a more sophisticated debate.[161]

---

[158] NAGL-DOCEKAL 2004, 129.
[159] NAGL-DOCEKAL 2004, 129.
[160] NAGL-DOCEKAL 2004, 130.
[161] NAGL-DOCEKAL 2004, 130 and 132.

FEMINIST PERSPECTIVES ON PRACTICAL PHILOSOPHY

Nagl-Docekal sets innovative impulses in the field of feminist ethics, explores philosophical foundations for a non-essentialist politics, and takes a closer look at Kant's concept of autonomy in order to show that this one term has found six different modes of application in current feminist discourse and to mark the respective shortcomings.

Feminist Ethics

The widely differing theoretical approaches in the field of feminist ethics share one common intention: "The starting point is the basic feminist concern to overcome the exclusion and oppression of women, which still characterizes all areas of life."[162] One of the central tasks of feminist ethics is to examine the classical texts on moral philosophy to find out whether they ignore the problem of gender injustice, whether they are partly responsible for this problem, and/or whether they offer categories that feminist ethics can employ in developing principles for overcoming gender injustice.

The impetus for a debate, that continues to this day, was Carol Gilligan's research on a specifically feminine morality, in the context of which Gilligan critically examines Kohlberg's developmental psychological theories of moral development.[163] "Taking Gilligan's remarks together with those of other authors who assume a gender-based internal differentiation of morality, three pairs of determinations are apparent. According to these, women's moral perceptions, compared to those of men, are, first, context-sensitive and narrative, not concerned with generality and not abstract; second, oriented toward relationships and relatedness, not toward separation from others or the principle of non-interference; and third, guided by feelings such as empathy and benevo-

[162] NAGL-DOCEKAL 1993, 7–8: "Den Ausgangspunkt bildet das feministische Grundanliegen, die Ausgrenzung und Unterdrückung von Frauen, welche nach wie vor alle Lebensbereiche prägt, zu überwinden."
[163] See GILLIGAN 1982.

lence, not by reason."[164] Based on Gilligan's theses, concepts of care ethics have been further developed, provoking a wide-ranging controversy.

With regard to the core of Gilligan's theory – the distinction between care ethics and justice ethics – feminist ethics needs to sort out the different topics involved. Firstly, the empirical observation of the "moral division of labor between the sexes" which reflects the traditional gender stereotypes: men allegedly tend toward a justice perspective, women toward a care perspective. The question arises, however, whether this cliché warrants Gilligan's claim that two types of moral judgment need to be distinguished. Nagl-Docekal first emphasizes the necessity of differentiating between morality and traditional customs. "Whoever orients his actions to traditional views of customs is not *eo ipso* morally justified. More precisely, it may be morally necessary to violate 'good customs', e.g. if they foster a hierarchical gender order."[165] Secondly, the difference between morality and law must be taken seriously: Orientation to abstract principles and the principle of non-interference form the basis of liberal conceptions of law, but not of a moral attitude. "The debate about Kant [...] conducted in this context made it clear that the way Kant determines morality as distinct from law contains core elements of 'caring'. In his explanations of the categorical imperative, for example, Kant elaborates the indispensability of context sensitivity and benevolence."[166]

---

[164] NAGL-DOCEKAL 1998, 46: "Nimmt man die Ausführungen Gilligans zusammen mit denjenigen anderer Autorinnen und Autoren, die von einer geschlechtsbezogenen Binnendifferenzierung der Moral ausgehen, so zeichnen sich drei Paare von Bestimmungen ab. Demnach ist die moralische Wahrnehmung von Frauen, verglichen mit derjenigen der Männer, erstens kontextsensitiv und narrativ, nicht auf Allgemeingültigkeit bedacht und nicht abstrakt; zweitens an Beziehungen und Verbundenheit orientiert, nicht an Abgrenzung gegenüber anderen bzw. am Prinzip der Nichteinmischung; und drittens von Gefühlen wie Empathie und Wohlwollen geleitet, nicht vom Verstand."

[165] NAGL-DOCEKAL 2008, 299: "Wer sein Handeln an überlieferten Tugendauffassungen orientiert, ist nicht eo ipso moralisch gerechtfertigt. Genauer gesagt, kann es moralisch geboten sein, gegen die 'guten Sitten' zu verstoßen, z. B. wenn diese eine hierarchische Geschlechterordnung befördern."

[166] NAGL-DOCEKAL 2008, 299. "Die in diesem Kontext geführte Debatte um Kant [...] ließ deutlich werden, dass die Weise, wie Kant die Moral im Unterschied zum

Thirdly, the concept of a "feminine morality" – that presents caring action as superior to all other moral attitudes, and claims that a developed caring attitude would better solve global problems (e.g. climate change, environmental degradation, and nuclear armament) – needs close examination. The problem for feminist ethics is the linking of caring action with femininity. That there is a need for a caring attitude in human social interaction, in dealing with nature and also in the economic sphere is undisputed. The problem arises in the linking of moral competencies with gender. Does the linking of care and femininity propagate the "European-Western design of gender characters once again? Should the traditional 'feminine virtues' be valorized but otherwise preserved unquestioned as an ideal?"[167] Positions that link the moral capacity of the caring attitude to femininity overlook or ignore the fact that these moral competencies have been developed under conditions of oppression. Thus, these positions serve to legitimize the ongoing exploitation or self-exploitation of women.[168] Marilyn Friedman calls for a "de-moralization of gender," as she points out that there are two theses at work in the approaches outlined above: on the one hand, the concept of feminine morality that is concerned with gender difference, on the other hand, the claim that two different conceptions of morality need to be distinguished.[169]

The starting point of the representatives of a theory of the two morals is the thesis that every moral conflict can be solved in two ways: either in the mode of justice or in that of care (Gilligan illustrates this with the tilt picture of Jastrow, which can be seen either as a duck or as a rabbit). These juxtapositions contain fuzziness that exposes the untenability of this thesis of two morals.[170] Under the umbrella term of an ethics of justice, it is assumed that moral norms are based on a contract between autonomous and equally entitled partners, whereby individuals are not perceived in their individual particularity,

---

Recht bestimmt, Kernelemente von 'Fürsorglichkeit' enthält. In seinen Erläuterungen zum kategorischen Imperativ arbeitet Kant z. B. die Unverzichtbarkeit von Kontextsensitivität und Wohlwollen heraus."

[167] NAGL-DOCEKAL 1998, 54.

[168] See NAGL-DOCEKAL 1998, 54.

[169] See FRIEDMAN 1997.

[170] See NAGL-DOCEKAL 1998, 58.

but merely as "generalized others" (e.g. Seyla Benhabib) under the aspect of abstract rationality. In this context, moral autonomy is defined by a set of rigidly defined principles with a universal claim of validity, and the principle of non-interference is considered a key guideline. Here, Nagl-Docekal diagnoses a lack of differentiation between morality and law. In the context of law, contract theory provides the basic elements of a theory of the modern liberal state that must be discussed in the philosophy of law. Recognition of all human beings as equal in dignity, equality of the person before the law, equality as counterparties, equal treatment – all these are indispensable elements of the modern state, behind which one must not regress.[171] The tilting picture of duck and hare is misleading, because, strictly speaking, there is no dilemma, as Nagl-Docekal explains: "It may indeed be that one and the same problem can be solved differently, depending on whether it is conceived as a question of justice or morality, but these are precisely two different levels and not a doubling of morality."[172]

The blurring of boundaries between conceptions of justice and caring also marks the critique of universalism that is pivotal in approaches to feminine morality. Ethics of care, as its proponents emphasize, is context-sensitive, relationally oriented, and guided by feelings. As Nagl-Docekal enlighteningly shows, all of these provisions contain universalistic implications. The demand to take individuals seriously and to support them in their individual particularity and specific life situation has a universalistic character: All individuals are obliged to act in such a way that they take every other individual seriously in his or her individual particularity. Similarly, the idea of taking relationships seriously contains a universalistic element.

Further deficiencies need to be exposed with regard to views that understand morality in terms of spontaneous sympathy. Those who define ethics by relatedness alone exclude far too many people and remain reduced to small groups.[173] One case in point is attachment

---

[171] See NAGL-DOCEKAL 1998, 59.

[172] NAGL-DOCEKAL 1998, 60: "Zwar mag es in der Tat sein, daß sich ein und dasselbe Problem unterschiedlich lösen läßt, je nachdem, ob es als eine Frage der Gerechtigkeit oder der Moralität aufgefaßt wird, aber es handelt sich dabei eben um zwei verschiedene Ebenen und nicht um eine Verdoppelung von Moral."

[173] See NAGL-DOCEKAL 1998, 63.

theory that maintains that people learn the behaviors necessary for successful relationships in the parent-child relationship, and that a proper mindset is further developed as norms and rules are removed from these primary relational contexts and elevated to a more general level. According to this view, the caring perspective consists in transferring the ability to relate to others, acquired in early attachments, to someone who is otherwise a stranger. In order to accomplish this transfer, a process of generalization is necessary. "Abstraction must be made from the distinctive character of particular relationships, individual elements of behavior must be extracted and thought of in paradigmatic form."[174] As care ethics demands action guided by feelings, philosophical differentiation is called for. It is self-evident that empathy is needed in the context of moral action, but it is also a clear moral duty to critically examine one's feelings. Am I harming the one I want to act morally toward with my feelings? "To act morally requires critically reflecting on one's own emotional reactions rather than blindly surrendering to them. This raises the question of what categories can be used as a yardstick for such criticism. And since we are dealing here with the problem of how I should or may treat other people, general concepts such as 'person' or 'human dignity' must also probably be brought into view."[175] Another problem of reducing morality to an ethics of feeling is that the appeal to follow one's own feelings leads into radical relativization and radical isolation. How can morality here "be determined at all, except through a perspective of 'do what feels good'."[176]

At this point, Nagl-Docekal suggests a rereading of moral philosophical universalism. "The term 'feminist ethics' denotes a project

---

[174] NAGL-DOCEKAL 1998, 64: "Es muss vom unverwechselbaren Charakter bestimmter Beziehungen abstrahiert, einzelne Verhaltenselemente müssen herausgelöst und in paradigmatischer Form gedacht werden."

[175] NAGL-DOCEKAL 1998, 65: "Moralisch handeln zu wollen erfordert, die eigenen Gefühlsreaktionen kritisch zu reflektieren, anstatt sich ihnen blindlings zu überlassen. Damit stellt sich die Frage, welche Kategorien als Maßstab für eine solche Kritik herangezogen werden können. Und da es hier um das Problem geht, wie ich andere Menschen behandeln soll respektive darf, müssen wohl auch allgemeine Begriffe wie 'Person' oder 'Menschenwürde' ins Spiel gebracht werden."

[176] NAGL-DOCEKAL 1998, 66: "Wie kann Moral überhaupt noch bestimmt werden, es sei denn durch eine Perspektive des 'do what feels good'."

clearly distinct from theories of a specifically 'feminine morality'. The central concern here is to demonstrate that discrimination on the basis of gender is incompatible with principles of morality. This argument refers to the core moral philosophical thesis that the point of moral obligation is to respect human dignity – that is, to treat all individuals equally as persons, i.e., as individuals with the competence of self-determination. These provisions offer a tool for exposing how women are not taken seriously as persons in multiple contexts."[177] Nagl-Docekal proposes to bring the moral philosophical concept of universalism back into view, in contrast to the notion that emerged from liberalist legal theory. Kant's moral universalism does not consist in a set of narrow and rigidly defined principles, but at its center is a single formal rule, the categorical imperative (which is formal and not abstract). The ends-in-itself formula of the categorical imperative commands never to instrumentalize others merely as a means, and it commands supporting people as well as possible in their endeavor for achieving their self-chosen ends in a non-paternalistic way, which Kant develops in more detail in his doctrine of virtue under the concept of duties of love. In his concept of duties of love, it becomes fully apparent "that Kant [...] is developing an ethics of caring. Thus it becomes clear how the aporia of particularism versus universalism, which is so burdensome for the present discussion, could be resolved: The one formal rule is at once strictly universalistic – it applies equally to all human beings, after all – and radically individualizing."[178] This formal-universalist basic

---

[177] NAGL-DOCEKAL 2008, 299: "Der Begriff 'Feministische Ethik' bezeichnet ein von Theorien einer spezifisch 'weiblichen Moral' klar unterschiedenes Projekt. Zentrales Anliegen ist hier nachzuweisen, dass Diskriminierung auf Grund des Geschlechts mit Prinzipien der Moral unvereinbar ist. Angeknüpft wird dabei an die moralphilosophische Kernthese, dass die Pointe moralischer Verpflichtung in der Achtung der Menschenwürde liegt – darin also, dass alle Einzelnen in gleicher Weise als Personen, d. h. als Individuen mit der Kompetenz der Selbstbestimmung zu behandeln sind. Diese Bestimmung bietet ein Instrument, um aufzudecken, dass Frauen in vielfältigen Kontexten nicht als Personen ernst genommen werden."

[178] NAGL-DOCEKAL 1998, 69: "[...] daß Kant eine Ethik der Fürsorglichkeit entwickelt. Damit wird nun deutlich, wie die Aporie von Partikularismus und Universalismus, die für die gegenwärtige Diskussion so belastend ist, aufgelöst werden könnte: Die eine formale Regel ist zugleich strikt universalistisch – sie gilt ja für alle Menschen gleichermaßen – und radikal individualisierend."

demand offers a category of analysis that can be applied to the position of women in all areas of the contemporary life world. The task of feminist ethics is, first, to show, "in what ways women are not taken seriously as individuals"; second, to develop concrete maxims of behavior, against the background of the question, "how everyday behavior must be changed so that both women and men can find the sympathy and support of others on their self-chosen paths to happiness."[179] Nagl-Docekal sees a desideratum in the redefinition "of love compatible with the moral requirement of reciprocal respect."[180] Would it also be possible – under the ethical perspective of finitude, suffering, and death – to a philosophy of religion "that is not limited to a critical analysis of the gender-hierarchical configuration of traditional religious ideas?"[181]

A Feminist Approach to Political Philosophy

The term 'feminist politics' is used, on the one hand, in a very broad sense and on the other in a much narrower meaning. In the broader sense, the entire practical field is included. "It covers all feminist-motivated efforts to change given gender relations, including individual efforts in the education of children and on the level of personal relations."[182] In the narrow sense, it refers to endeavors in legal and economic decision making in public deliberative processes.

Feminist politics in a narrower sense opens questions about, for example, a feminist "we." Who belongs to the feminist "we": all women, particular groups, differentiated individuals? Who is entitled to speak

[179] NAGL-DOCEKAL 1998, 70: "[…] aufzudecken, in welcher Weise Frauen nicht als Individuen ernst genommen werden. Im antizipatorischen Teil geht es indessen um Ethik im Sinne konkreter Verhaltensmaximen. Den Ausgangspunkt bildet dabei die Frage, wie die alltäglichen Umgangsformen verändert werden müssen, damit sowohl Frauen als auch Männer auf ihren selbstgewählten Wegen zum Glück die Anteilnahme und Unterstützung anderer finden können."

[180] NAGL-DOCEKAL 2008, 300.

[181] NAGL-DOCEKAL 2008, 300.

[182] NAGL-DOCEKAL 2004, 133.

in the name of whom?[183] What is the problem that feminist politics is supposed to overcome? Is the problem the subordination of women in all areas of society? Or the lack of recognition of difference? Nagl-Docekal emphasizes that the outcome of these questions also influences the formulation of feminist objectives. For many women in the world, it is true that they are discriminated against, not only on the basis of belonging to the female gender, but also by (post-)colonial conditions, class antagonisms, ethnocentric and racist structures, on the basis of age, and so on. Women are not excluded as participants involved in discrimination against women.

While there exist different forms of discrimination, different mechanisms of oppression, it is important to focus on the core of the problem. "Crucial to feminist politics is the shared confrontation with disadvantage, not a shared 'female' identity. In the case of women, therefore, an end to discrimination means precisely the dissolution of their (imposed) group status. Central to this is the idea that 'gender' as a category of the social order is to be abandoned altogether."[184]

In order to create certain measures of emancipatory politics, it is necessary to examine exactly what mechanism of oppression is involved in each case. Nagl-Docekal draws on a differentiation by Iris Marion Young, who distinguishes five different forms of oppression: exploitation, marginalization, powerlessness, cultural imperialism, and violence. Women, as Young argues, suffer from all five forms of oppression.[185] The task of philosophy is to differentiate and disentangle these intertwined aspects.

Feminist politics has to negotiate as to where concrete measures must be decided, e.g. with regard to state subsidies for the targeted support of women's education. Such negotiations are about feminist concerns – but, and this is very important: the striving to overcome gender injustice and the commitment to gender justice must not be considered "a policy

---

[183] See NAGL-DOCEKAL 2004, 134.

[184] NAGL-DOCEKAL 2008, 301: "Ausschlaggebend für feministische Politik ist die geteilte Konfrontation mit Benachteiligung, nicht eine gemeinsame, 'weibliche' Identität. Im Falle der Frauen bedeutet daher ein Ende von Diskriminierung gerade die Auflösung ihres (aufoktroyierten) Gruppenstatus. Zentral ist der Gedanke, dass 'Geschlecht' als Kategorie der sozialen Ordnung zu verabschieden ist."

[185] See YOUNG 1990.

oriented to particular interests and compromises" – for two reasons. Firstly, discrimination is a problem that cannot be negotiated in the mode of more or less (more or less justice), for this would be cynical. Secondly, gender discrimination is an injustice that affects not only those directly affected, but the whole society. Here, feminist engagement leads beyond law to the moral foundations of law. Gender justice is a fundamental right. "Contemporary debate on the philosophy of law acknowledges that it is inadmissible to negotiate or vote on whether or not fundamental rights are granted to individuals. The state does not provide this kind of rights; only their concrete implementation requires legislative action."[186] In Kant's sense, as Nagl-Docekal highlights: "I have already always had it through the fact that I am a human being (i.e., that I have the competency for self-determination)."[187]

Two guidelines arise from the categorical imperative with regard to the topic of discrimination: Firstly, every person has to ask themselves to what extent they contribute to the disrespect and oppression of women – not only men have to ask themselves this question.[188] "I must examine who will be affected by the action I have in mind, and whether or not those individuals will be respected in the way I intend to treat them, as persons who themselves have the competency to decide and to act."[189] Secondly, the categorical imperative implies the duty to respect my own human dignity as well. "[N]ot only that we are not allowed to diminish the freedom of others without good reasons. We are obliged to help others as far as possible (and compatible with the moral imperative) where they are unable to realize their self-chosen ends on their own."[190] Kant explains this in a more detailed way in his theory of duties of love. Furthermore, for those affected by discrimination, there is a duty to resist: "[I]t is morally imperative to object to discrimination against women on account of their sex."[191]

The human right is not given to me by the state to which I belong, but it always comes to me inherently due to the fact that I am a human

---

[186] NAGL-DOCEKAL 2004, 135.
[187] NAGL-DOCEKAL 2004, 140.
[188] See NAGL-DOCEKAL 2004, 139.
[189] NAGL-DOCEKAL 2004, 136.
[190] NAGL-DOCEKAL 2004, 137.
[191] NAGL-DOCEKAL 2004, 141.

being, i.e. that I have the competence for self-determination. "It is the experience that we – from the perspective of the first person – have the freedom to take a position toward given conditions generated by nature and history […]. If we are impeded without good reason from making a free decision in that sense, we suffer an injury."[192] By being a person, I have the right to demand that others respect me, i.e., the right that I obligate others to respect me as a person. The concept of person, as Nagl-Docekal highlights, "belongs to the inalienable foundations of feminist political theory."[193]

Since, as Kant notes, "out of such crooked wood as the human being is made, nothing entirely straight can be fabricated,"[194] from the categorical imperative arises the duty to enter "in such a precinct as the civil union is,"[195] i.e., we are morally obligated, to establish just legal structures in the sense of positively stated law. "How do we have to conceive the state so that it provides the legal preconditions for all individuals to be respected in the same manner as human beings?"[196]

One central component of feminist theory is the concept of equality. It is important to distinguish between "sameness" and "equality." The philosophical concept of equality concerns a matter of formal equality, as it is based on what Kant formulates in the categorical imperative: the duty to respect the personal dignity of every human being everywhere in the world, at all times. This implies the duty to respect all human beings as persons who set their own purposes, to recognize every human being as a person endowed with the competence to act. "If we are prevented from freely choosing in this way without good reason, it means that we suffer a violation. We are curtailed in our very own competence, in the worst case deprived of it altogether, i.e., we are not taken seriously as human beings."[197]

However, the instrument of formal equality is not a sufficient means for implementing feminist aims; achieving equality *de jure* does not necessarily mean to achieve it *de facto*. Therefore it proves necessary to

---

[192] NAGL-DOCEKAL 2004, 136.
[193] NAGL-DOCEKAL 2004, 138.
[194] KANT 2014, 113; see KANT 1923, 23.
[195] KANT 2014, 112; see KANT 1923, 22.
[196] NAGL-DOCEKAL 2004, 141.
[197] NAGL-DOCEKAL 2004, 181.

introduce special programs for the advancement of women: state social and welfare programs, quota regulation, reverse discrimination for those areas that are still the domain of men.[198] Such programs are most important, because otherwise "only those women can make use of the opportunities given *de jure* also *de facto*, whose living conditions are largely aligned (in the sense of sameness) with those of men."[199] "Gender mainstreaming," as a principle of EU law, demands that attention must be paid to gender symmetry in the workplace and the labor market.

Feminist political philosophy also has to examine the difference, as well as the relation, between public and private spheres. The world of work and the family are closely interwoven. "If social relations in the private sphere are characterized in an undifferentiated way by the term 'love', it obscures the fact that we are dealing with multiple distribution structures – in addition to the multiplicity of emotional ties, the family is a place of the distribution of money and other goods, of decision-making authority, freedom and work [...]."[200] What is also needed is a redefinition of the concepts of "work" and "labor."

Feminist political philosophy would be well advised to reformulate contract theory. To begin with, it is necessary to investigate where the source of given injustices lies. The problem often resides not necessarily in the laws themselves, but is generated through the application of the laws. Turning to the laws themselves, a distinction must be made between problems arising from the formulations of the laws and

[198] See NAGL-DOCEKAL 2004, 192.

[199] NAGL-DOCEKAL 2008, 301: "Einen Schlüsselbegriff bildet 'Gleichheit', wobei freilich die unterschiedlichen Bedeutungen zu beachten sind, die im Englischen durch zwei spezifische Termini ausgedrückt werden: 'equality' und 'sameness'. Die Tatsache, dass eine formalrechtliche Gleichstellung (equal rights) nicht ausreicht, um alle bestehenden Geschlechterasymmetrien zu eliminieren, wurde daraus erklärt, dass nur diejenigen Frauen von den de jure gegebenen Möglichkeiten auch de facto Gebrauch machen können, deren Lebensumstände denen der Männer weitgehend angeglichen (im Sinne von sameness) sind."

[200] NAGL-DOCEKAL 2008, 301: "Werden die sozialen Beziehungen in der Privatsphäre undifferenziert durch den Begriff 'Liebe' charakterisiert, so wird verschleiert, dass es sich um multiple Verteilungsstrukturen handelt – neben der Vielfältigkeit emotioneller Bindungen ist die Familie ein Ort der Distribution von Geld und Gütern, von Entscheidungskompetenz, Freizeit und Arbeit [...]."

those arising from the basic assumptions of state theory.[201] Common feminist ways of challenging the foundations of legal theory address this core issue: Does the modern state inherently have a masculine character in its foundations? From this perspective, the conception of the social contract moves to the center of attention.[202] Nagl-Docekal seeks to demonstrate that there is no plausible reason for feminist legal theory to reject the concept of the contract *toto genere*. "I will show that feminist legal theory is well advised if it does not reject the social contract approach in toto but reformulates it from the viewpoint of justice between the sexes."[203]

Feminist demand for the reconceptualization of contract theory addresses central concerns, such as the demand that women must be assured their civil, political, and social rights to the fullest extent. A rethinking of the domestic sphere is indispensable: for example, by evaluating child-rearing as work it becomes evident that regulations calling for the sharing of domestic work between partners are urgently needed. Confronting those authors who suggest a complete dismissal of contract theory, Nagl-Docekal underscores that the core elements of the contract conception do not logically imply the subordination of certain persons.[204] Rather, the point of the contract theory lies precisely in the concern that all individuals must have the same opportunity to follow their particular path in life and to form groups of their own choosing. In short, it would be a serious misunderstanding to interpret the counter-concepts "autonomy" and "heteronomy" in the sense that the self-determination of some necessarily presupposes the heteronomy of others. In view of the concern to formulate feminist theory as precisely as possible, it seems downright disastrous that a vagueness on this point has become so widespread in the context of postmodern approaches to political theory.[205]

It is important to distinguish the concepts of citizen as *citoyen* and bourgeois: the classics of contract theories are shaped patriarchally,

---

[201] See NAGL-DOCEKAL 2004, 152.
[202] See NAGL-DOCEKAL 2004, 156.
[203] NAGL-DOCEKAL 2004, 157.
[204] See NAGL-DOCEKAL 2004, 164.
[205] See NAGL-DOCEKAL 2004, 165.

because notions of the bourgeoisie have been incorporated into contract theory. "Obviously those theorems of the classics, which deny women the right to self-determination to a great degree, correspond with the normative ideas of the bourgeoisie of the eighteenth century and also with the economic realities of bourgeois society."[206] This leads to inconsistencies within contract theory, which must now be critically addressed by feminist theorists. It is important to consider that there exists no indissoluble link between the contract among equal citizens and gender hierarchy. On the contrary, patriarchal notions run counter to the core of contractualist thought. Once this disentanglement has been accomplished, the way opens to examine the relevance of contract thought to a feminist-motivated conception of citizenship.

Some feminist authors criticize Rawls' main work *A Theory of Justice*, focusing on the conception of the original position. "According to them, Rawls' argument that the contract partners have to deliberate under a 'veil of ignorance' when making decisions on fundamental principles of justice leads inevitably to the well-known problem of gender blindness."[207] But is this a convincing criticism? Nagl-Docekal again suggests a differentiation at this point.

One should be cautious in making an overly hasty identification of the veil of ignorance with gender blindness. In Rawl's theory, the individual contracting parties are only denied the view of how they themselves will be positioned in the community whose normative regulation is at issue. "Otherwise, the individuals are quite aware of the problems that living together typically entails, including possible structural asymmetries. Therein lies the point of the whole hypothetical construction."[208] The contracting parties are well aware of the forms of injustice and possibilities of injury that exist in social coexistence, but they do not know, behind the veil of ignorance, what position they themselves will hold in the state to be constituted. Nagl-Docekal continues: "Accordingly, everybody deliberating in the original position must tackle the question that starts as follows: Assume I am an individual belonging to the female sex. Which principles would appear to

[206] NAGL-DOCEKAL 2004, 166.
[207] NAGL-DOCEKAL 2004, 167.
[208] NAGL-DOCEKAL 2004, 167.

me in this condition appropriate as a foundation for an order of the community? With this in mind, the problem of gender blindness can be addressed more precisely. […] It would be counterproductive as well as erroneous to raise the reproach of gender blindness in regard to the veil of ignorance, since it is through this part of Rawls' conception that all single contract partners can take discrimination seriously as a problem of justice."[209]

What is the potential of contract theory for feminist politics? Referring to the recent debate in legal theory that has shown "that the principle of equality, central to contract theory, also implies that underprivileged individuals and groups have to be promoted specifically to ensure substantial as well as formal equality of opportunity," Nagl-Docekal notes, "I am emphasizing this aspect of contract theory because it provides a sound way of reasoning for feminist politics."[210] In the general public discourse, massive critique is being articulated in relation to the terms "reverse discrimination" and "recognition of difference." Nagl-Docekal points out the importance of a different line of argument: "On the basis of contract theory, however, a different path of argumentation opens up. Now it can be shown that such plans do not diverge from the principle of equal treatment."[211]

A political theory that is interested in overcoming discrimination would be well advised to use the tools provided by contract theory. "But contract theory can only provide the necessary foundations if the asymmetries defined by gender or sexual orientation are included in the reflections of the individual who is deliberating in the original position. Therefore, from a feminist perspective, we must strive for a reformulation of contract theory."[212]

---

[209] NAGL-DOCEKAL 2004, 169.
[210] NAGL-DOCEKAL 2004, 169.
[211] NAGL-DOCEKAL 2004, 170.
[212] NAGL-DOCEKAL 2004, 170.

Rereading Kant's Concept of Autonomy as a Feminist

The following concluding section of this Introduction comprises a concise summary of Nagl-Docekal's critical discussion of feminist references to Kant's notion of autonomy and to what is called the "Kantian Approach."[213]

Nagl-Docekal has first problematized the reduction of the concept of autonomy to self-determination and the omission or ignorance of the notion of self-legislation in her essay "Autonomy between self-determination and self-legislation" in 2002.[214] She argues, e.g., that the restricted definition of autonomy in terms of self-determination fails to take adequately into account the dependence of human beings on care and help from others. Discussing this problem, she brings into view another understanding of the term autonomy, which lies in the realm of morality, as elaborated by Kant in his definition of autonomy as self-legislation.[215]

She first addresses widely shared objections to "Kantian" notions of autonomy raised by feminist authors. In doing so, she also discusses alternative feminist conceptions of autonomy proposed by feminist authors, e.g. the concept of a "relational autonomy." In a second step, Nagl-Docekal details six distinct meanings of the term "autonomy," explaining how these different notions are applied in moral philosophy, justice theory, social theory, and moral psychology. She claims that a distinction must also be made between Kant's original theory and what is called the "Kantian" tradition in the feminist debates cited. In a third step, Nagl-Docekal explains Kant's definition of autonomy as self-legislation, to illustrate to what extent his conception can be made fruitful for feminist theorizing.

Contemporary feminist critics interpret Kant's concept of autonomy as impartial, impersonal, universal, and principle based, as already mentioned above. The main point of critique is that Kant's ethics ignores human relationships, the particularity of the individual, and private domains of life (e.g. sexuality, family, and friendship). Some theorists

---

[213] See NAGL-DOCEKAL 2022.
[214] See NAGL-DOCEKAL 2002.
[215] See NAGL-DOCEKAL 2002, 298–300.

challenge the so-called metaphysical idea of atomistic personhood.[216] It is relevant to emphasize that in feminist critiques, references are made to Kant on the one hand and "Kantian ethical tradition" on the other. "It is important to note these two distinct points of reference and to bear in mind the question whether one and the same critical account may indeed cover both."[217]

A different trend in the feminist critique of the concept of autonomy, influenced by postmodern theories following Nietzsche, Freud, and Foucault, rejects the strong emphasis on free will in Kant's moral theory. "[T]hey are unified in the charge 'that defenders of autonomy still cling to the Cartesian idea that consciousness can be transparently self-aware or to the Kantian view of persons as rational self-legislators', and consider this view to be 'complicit with structures of domination, in particular with the suppression of others – women, colonial subjects, blacks, minority groups – who are deemed incapable of achieving rational self-mastery'."[218] Central elements of these rejections of Kant's concept of autonomy are still defended today, and are also present in feminist bioethics. Furthermore, it is worth noting that many critics of the concept of autonomy refer to findings of moral psychology rather than philosophy. As Nagl-Docekal demonstrates, many of these critiques are based on blatant misinterpretations of Kant's practical philosophy that seem to be mostly due to a refusal of a thorough reading of Kant's works. By contrast, support for feminist rereadings of Kant's practical philosophy that are avoiding overly sweeping dismissive comments is provided, for instance by "research published by Marcia Baron, Barbara Herman, Onora O'Neill, Pauline Kleingeld and Christine M. Korsgaard."[219]

Authors who represent the current, lively discussion on post-humanist positions reject Kant's concept of autonomy *toto genere*. "Post-humanism" is "an umbrella term that is commonly defined with reference to other schools of thought such as 'trans-humanism', 'anti-humanism' and 'meta-humanism'. The term 'feminist post-humanism'

[216] See NAGL-DOCEKAL 2022, 3 [unpublished manuscript, forthcoming].
[217] NAGL-DOCEKAL 2022, 2.
[218] NAGL-DOCEKAL 2022, 4, with reference to MACKENZIE & STOLJAR 2000, 3.
[219] See NAGL-DOCEKAL 2022, 4.

also covers a broad range of theories that include, for instance, 'new materialisms'. One shared claim concerns the traditional understanding of 'the human', that is challenged for promoting 'anthropocentric ideals of the human as uniquely sovereign over the world and binary thinking that separates nature from culture, human from animal, the animate from the inanimate, subject from object, self from environment, the living from nonliving."[220] From this perspective, Kant's practical philosophy is blamed for defending "transcendental, ahistorical, cross-cultural, abstract laws," which would "define the possibilities of experience."[221] All these theories dismiss the "liberal subject" in general, as Nagl-Docekal highlights. Examining this approach, she focuses on central theses held by Karen Barad and Rosi Braidotti.

In humanist theories, Barad argues, the capacity of intelligence presupposes an agent competent to act; intelligence and agency are tied back to a subject of action. Consequently, intelligence would be considered a specifically human capacity, as maintained in the humanist tradition. Against this tradition, Barad sets her own theoretical considerations by arguing that intelligence is an ontological competence of the world itself, the world acts in intelligent articulations. Nature, technical artefacts, and the world itself are assumed to be capable of responsible agency. There is also an intelligent relationship of the world to itself. Action is understood by Barad as efficacy, and this is not limited to humans, there are also non-human agents.

In the context of a posthumanist conception of ethics, Barad rejects the humanist idea of an autonomous subject, endowed with free will, who assumes the consequences of his or her own actions in a responsible attitude. In Barad's view, the human being is part of the dynamics of the world-body-space, therefore the human being is not exclusively morally or legally responsible. Ethicality is part of the fabric of the world. But, as Nagl-Docekal notes, "the question arises which criteria might allow us to distinguish 'ethics' and 'responsibility' from any other 'self-articulation' of the material world. Specific issues arise with regard to feminism. While Barad clearly shares the rejection of Enlightenment conceptions of universal principles, she does not show

[220] NAGL-DOCEKAL 2022, 6.
[221] NAGL-DOCEKAL 2022, 7.

how women who are confronted, in concrete situations, with discrimination, oppression and violence, and who strive to overcome given gender hierarchies, might find a satisfactory moral foundation for their cause in the claim that accountability must not be attributed specifically to humans."[222]

In a very lucid fashion, Nagl-Docekal refers to Leibniz, who, in *Monadology*, places humans in interrelations among all the other elements of the universe. Leibniz differentiates, however, between various competences, distinguishing between unconscious perceptions shared by all elements of the universe, perceptions shared by all living creatures, and apperceptions, of which only human beings are capable. A rereading of Leibniz would be advisable in light of the current debate in posthumanist theory.[223]

Braidotti calls for a new concept of human beings beyond "the human."[224] Her line of argument takes issue with the dangers which accompany unrestrained capitalism; everything is commodified: animals are manipulated, mistreated, and tortured, women and children are victims of human trafficking and are commodified for profit, people are exploited, tortured, and dehumanized as sexualized and racialized others within the framework of neoliberal capitalism. With her concept of posthumanism, Braidotti searches for a way out of this problem and asks: Should we not abandon the old concept of "the human" to thoroughly overcome it, in order to be able to solve these current world political problems? Isn't it a matter of thinking post-anthropocentrically to make it comprehensible that human beings are part of nature and that we are connected to everything organic and anorganic, but also to technological artefacts in a way that they must not be exploited? Braidotti asks: What comes after the anthropocentric subject? "In my view, the common denominator for the posthuman condition is an assumption about the vital, self-organizing and yet non-naturalistic structure of living matter itself. This nature-culture-continuum is the

---

[222] NAGL-DOCEKAL 2022, 8.
[223] See NAGL-DOCEKAL 2022, 8, n. 40. In particular, Nagl-Docekal refers to *Monadologie* §§ 14–17.
[224] See BRAIDOTTI 2013.

shared starting point for my take on posthuman theory."[225] In this manner, Braidotti develops a "nature-culture-continuum" to confront political distortions such as colonialism, which has produced the perception of "sexualized and racialized others." In her understanding, the "humanist human" elaborated in the concept of Eurocentric transcendental reason is the source of all these abuses of power. But, this question has to be addressed to Braidotti: Do we have to invent new theories such as "zoe-egalitarianism," to speak of the intelligent flesh, or unfold a vitalistic materialism to solve today's world political problems?

In terms of social relations, Braidotti calls for a new way of combining ethical values with the well-being of an expanded sense of community, that is, a grounded, partial form of accountability based on a strong sense of collectivity and relationship. Discussing her approach, Nagl-Docekal notes that "core questions concerning the notion of 'ethical values' remain open here. For instance, what is supposed to happen in the event of clashes between communities defending different 'locally situated micro-universalist claims'? Does this approach imply, albeit in a tacit manner, an appeal to a competence of reasonable moral argument shared by humans across the globe?"[226]

Six different notions of autonomy[227]

In her current research, Nagl-Docekal identifies six different ways of using the term autonomy in feminist debates, suggesting that these differences call for careful examination. She distinguishes the following notions: 1. Moral autonomy as self-legislation, as explained in Kant's conception of the categorical imperative; 2. The autonomy of the contract parties assembled under the veil of ignorance, as explained by Rawls; 3. Moral autonomy in the sense of the procedural postmetaphysical conception; 4. Rational autonomy, as the capability of individuals to design their lives themselves according to their preferences in order to

[225] BRAIDOTTI 2013, 2.
[226] NAGL-DOCEKAL 2022, 9.
[227] See NAGL-DOCEKAL 2022, 9.

lead a successful life; 5. Autonomy as masculine identity in traditional asymmetrical gender relations; 6. *Homo economicus*, conceived as egoistically following one's own interests of success.[228] It is obvious that a well-founded reference to Kant is not at all possible, without carefully distinguishing the different notions listed above, as Nagl-Docekal underlines.

1. Kant clearly and distinctly differentiates the spheres of law and morality, as he elaborates his studies on philosophy of law and philosophy of morality. It is only on the basis of this distinction that the relations between the two spheres can be analyzed consistently, Nagl-Docekal shows.

2. Autonomy in the sense of the decision making of the parties to the ideal contract, as the basis for the constitutional state, is currently discussed mainly with reference to John Rawls. While Rawls repeatedly emphasizes that his concept of justice as fairness is based on Kant's theory of contract, his theory has often been interpreted as a "Kantian" approach to morality.

3. In the field of moral philosophy, Rawls interprets Kant's theory in a way that declares obsolete the central aspect of autonomy as self-legislation. As he claims that his concept of the ideal contract provides a procedural interpretation of Kant's concept of autonomy and the categorical imperative, he eliminates the distinction between law and morality, which is, however, indispensable for Kant.[229] Jürgen Habermas draws on Rawls in his discourse-theoretical theory of morality and autonomy that seeks to elaborate a "post-metaphysical" approach. He argues that, in the absence of metaphysical principles, moral principles can only be justified in a process of reciprocal rational argumentation.

4. In debates on political liberalism, autonomy is often understood as individual freedom of choice. In this context, it is relevant to keep in mind that Rawls ascribes two basic capacities to the moral person, namely, to have an individual life design and a sense of justice. Based on this, Rawls develops the concepts of "rational" and "reason" and links them to "good" and "just." The term "rational autonomy" means the ability to form, revise, and realize one's individual conception of

---

[228] See NAGL-DOCEKAL 2022, 9.
[229] See NAGL-DOCEKAL 2022, 11.

the good life.[230] The term "reasonable" refers to the shared interest of citizens to cooperate under fair conditions and articulates an idea of reciprocity and mutuality. It draws on Kant's considerations of the protective enclosure of the constitutional state. In Kant's sense, the original contract is the basis for a civil legal constitution, which gives the principles for the coercive laws under which each person is protected from damaging encroachments by others. Law creates that free space in which each person can freely pursue his or her own ideas of a successful life without harming others in the course of doing so. Liberal theory, including Kant's theory of the constitutional state, by distinguishing the two spheres of the good and the just, is able to provide a basis for people to realize both their respective individual conceptions of the good life, of happiness, and also to pursue shared values and enduring relationships.

5. Authors who take issue with Kant's concept of autonomy, often refer to the understanding of autonomy in terms of masculine identity that is elaborated in the psychoanalytical and developmental psychological context, as has already been shown. However, a thorough reading of Kant's practical philosophy leads to the conclusion that his concept of autonomy is not inextricably entangled with an idea of masculine character, as has been demonstrated by Nagl-Docekal.

6. Authors who criticize the harmful effects of neoliberal market economy and postcolonial conditions sometimes refer to the construct of a "Kantian agent" when they criticize the *homo oeconomicus* (acting merely for maximization of profit). In doing so, they ignore the careful distinction in Kant's maxim ethics, where he clearly distinguishes the hypothetical (technical) principles (level of rationality) and the moral law (level of reason).[231]

Only by considering these distinctions does it make sense to refer to Kant's concept of autonomy from a feminist perspective. First of all, it is important to consider that a rereading of contract theory provides a helpful tool to analyze and reject injustice, oppression, and exploitation on the grounds of being female or LGBTIQ. With respect to Rawls' idea of the veil of ignorance, it should be noted that its point

---

[230] See NAGL-DOCEKAL 2022, 12.
[231] See NAGL-DOCEKAL 2022, 13.

is "to specify basic principles for a constitution that proves truly universal by applying to all citizens on equal terms, regardless of their social standing, gender, race, ethnicity, sexual orientation, etc."[232] Those who criticize contract theory because it defines parties in the original position as free of particular needs and interests, and who misunderstand this theory as a psychological conception of humans disconnected from their needs, have completely missed its point. Rawls conceives of the original position as a 'hypothetical situation' whose goal is to facilitate a fair process, through which just and equitable constitutional principles can be arrived at.[233] Furthermore, the objection that blames contract theory for operating with a notion of atomistically isolated individuals is also untenable, because the contracting parties are conceived as persons who come together with the shared goal of developing the foundations of a just state. The social contract is based on a union of all citizens, for the common goal that they all share.

Likewise, regarding the objection that challenges contract theory for promoting a concept of individualism, it is advisable to proceed in a differentiated way. It is certainly imperative to reject an understanding of individualism that envisions individuals as merely striving for their own interests, for the achievement of their own success, without regard for other people. This is, as Jürgen Habermas has clearly evinced, a very common idea of individuality today. From a feminist perspective, there are good reasons to reject such an idea of individualism. But, and this is essential to keep in mind, contract theory does not operate with a concept of individuality narrowed in this sense. The point of contract theory is rather to create a protective force, i.e., a framework of basic principles which enables individuals to live lives of freedom, according to their own ideas of happy forms of life that may include conceptions of close communities.

Secondly, as regards the topic of morality, it is important for a feminist approach to be cautious where the categorical imperative is conceived in the logic of the procedural conception of the contract. Here Nagl-Docekal again refers to Kant's distinction between law and morality. In the deliberative process, only rules for the external coex-

[232] NAGL-DOCEKAL 2022, 14.
[233] See NAGL-DOCEKAL 2022, 14.

istence of people can be laid down; such rules concern our "external freedom." Kant contends, however, that every action can be viewed from two different angles – we need to distinguish between the external perspective and the internal one, i.e. the perspective of the first person. The point of his conception of "internal freedom" is this: only I can decide for myself the ends of my action, only I can know what is the motive and the aim of my action. Kant's concept of the categorical imperative addresses this internal perspective.[234]

One important implication of the moral law concerns consideration for those persons who are affected by my action: I am obligated to always ask myself how the persons affected by my action are faring. This also means that, with regard to human interaction, we have to become increasingly sensitive to the manifold dimensions of violation that may occur. In this sense, it is important to enter into conversations and to actively listen to each other, as Nagl-Docekal emphasizes.

What does self-legislation mean in Kant's sense? Nagl-Docekal notes the importance of Kant's distinction between rationality and reason. Reason is the competence of principles.[235] Pure reason is practical for itself and gives to every human being the universal moral law. As the competence of practical reason is shared by all humans, it does not mean an arbitrary, individualized form of self-regulation. The moral law expresses nothing more than the autonomy of pure practical reason, i.e. freedom. In this sense, autonomy is the basis of human dignity. As Kant expresses in one of the formulations of the categorical imperative: "So act that you use humanity, whether in your own person or in the person of any other, always at the same time as an end, never merely as a means."[236] We have the obligation to treat every human being as a person, and this also applies to "every action toward oneself." To implement this demand of the categorical imperative in our lives requires a lifelong practice of virtue. Humans must train themselves to act virtuously.

Based on the categorical imperative, my moral responsibility is to ensure that others do not instrumentalize me as a thing, but respect and

---

[234] See NAGL-DOCEKAL 2022.
[235] See NAGL-DOCEKAL 2022, 17.
[236] KANT 1998, 38; KANT 1911, 429. See also NAGL-DOCEKAL 2022, 17.

esteem me as an end in myself. “Do not make yourself a mere means for others but be at the same time an end for them.”[237] In this manner, moral philosophy provides feminist political theory with a foundation for the moral justification of resistance against all relations of exploitation, oppression, instrumentalization, and violence. Furthermore, the categorical imperative implies duties of love to others, in the sense of an active practical beneficence, which I make the welfare of others my end. This requires supporting other people in non-paternalistic ways. “It is impossible that I can act kindly toward others […] by force of my idea of happiness, but only by studying his ideals of welfare […].”[238] Fostering the well-being of others also means being sensitive to the specific needs of other humans, which requires that we have to learn to listen to each other. “We must learn to listen if we intend to cultivate a moral disposition.”[239] But whose voice do we hear when we listen? It is important that people find it possible to speak for themselves, to express their own fears, plans, and suffering, without fear of repression. “Thus there is a need for a global legal framework that protects the equal rights of everybody to express his/her opinion in an unrestricted manner.”[240]

Following Kant’s understanding, Nagl-Docekal emphasizes very clearly, that people would not be able to fully realize the implementation of the demand of the categorical imperative if they were left alone with this duty. Although the demand of the categorical imperative is addressed to each individual, and although each person can only make moral decisions on their own, people need human communities of solidarity to strengthen each other in moral terms, to educate and to develop a culture of sincerity. Therefore, we are obligated by the categorical imperative to become members of a worldwide ethical community. Kant’s differentiation between ethical and political state is important here. Based on the definition of the ethical state as a worldwide community “under the law of virtue,” he explains that the duty to establish such a state concerns humanity as a whole. The task is that people

---

[237] NAGL-DOCEKAL 2022, 18.
[238] KANT 1886, 273; see KANT 1907, 454.
[239] NAGL-DOCEKAL 2022, 23.
[240] NAGL-DOCEKAL 2022, 23.

support each other in moral self-education. These reflections contain valuable insights that may be appropriated in a feminist theory of worldwide solidarity. The task is that people support each other in moral self-education. Moreover, considering that Kant regards his conception of the ethical community as an adequate philosophical assessment of what a "church" is all about, we find that this conception lends itself as a linking point for a feminist philosophy of religion.

Herta Nagl-Docekal's pioneering differentiations[241] have relevance for the controversy about "moral-theoretical universalism," the debate which focuses on the dyad abstract universalism versus context sensitivity. She counters the long-lived criticism (since Hegel's objection to an abstract universalism) of Kant's moral philosophy with the argument, that the categorical imperative is formal and precisely not abstract, because the categorical imperative has no specific content, whereas abstract rules formulate specific instructions. In Kant's moral philosophy, as she reaffirms, the "maxim" is the starting point: maxims are our subjective principles of action, which we have to examine, if they would pass the test on the bare formula of the categorical imperative. The one and only formal law provides the critical yardstick, which can claim validity in every situation. The term "universalism" refers to the moral duty to question if everyone who is affected by my actions could agree with them. Crucially, the concept of the categorical imperative also opens a space for self-critique, for the possibility to correct decisions already made, inasmuch as I can judge my choices in hindsight. This reading demonstrates that Kant's moral philosophy indeed relates to specific, concrete circumstances and the daily living-conditions of individuals. The formula of humanity specifies this one moral law in terms of respect for the dignity of every human being. This also implies taking each person seriously in their individual particularity, which means not seeing others merely as a generalized "Other." Thus, it turns out that this one formal rule is, on the one hand, strictly universalistic and at the same time radically individualizing.[242]

[241] See BUCHHAMMER 2019, 13–14.
[242] See NAGL-DOCEKAL 1998, 69–70.

In her essay "Film als Tugendlehre?" (2016) Nagl-Docekal insists on the importance of Kant's moral philosophy in critical examination of shortcomings currently marking the common understanding of morality. "On the one hand, we are inclined to listen to the prevailing view, according to which our moral obligation is satisfied if we adhere to the 'golden rule' – that is to say that it is crucial not to hurt anyone without good reason or to interfere with their self-determination, while all forms of support and charity granted to others are to be regarded as voluntary actions, above and beyond one's own moral obligation. We are even more familiar with this 'common sense' in its more moderate form, according to which a certain degree of assistance – not only within one's immediate personal sphere, but also vis-à-vis 'distant strangers' – is quite commendable, while altruism going beyond this degree is to be regarded as excessive."[243]

In the recent philosophical debate a way of thinking has developed, in which the term "supererogatory" is used to characterize a mode of action which goes beyond what is considered the generally binding duty – as a kind of voluntary moral excellence. Saints and heroes are often used as paradigms of such actions, as Nagl-Docekal explains.[244] Based on Kant's *Doctrine of Virtue*, Nagl-Docekal reveals the limited understanding of morality in the conception of the supererogatory, which, in fact, does not do justice to the reflected experience of lived human morality. Kant stresses that the idea of a richer, more encompassing morality has always been perceived in the human soul: a more encompassing form of morality "is really an obscurely thought metaphysics that is inherent in every human being because of his ra-

---

[243] NAGL-DOCEKAL 2016, 208: "Geläufig ist uns zum einen die Neigung, auf die verbreitete Auffassung zu hören, derzufolge unsere moralische Verpflichtung abgegolten ist, wenn wir uns an die 'goldene Regel' halten – die Auffassung also, dass es darauf ankomme, niemanden ohne guten Grund zu verletzen oder in seiner/ihrer Selbstbestimmung zu beeinträchtigen, während alle Formen von Unterstützung und Wohltätigkeit, die anderen gewährt werden, als freiwillige Mehrleistungen jenseits der eigenen moralischen Verpflichtung zu betrachten seien. Noch vertrauter ist uns dieser 'common sense' in der moderateren Form, wonach sich ein gewisses Maß an Hilfeleistungen – nicht nur im nahen persönlichen Umfeld, sondern auch gegenüber 'distant strangers' – durchaus schicke, während ein über dieses Maß hinausgehender Altruismus als überzogen zu betrachten sei."

[244] See NAGL-DOCEKAL 2016, 209.

tional disposition."[245] When Kant transcribes the core of our shared understanding of morality he states explicitly that the categorical imperative is not just about the "golden rule," but also implies the duties of love towards others. Respecting others as autonomous persons also implies giving them benefits to the best of our ability (and as much as is morally permissible). In addition to the strict prohibitions that do not allow for exceptions, we have duties of wide obligation, which are also veritable duties, although "it is up to the individual agents to decide whom to give help and support to, and to what extent."[246] Using the example of central themes in the movie *La Fils* by the brothers Dardenne and Robert Pippin's interpretation, she exemplifies the crucial difference between the moral theory of the "supererogationists" and Kant's approach, which reflects a richer everyday conception of moral action.

Herta Nagl-Docekal asks: "How can one be a democrat and not be committed to feminism?"[247]

ജ

REFERENCES

BRAIDOTTI Rosi, 2013, *The Posthuman*, Cambridge, UK – Malden, MA: Polity Press

BUCHHAMMER Brigitte, 2011, *Feministische Religionsphilosophie. Philosophisch-systematische Grundlagen*, Vienna: LIT

BUCHHAMMER Brigitte, 2019, Introduction: The Philosophical Works of Herta Nagl-Docekal, in: Brigitte BUCHHAMMER (ed.), *Freiheit – Gerechtigkeit – Liebe, Freedom – Justice – Love. Festschrift zum 75. Geburtstag von Herta Nagl-Docekal. Celebratory Volume for Herta Nagl-Docekal's 75th Birthday*, Vienna: LIT, 9–40

BUTLER Judith, 1999, *Gender Trouble. Feminism and the Subversion*

[245] KANT 1996, 510. See KANT 1907, 376.

[246] NAGL-DOCEKAL 2016, 211: "[...] wobei freilich alle Einzelnen selbst entscheiden müssen, wem sie in welchem Ausmaß Hilfe und Unterstützung angedeihen lassen."

[247] BUCHHAMMER 2011, 2.

of Identity, New York, NY – London, UK: Routledge

CIXOUS Hélène, 1981, The Laughter of Medusa, in: Elaine MARKS & Isabelle de COURTIVRON (eds.), *New French Feminism: An Anthology*, New York: Schocken, 245–264

FREUD Sigmund, 1933, *New Introductory Lectures on Psychoanalysis*, trans. Walter J. H. Sprott, New York, NY: W.W. Norton

FREUD Sigmund, 1935, *A General Introduction to Psycho-Analysis. A Course of Twenty-Eight Lectures Delivered at the University of Vienna*, trans. Joan Riviere, New York: Liveright Publ.

FREUD Sigmund, 1969, *Vorlesungen zur Einführung in die Psychoanalyse und Neue Folge der Vorlesungen zur Einführung in die Psychoanalyse. Studienausgabe*, 1, ed. Alexander Mitscherlich & James Strachey, Frankfurt/M.: Fischer

FRIEDMAN Marilyn, 1997, Autonomy and Social Relationships: Rethinking the Feminist Critique, in: Diana T. MEYERS (ed.), *Feminist Rethinking the Self*, Boulder, CO: Westview Press, 40-61

GILLIGAN Carol, 1982, *In a Different Voice: Psychological Theory and Women's Development*, Cambridge, MA: Harvard University Press

HUTFLESS Esther, 2022, Von Identität zu Differenz zu Alterität. Jean Laplanche und das Denken nicht-normativer Geschlechtlichkeit in der Psychoanalyse, *Kinderanalyse. Psychoanalyse im Kindes- und Jugendalter und ihre Anwendungen*, 30. Jahrgang, 1/2022, 4–27, https://doi.org/10.21706/ka-30-1-4

HUTFLESS Esther & ZACH Barbara, 2017, *Queering Psychoanalysis. Psychoanalyse und Queer Theory. Transdisziplinäre Verschränkungen*, Vienna: Zaglossus

KANT Immanuel, 1886, *The Metaphysics of Ethics*, trans. J. W. Semple, 3rd ed., Edinburgh: Clark

KANT Immanuel, 1907, *Die Metaphysik der Sitten*, in: Immanuel KANT, *Gesammelte Schriften. Akademieausgabe*, VI: *Die Religion innerhalb der Grenzen der bloßen Vernunft; Die Metaphysik der Sitten*, Berlin: Reimer, 203–492

KANT Immanuel, 1911, *Grundlegung zur Metaphysik der Sitten*, in: Immanuel KANT, *Gesammelte Schriften. Akademieausgabe*, IV: *Kritik der reinen Vernunft; Prolegomena; Grundlegung zur Metaphysik der Sitten; Metaphysische Anfangsgründe der Naturwissenschaft*, Berlin: Reimer, 385–463

KANT Immanuel, 1923, Idee zu einer allgemeinen Geschichte in weltbürgerlicher Absicht, in: Immanuel KANT, *Gesammelte Schriften. Akademieausgabe*, VIII: *Abhandlungen nach 1781*, Berlin: De Gruyter, 15–31

KANT Immanuel, 1996, The Metaphysics of Morals, in: Immanuel KANT, *Practical Philosophy*, trans. and ed. by Mary J. Gregor, Cambridge, UK: Cambridge University Press, 353–604

KANT Immanuel, 1998, *The Groundwork of the Metaphysics of Morals*, trans. and ed. by Mary J. Gregor, Cambridge, UK: Cambridge University Press

KANT Immanuel, 2014, Idea for a universal history with a cosmopolitan aim, in: Günter ZÖLLER & Robert B. LOUDEN (eds.), *The Cambridge Edition of the Works of Immanuel Kant*, 7: *Anthropology, History and Education*, trans. Mary Gregor, Paul Guyer, Robert B. Louden, Holly Wilson, Günter Zöller & Arnulf Zweig, 4th printing, Cambridge: Cambridge University Press, 107–120

MACKENZIE Catriona & STOLJAR Natalie, 2000, Introduction: Autonomy Refigured, in: Catriona MACKENZIE & Natalie STOLJAR (eds.), *Relational Autonomy. Feminist Perspectives on Autonomy, Agency and the Social Self*, New York – Oxford: Oxford University Press, 3–31

NAGL-DOCEKAL Herta, 1982, *Die Objektivität der Geschichtswissenschaft. Systematische Untersuchungen zum wissenschaftlichen Status der Historie*, Vienna – Munich: Oldenbourg (Überlieferung und Aufgabe 22)

NAGL-DOCEKAL Herta, 1990, Was ist Feministische Philosophie?, in: Herta NAGL-DOCEKAL (ed.), *Feministische Philosophie*, Vienna – Munich: Oldenbourg, 7–39 (Wiener Reihe 4)

NAGL-DOCEKAL Herta, 1993, Jenseits der Geschlechtermoral. Eine Einführung, in: Herta NAGL-DOCEKAL & Herlinde PAUER-STUDER (eds.), *Jenseits der Geschlechtermoral. Beiträge zur feministischen Ethik*, Frankfurt/M.: Fischer, 7–32

NAGL-DOCEKAL Herta, 1998, Feministische Ethik oder eine Theorie weiblicher Moral? in: Detlef HORSTER (ed.), *Weibliche Moral – ein Mythos?*, Frankfurt/M.: Suhrkamp, 42–72

NAGL-DOCEKAL Herta, 2002, Autonomie zwischen Selbstbestimmung und Selbstgesetzgebung oder Warum es sich lohnen könnte, dem

Verhältnis von Moral und Recht bei Kant erneut nachzugehen, in: Herlinde PAUER-STUDER & Herta NAGL-DOCEKAL (eds.), *Freiheit, Gleichheit und Autonomie*, Vienna – Munich: Oldenbourg – Berlin: Akademie Vlg., 296–326 (Wiener Reihe 11)

NAGL-DOCEKAL Herta, 2004, *Feminist Philosophy*, trans. Katharina Vester, Boulder, CO – Oxford, UK: Westview Press

NAGL-DOCEKAL Herta, 2008, Feministische Philosophie: Wie Philosophie zur Etablierung geschlechtergerechter Bedingungen beitragen kann, in: Ruth BECKER & Beate KORTENDIEK (eds.), with the collaboration of Barbara Budrich, Ilse Lenz, Sigrid Metz-Göckel, Ursula Müller & Sabine Schäfer, *Handbuch Frauen- und Geschlechterforschung. Theorien, Methoden, Empirie*, 2nd ed., Wiesbaden: VS Verlag für Sozialwissenschaften, 295–304

NAGL-DOCEKAL Herta, 2010, Zur Aktualität dieses Buches, in: Maria Isabel Peña AGUADO & Bettina SCHMITZ (eds.), *Klassikerinnen des modernen Feminismus*, Aachen: ein-FACH-verlag, 112-117

NAGL-DOCEKAL Herta, 2016, Film als Tugendlehre? Eine Diskussionsbemerkung zu Robert Pippins Deutung von *Le Fils*, in: Ludwig NAGL & Waldemar ZACHARASIEWICZ (eds.), *Ein Filmphilosophie-Symposium mit Robert B. Pippin. Western, Film Noir und das Kino der Brüder Dardenne*, Berlin: De Gruyter, 205–215

NAGL-DOCEKAL Herta, 2022, Feminist Perspectives on Kant's Conception of Autonomy: On the Need to Distinguish between Self-determination and Self-legislation, in: Susanne LETTOW & Tuija PULKKINEN (eds.), *Palgrave Handbook on German Idealism and Feminist Philosophy*, Basingstoke: Palgrave Macmillan (forthcoming)

YOUNG Iris Marion, 1990, *Justice and the Politics of Difference*, Princeton, NJ: Princeton University Press

BETTINA ZEHETNER

FEMINIST PHILOSOPHY GETS PRACTICAL

DIFFERENTIATED PARTIALITY (PARTEILICHKEIT) FOR COUNSELING WOMEN IN VIOLENT RELATIONSHIPS

Herta Nagl-Docekal's philosophy has been an important basis for my feminist engagement from the beginning of my studies at the University of Vienna in the 1990s, during my work in different women's shelters, right up to the present day in my work in a feminist counseling center. In the following, I would like to outline some basic theses of Herta Nagl-Docekal's influential book *Feminist Philosophy*[1] and connect them with my practice of feminist psychosocial counseling, namely the principle of "differentiated partiality" ("differenzierte Parteilichkeit") in counseling processes with women who experience violence by their partner.

FEMINIST PHILOSOPHY

One important aim of feminist philosophy is to overcome the hierarchical opposition of mutually exclusive gender roles that confront individuals with the norm to identify themselves as either male or female and develop a non-reductive conception of the human subject. How can we think differentially without polarizing and without creating a hierarchy between the two poles?

1) Feminist philosophy is motivated and initiated by feminism as a political movement. It is based on the critique of a patriarchal society

[1] See NAGL-DOCEKAL 2004.

and relations of dominance and the will to create equality between human beings, regardless of their gender.

2) The accusation leveled against feminist philosophy as "just another ideology" is not justified – quite the opposite: feminist philosophy means criticism of ideology, namely the androcentric ideology that masks itself as gender-neutral universal truth – this so-called neutrality is full of ideologies. Feminist philosophy is a critique of the ideology that has become the allegedly "normal" perspective, which disguises relationships of domination and discrimination. Feminist philosophy has developed the alternative concepts of the "situatedness of knowledge" (Harding) and the explicit "positionality of knowledge" (Haraway). There is no god-like point of view from "above and outside" possible for humans, the position of the researcher or speaker must be made explicit; motivation, interest, his or her social and cultural background, and experiences influence his or her perception and judgment.

We need to revise the meaning of the term "objectivity": an argumentation based on the current, most plausible theories. For example, in the present state of philosophical discourse we have elaborate theories of justice and equality between all human beings, therefore a theory which argues that women are inferior to men would have to counter these existing theories and would fail because it would not produce better arguments for gender-based discrimination than for gender equality (or indeed suppression or exploitation).

Feminist thinking sharpens our view on society, it discovers the often-invisible gender-bias (for instance, the never mentioned but very effective male quota: "Look at this guy, he is white, heterosexual, middle class, he is like us, let's give him the job!" – only this implicit and invisible quota renders an explicit female quota necessary). "Objectivity" in this new, non-scientific, non-reduced positivist sense does not mean the resignation and withdrawal of the original claim, but the quality of situatedness of thoughts and knowledge is reflected, in order to produce an even "stronger" objectivity than before. However, the term is rather loaded and we also could look for other terms before the process of resignification has been effective.

Parallel to "objectivity," the "non-normativity," freedom of values, ethical neutrality is not only an impossible aim, but also counterproductive. To be free of values is not desirable in philosophy, nor in any other science.[2] When we are conducting research, we do not want mere neutral information; rather, we are looking for some kind of orientation, we want answers to important questions in our actual lives – as temporary and provisional as they may be.[3]

3) Feminist philosophy is not merely one new, additional part of philosophy – it questions the entire canon at its core, including its gendered categories and dichotomies. There are not just some blank spaces on the map of the history of philosophy, rather the whole system is distorted; for example, the ignorance of gender-based discrimination (the illusory meaning of "human beings," which actually refers only to male beings and renders men as the subject of philosophy) or the pseudophilosophical "justification" of differences between men and women on grounds of their essence or biology ("women are less rational/ethical than men because of their different nature or brains"). Therefore, the whole history of philosophy has to be critically revised with respect to its implicit misogyny and androcentrism, masked as gender-neutrality.

Feminist philosophy is a philosophy aligned with the interest of women's emancipation from discriminating conditions. "Feminist philosophy is thus philosophizing along the guidelines of interest in women's liberation."[4]

4) The importance of plurality: Feminist philosophy is not one homogenous philosophical position but lives from the differences between diverse concepts and positions – as there is not just one feminism ("the real one or the only right one"), but a plurality of many diverse feminisms. We should encourage the productive development of many different feminist philosophies by promoting a culture of open dialogue between the diverse positions and develop a politics of solidarity and alliances.

5) And last but not least, women philosophers throughout history must be recognized, studied, and included in the philosophical canon, rather than being hidden and forgotten.

---

[2] See NAGL-DOCEKAL 2004, 104–105; see also NAGL-DOCEKAL 1982, esp. 227–243.

[3] I will explain below the practical relevance of this critique of the traditional use of the terms "objectivity" or "neutrality" for feminist psychosocial counseling.

[4] NAGL-DOCEKAL 1990, 11.

The subject of rationality in Western philosophy has a definite male bias, resting on the equation of man as human being and human being as male. Western philosophy has separated the realm of the body, of gender, and of contingency from the implicitly male-connotated subject of rationality and ascribed these irritations to "the female": "Man" and "the second sex" (de Beauvoir), logos and rationality versus body and emotions.

Who is this subject when we speak of man/human? Who is addressed and who is excluded? When the French revolutionaries wrote "Les droits de l'homme et citoyen," Olympe de Gouges challenged their approach by publishing "les droits de la femme et citoyenne": she was beheaded, a punishment of the highest symbolic significance; cutting the head off a woman who demands the same rights as a man and campaigned against the death penalty.[5]

The 18th and 19th centuries saw the rise of theories that claimed a fundamental difference between men and women. The belief in an essentially different "nature" or biology, a difference in body and soul, so to speak, became the recognized paradigm in Europe. Karin Hausen calls the result of this development "different characters of gender" ("unterschiedliche Geschlechtscharaktere")[6] – a form of polarization, with women and men being complementary to each other in the sense that woman is the other to the male norm. With the shift from the theological to the scientific paradigm, the differences between the sexes were constructed as completely opposite "natures" of body and soul, which resulted in the ideology of different tasks – women should be confined to the household, removed from the male public sphere of political life. Thus, a foundation and pseudoscientific justification for these different worlds and values was provided.

One of many examples is Jean-Jacques Rousseau's theory of gender specific education. Rousseau, who developed decisive foundations for the contract-theoretical basis of the modern state with his seminal work *The Social Contract*, simultaneously designed a naturalistic concept of gender character – how gender-differentiated education should

[5] Cf. ZEHETNER 2020.
[6] HAUSEN 1976.

proceed was developed by Rousseau in his book *Emile, or On Education.*[7] I would like to quote a famous passage from Rousseau's *Emile*:

> *I would prefer a simple and roughly educated girl a hundred times over a blue stocking and aesthete who installs a literary court and make(s) herself the president. An aesthete is a scourge for her husband, her children, her friends, her servants, for the entire world. From the height of her genius she despises all her feminine duties and only thinks of becoming a man of the kind of Mademoiselle l'Enclos. Outside she always appears ridiculous and is rightfully criticized since criticism cannot stay away as soon as you desert your status and adopt a new one for which one is not made ... even if she would indeed have talents she would devaluate them by her arrogance. Her dignity consists in remaining unknown; her fame is the respect of her spouse; her pleasure consists in the happiness of her family ... If there were only reasonable men, every educated girl would remain spinsters their entire lives.*[8]

For Rousseau, it is a given fact that men and women are different in character and temperament. He developed his theory of gender character: men and women are not and should not be of the same essence, a position that perpetuates and reiterates the conventional misunderstanding or faulty logic of deducing a norm of ought from being (being-ought fallacy).

Rousseau develops a totally different theory of education for Sophie, the potential spouse for his protagonist Emile, consisting of literally the opposite principles for girls than for boys: The girl shall be educated in a way to please her future husband.[9] What is the genuine role of a woman?

> *Thus the whole education of women ought to relate to men. To please men, to be useful to them, to make herself loved and honored by them, to raise them when young, to care for them when grown, to counsel them, to console them, to make their lives agreeable and sweet – these*

---

[7] See NAGL-DOCEKAL 2004, 128.
[8] ROUSSEAU 1979, 447–448, as cited in NAGL-DOCEKAL 2004, 128.
[9] Cf. ROUSSEAU 1979; see also SCHMID 1992.

> *are the duties of women at all times, and they ought to be taught from childhood.*[10]

In many of today's counseling sessions I get the impression that these principles have been deeply effective and incorporated by men and women alike – "In every gesture lies the whole society."[11] According to this paradigm, man equals the human being, he is the center of thinking, the normative benchmark; woman, on the other hand, has to adapt herself to his needs – the female partner as mother of her husband which, in my view, is one of the most common causes for the failure of marriages.

GENDER SPECIFIC ASPECTS OF VIOLENCE AND VULNERABILITY

Only the separation of the female-connotated particularity allows the male philosophizing subject to define itself as universal. Only the denial of one's own finitude allows the subject to imagine itself as a thoroughly rational, autonomous, morally competent, sovereign being. This conception of the human being as sovereign subject eliminates the foundation of human relatedness and interdependence, including our vulnerability. I would like to confront this conception of man as sovereign subject with the foundation of human relatedness and interdependence, with our vulnerability.

Vulnerability is an essential part of the human condition. But the connotations of vulnerability are gender specific: phantasmatic impenetrability and the power to hurt are symbolically assigned to masculinity, the openness to being hurt, the need for protection are symbolically ascribed to femininity. Women are symbolically conceived as passive objects of (at least potential) violation and fear, men as active subjects with full (aggressive) agency ("Verletzungsoffenheit" and "Verletzungsmächtigkeit"). This is obviously a disciplinary discourse with the message to women: "For your own safety you should not walk

[10] ROUSSEAU 1979, 477.
[11] KAUFMANN 1994, 293.

alone, without a male protector, at best you should let yourself be protected by a male partner who can defend you against the potential violation of other men." Of course, this is a rather paradoxical and cynical message, considering that for a woman the place with the highest risk to experience violence is her own home, her own relationship.[12] In the current right-wing discourse, sexism intersects with racism: "We," Western men, have to protect "our" women from aggressive and dangerous foreigners (for example at New Year's Eve in Cologne, Germany). This discourse is to distract from one's own violent structures and actions by projecting all the "dark sides" onto the Other, men of color, refugees etc. – thereby establishing white women as the property of white men.

So once again: The hegemonic construct of masculinity is marked by the denial of vulnerability (and fear), whereas the construct of femininity is essentially identified with violability (and fear). The emancipatory potential of a critical philosophy of gender can be realized in the psychosocial field by opening up perspectives of creating gender relations in a new way. How can we embody "masculinity" and "femininity" in a less restrictive, less violent way?

As background information, it is important to know that the forms and contexts of violence are not gender-neutral. Violence against women is mostly violence from male partners or ex-partners and is executed in most cases in their own home. Violence against men is mostly violence executed by other men and mostly in public spaces.[13]

"PARTEILICHKEIT" AS A PRINCIPLE OF FEMINIST COUNSELING

The German term "Parteilichkeit" is commonly translated as "partiality," but also as "commitment," "partisanship" or "bias." "Parteilichkeit" is an important principle of feminist counseling, understood as gender sensible or gender reflective counseling, or also emancipatory counseling.

---

[12] See FRA 2014.
[13] See SCHRÖTTLE & ANSORGE 2012; FRA 2014.

Partiality as a principle of feminist counseling is based on a critical perspective of society, especially regarding structures of dominance and oppression. It involves explicit positionality and interest, with the goal of giving back the power of defining violence to the one who has been exposed to it and to strengthen, support and empower her in her own agency.

A common point of critique of feminist thinking is the accusation of partiality and the alleged subjectivity of its arguments – expressed mostly by those who want to declare their own standpoint as a universal one. To counter these accusations, we can point to the illusory quality of this demand of a god-like "objectivity" or "neutrality."[14] I want to show the necessity of a partial standpoint through the example of counseling sessions with women who have suffered violence by their partner.

In these sessions, the connection of structural, cultural, and personal violence becomes obvious; no problem of women who seek counseling is just an individual problem. It is always part of social, economic, and political relations and conditions. For example, economic dependency on one's husband due to an unjust division of unpaid care work furthers violence in the relationship and aggravates an autonomous decision to end such a relationship.

Women who experience violence from their partners often feel shame and guilt instead of their partners. A non-partial – allegedly "neutral" – attitude establishes the violent structure once more, as the phenomenon of victim-blaming clearly demonstrates (for instance, questions such as: "What did you do to enrage him like this?" Or: "Have you provoked him in any way?"). We have to differentiate between the illusion of agency ("If I do everything the right way, if I fulfill his wishes, then the violence will stop" – this is a completely wrong assumption, a trap, because the violent behavior of the partner is not a rational reaction to something that the woman has done "wrong") and the fact that the violent behavior is most definitely a problem of the person who is acting violently, instead of using other strategies, such as verbalizing feelings of anger, fear of helplessness, or fear of losing one's partner. The urge to control and possess one's

[14] See above pp. 84–85.

partner results from some sort of subconscious deficit in one's own self-esteem – too threatening if it ever were to become conscious. It is due to this unbearable unknown that the abuser acts out violently against his partner. Vulnerability and fear question the man's masculinity in our symbolic order. Obviously, it is necessary to change this double standard towards more openness, so as to develop the whole range of "human" behavior for all genders.

A partial attitude relieves the victim of guilt and stops her from blaming herself for the violence she has experienced. It is helpful and necessary to state this position very clearly: "Violence is the responsibility of the person who acts violently," and "There is no justification for the violence that you have suffered." "Every human being has the right to live a life that is not threatened by violence."

The pseudoneutral assumption that violence is just an imbalance of power and that the woman could end the relationship any time is a misunderstanding of the difference between violence and power and the dynamics and effects of violence on the victim. Any kind of violence weakens a woman's self-esteem and the trust in her own agency; it limits her ability to change the situation, to act independently from her partner, and to live her own life in freedom. Violence is *not* a mere imbalance of power between two people. Power is something that demands affirmation and consent, it is an inter-relational process, open to negotiation, whereas violence is one-sided, it threatens and silences. There is no easy way out of a long-term violent relationship, because it weakens the victim in her self-esteem and her agency. She does not perceive herself as worthy or capable of living by herself any more, often a paradoxical dependence has developed. All of this is ignored by a so-called "neutral" or allegedly objective standpoint, which by ignoring the dynamic and the effects of violence stabilizes the underlying inequalities.[15]

"Reflective" or "differentiated partiality" does not mean supporting any aim of the person receiving counseling (for example, self-harming

[15] Similar pseudoneutral assumptions are that everybody has the same chances in the labor market, that every person is treated equally with respect to his or her competencies, or the neoliberal myth that everybody can achieve everything if s/he only tries hard enough.

tendencies), but to be a serious and, if necessary, critical partner for a dialogue. The most important general aim of feminist counseling is to support the counseling-seeking person in the widening of her own range of agency, to develop new possibilities to think and speak about themselves and their situation (and situatedness) and to act in a less restricted way, to gain more freedom of acting.

CONCLUSION

Psychosocial counseling is not a repair shop or service center for better adaptation to stressful environments and economic demands. On the contrary, emancipatory counseling helps to develop a wider perspective in order to overcome the individualization of structural problems. Instead of pathologizing women in their role as victims, feminist counseling strengthens women in their agency and autonomy. Feminist counseling provides a space for critical thinking so as to expand the possibilities for all genders. I argue for a feminist attitude in psychosocial counseling with the aim of expanding the possibilities for all genders. I am arguing for a feminist attitude in psychosocial counseling, with the aim of liberation from the restricted perspective of gender polarization, i.e., of from the pressure to define oneself as *either* male – *or* female. In this way, feminist philosophy as it has been developed by Herta Nagl-Docekal allows to establish an emancipatory practice in all areas of human co-existence. In the field of counseling, feminist philosophy must create an emancipatory practice of counseling, based on a non-reductive concept of human beings for the emancipation of all genders!

ຄ໙

REFERENCES

FRA, 2014, *Violence against Women: an EU-Wide Survey. Results at a Glance*, Vienna: FRA – European Union Agency for Fundamental Rights, http://fra.europa.eu/en/publication/2014/violence-against-women-eu-wide-survey-results-glance, accessed 9/2/2021

HAUSEN Karin, 1976, Die Polarisierung der "Geschlechtscharaktere." Eine Spiegelung der Dissoziation von Erwerbs- und Familienleben, in: Werner CONZE (ed.), *Sozialgeschichte der Familie in der Neuzeit Europas. Neue Forschungen*, Stuttgart: Klett, 363–393

KAUFMANN Jean-Claude, 1994, *Schmutzige Wäsche. Zur ehelichen Konstruktion von Alltag*, Konstanz: Universitätsverlag

NAGL-DOCEKAL Herta, 1982, *Die Objektivität der Geschichtswissenschaften*, Vienna – Munich: Oldenbourg

NAGL-DOCEKAL Herta, 1990, Was ist Feministische Philosophie?, in: Herta NAGL-DOCEKAL (ed.), *Feministische Philosophie*, Vienna – Munich: Oldenbourg, 7–39 (Wiener Reihe 4)

NAGL-DOCEKAL Herta, 2004, *Feminist Philosophy*, trans. Katharina Vester, Boulder, CO – Oxford, UK: Westview Press

ROUSSEAU Jean-Jacques, 1979, *Emile, or On Education*, trans. Allan Bloom, New York: Basic Books

SCHMID Pia, 1992, Rousseau Revisited. Geschlecht als Kategorie in der Geschichte der Erziehung, *Zeitschrift für Pädagogik* 38 (6), 839–854

SCHRÖTTLE Monika & ANSORGE Nicole, 2012, *Gewalt gegen Frauen in Paarbeziehungen – eine sekundäranalytische Auswertung zur Differenzierung von Schweregraden, Mustern, Risikofaktoren und Unterstützung nach erlebter Gewalt. Kurzfassung*, 4th ed., Berlin: Bundesministerium für Familie, Senioren, Frauen und Jugend, https://pub.uni-bielefeld.de/download/1859151/2653842/gewalt-paarbeziehungen_kurzfassung.pdf, accessed 9/2/2021

ZEHETNER Bettina, 2020, Freiheit in der feministischen politischen Philosophie, in: FRAUEN* BERATEN FRAUEN* (ed.), *Freiheit und Feminismen. Feministische Beratung und Psychotherapie*, Giessen: Psychosozial-Verlag, 21–43

WALTRAUD ERNST

NORMS – REASON – JUSTICE: HERTA NAGL-DOCEKAL'S CONTRIBUTION TO A THEORY OF TRUTH

Herta Nagl-Docekal's rich philosophical work rests on two related presuppositions: a reason-based examination of legal and social norms as the basis for critical scholarship and discourse; a demand for justice and equality as the foundation of democracy. Relating these two presuppositions serves as the foundation for her understanding of feminist philosophy. Moreover, the demand for justice and equal rights for all human beings is not only the guiding principle for Nagl-Docekal's political philosophy, but affects also other areas of her philosophical oeuvre, especially ethics and epistemology.

As I have outlined elsewhere,[1] I believe that epistemic claims are always deeply entangled with political and ethical concerns. For this reason, I want to explore in the following some specific insights and arguments, which Herta Nagl-Docekal has developed and which constitute – in my view – a valuable contribution to a theory of truth. I will accomplish this by way of a close reading of three of her texts: a recent paper on feminist philosophy in a post-feminist context,[2] her earlier book on the objectivity of the historical sciences,[3] and the chapter on reason from her book *Feminist Philosophy* which has been translated into many languages and was issued in a second edition in 2001 and reprinted in 2016.[4]

---

[1] ERNST 1999.
[2] NAGL-DOCEKAL 2012.
[3] NAGL-DOCEKAL 1982.
[4] NAGL-DOCEKAL 2000; 2004; 2016.

NORMS AND JUSTICE

In her paper on "Feminist Philosophy in a Post-Feminist Context,"[5] Nagl-Docekal argues against four different variations of the claim that feminism is an unpopular or outdated concept.

1) Against the assertion that young women in particular would prefer to adhere to an "aggressive individualism" rather than identify with feminism (although they report e.g. gender-based discrimination in the workplace and in the labor market overall), Nagl-Docekal holds that it is important to realize that a sustainable struggle against asymmetric structures cannot be won by isolated individuals, but only through cooperative efforts and with politics aiming for gender justice.[6]

2) Counter to the claim that feminism relates to a simplifying critique of patriarchy and neglects intersections of gender asymmetries with other forms of discrimination, e.g. privileging middle class, whiteness, heterosexuality, Christianity, etc., Nagl-Docekal maintains that the demand for implementation of the equality principle is in itself a manifestation of intersectionality. Demands for "equal pay for equal work!" or for equal participation in the formation of public opinion or in decision-making processes[7] are not only issues of patriarchy and they certainly do not belong to the past.

3) Paradoxically, as Nagl-Docekal notes, even women who, for decades, tirelessly worked for gender justice within powerful institutions of education or in the (labor) unions frame their demands in terms of distancing themselves from the label "feminism," as a strategy towards success of their initiatives.[8]

4) According to Nagl-Docekal, the dominant repudiation of feminism rests on the claim that the era of feminism is over and that traditional gender hierarchies should be accepted to inform the lived experience of women.[9] This last argument manages to establish sufficiently

[5] NAGL-DOCEKAL 2012.
[6] NAGL-DOCEKAL 2012, 231–232.
[7] NAGL-DOCEKAL 2012, 232–233.
[8] NAGL-DOCEKAL 2012, 233.
[9] NAGL-DOCEKAL 2012, 233.

intimidating public pressure to be supported by groups who adhere to the first and third arguments above.

In this context, Nagl-Docekal defines feminism as the struggle against all forms of discrimination or subordination of women. This struggle does not have to be carried out only by those affected by discrimination. On the contrary, she clarifies that all those concerned with issues of justice and democracy cannot give up on the demand for the abolition of every kind of discrimination and subordination, without losing credibility.[10] For Nagl-Docekal, feminism or feminist philosophy function as umbrella terms and her main question is how philosophical research can contribute in the advancement of the aim of gender justice in the contemporary context.[11]

In Nagl-Docekal's view, this is not the task of feminist philosophy of law alone. Among others, the field of philosophical anthropology also has to contribute to this endeavor. Here, one must distinguish neatly between social or cultural norms and biological differences of the gendered body. This is not to deny any interconnection of social and bodily existence. In Nagl-Docekal's view, the normative functions of gender images and stereotypes conveyed through a visual culture affirm this interconnection. Already small children are educated to become a "real girl" or a "real boy" and are trained to incorporate typical stereotypical postures, gestures and facial expressions into their bodily existence.[12]

However, it seems important for Nagl-Docekal to maintain a conceptual distinction between sex and gender in feminist theory. This is particularly because conservative circles (and not only from within the clerical context) still argue that traditional gender norms are derived from the general idea of a binary, natural bodily difference between women and men. To illustrate this, she reminds us that it is still a publicly defended position that certain care practices are founded on female instinct. In order to move this debate of how vital social care work has necessarily to be organized to a different level, it is important to note that care practices rely on a question of norms which

[10] NAGL-DOCEKAL 2012, 234.
[11] NAGL-DOCEKAL 2012, 237.
[12] NAGL-DOCEKAL 2012, 238.

must be argued on grounds of moral principles and justice. Therefore, Nagl-Docekal opposes a naturalist fallacy, which questions in general the distinction between nature and culture or sex and gender. In her view, such a position endangers the foundation of arguing consistently for political change in general and for gender justice in particular.[13]

In the realm of philosophy of law and political theory, Nagl-Docekal contends that arguments from feminist legal scholars on the principles of freedom and equality within the liberal constitutional state have had effects, but that the process of actually improving laws is still far from being accomplished. Therefore, it is important that feminist legal theory continues to point out problems, in order to find a just solution. For her, it is an inherent quality of emancipatory movements that social asymmetries are brought to light and are examined with scrutiny by those concerned.[14] Against the suspicion that claims to gender equality entail that women would like to mimic or become alike men or even transform into men, Nagl-Docekal argues that equality before the law and equal opportunities never implies sameness. On the contrary, it means that the state must treat everyone equally in spite of human diversity,[15] and has to establish measures to secure equal participation in education and the formation of public opinion for everyone.[16]

In the field of social philosophy, Nagl-Docekal points out that a feminist perspective can bring to light the negative consequences of globalized neo-liberal economies, e.g. the worldwide increases in the feminization of poverty and human-trafficking involving women.[17] In moral philosophy and the philosophy of history, she argues in favor of exploring forms of living together that transcend the liberal quest for autonomy as individual self-determination. In her view, feminist approaches offer models of friendship and love to meet the need for non-hierarchically organized ways of living.[18] Nagl-Docekal has elaborated further on this topic in her most recent book, *Innere Freiheit: Grenzen*

[13] NAGL-DOCEKAL 2012, 240.
[14] NAGL-DOCEKAL 2012, 241.
[15] NAGL-DOCEKAL 2012, 242.
[16] NAGL-DOCEKAL 2012, 243.
[17] NAGL-DOCEKAL 2012, 244.
[18] NAGL-DOCEKAL 2012, 247.

der nachmetaphysischen Moralkonzeptionen.[19] Stressing the role of feminist theory for promoting the dimensions of personal bonding and solidarity, she suggests that a collective struggle for gender justice, which transcends national borders, can also be argued for in moral theory.[20]

THE TRUTH OF HISTORY

In her substantial study of the objectivity of history as a scientific discipline, Herta Nagl-Docekal argues against the postulate of value-freedom in the sciences.[21] Moreover, she relates the truth of history to value judgments, in particular to justice. There, she defines objectivity as "the binding nature of statements based on arguments."[22] Going back to the beginning of historical science in the nineteenth century, Nagl-Docekal aims in this text to establish history as a scientific discipline on the basis of the possibility for objectivity via true propositions. In this process, she discusses the leading approaches of the hermeneutic tradition from Dilthey to Gadamer and Nietzsche by delineating their respective fallacies but also incorporating the strength of each position.

On grounds of this thorough and subtle argumentation, Nagl-Docekal develops her own account of historical objectivity as unique and specific. In this view, historical research neglects neither the researcher as the epistemic subject nor the research as something transcending the subjectivity of the historian. The unique character of this kind of objectivity typical for historical science is established as a form of liability or commitment resulting from a process of argumentation on four levels and guided by four criteria. The binding character of the historical sciences results, first, from the empirical level, from the accurate correspondence between given propositions and the factuality of the past. This can be established via reference to linguistic and nonlinguistic sources or any other available evidence. The propositions of history

[19] NAGL-DOCEKAL 2014.
[20] NAGL-DOCEKAL 2012, 248.
[21] NAGL-DOCEKAL 1982.
[22] NAGL-DOCEKAL 1982, 10: "die durch argumentatives Ausweisen begründete Verbindlichkeit von Aussagen."

have to be confirmed by such sources and their refutation should be impossible. Secondly, the empirical work relies on the questions posed by the historian, which are not to be arbitrary, but can and must be legitimized. Rather than being personal, these research questions have to represent the conception that the present has of itself in its relevant moments. Criteria for the justification of the research questions are the disputes about the analyses and subsequent receptions of a given understanding of the present.[23] However, those questions are not justified once and for all, rather, a new era generates novel questions that have to be answered by historical research. Nevertheless, they can and must be justified.

Third, not only research questions and empirical facts need to be critically examined, but also truth claims formulated in the past, for instance in art, religion, and philosophy. The validity of such claims needs to be investigated in the light of the most advanced discourse on the relevant issues. Philosophical truth claims, for instance, need to be judged in terms of currently elaborated arguments regarding the respective topic. Furthermore, fourth, the involved practical principles have to be judged. This means that the moral principles guiding the historian are not arbitrary either but can be and therefore must be legitimized as well. The criterion for justification of practical principles in historical research Nagl-Docekal relates to is Kant's "Categorial Imperative," as explicated in his practical philosophy.[24] Practical argumentation can achieve binding character and therefore objectivity. So, it is the dispute through arguments which leads to objectivity in the historical sciences, including arguments for moral judgment. In this regard, Nagl-Docekal borrows the model for the judge of history from Nietzsche, whose figure of the judge reaches a true judgment on the basis of justice. Only if historians follow the principles of justice, can their judgment claim to be true.[25] Thorough examination is required in this context as well, as the principles of justice need to be legitimized by argumentation. From all this follows that objectivity in history is to be understood as a process of argumentation and that truth

[23] NAGL-DOCEKAL 1982, 238.
[24] NAGL-DOCEKAL 1982, 240.
[25] NAGL-DOCEKAL 1982, 242.

about history can be achieved only if historical research is guided by concerns of justice.

THE TRUTH OF FEMINISM

In her book *Feministische Philosophie*,[26] especially in the chapter on reason, Herta Nagl-Docekal relates her own contributions to a theory of truth in history to feminist epistemology as developed within the US context e.g. by Sandra Harding. Sharing Harding's critique of the positivist concept of objectivity,[27] Nagl-Docekal confronts Harding's approach with her own account of objectivity in history and warns feminist epistemology about implicitly accepting the scientific paradigm that upholds value-freedom and negates the normative aspect of science. For a feminist approach to science in general, Herta Nagl-Docekal holds that the motivation for such an approach should be based on the equal relevance of all genders for the research process.[28] This idea can and must be justified on the basis of justice, which again relates to the normative level. Therefore, feminist epistemology, in her view, has to and can be legitimized by way of argumentative verification of normative propositions.[29] Thus, Nagl-Docekal relates the epistemological debate in feminist philosophy to practical reason, comparable to the way she argued for justice as the guiding principle for historical research.

In the same chapter, in regarding the feminist critique of reason, Nagl-Docekal criticizes the usurpation of the concept of reason by masculinity, starting in the first half of the eighteenth century. She cautions contemporary feminist approaches from accepting this gender dichotomy and consequently rejecting reason as a useful concept for feminist philosophy. Instead, Nagl-Docekal suggests retaining reason as a useful and powerful means for feminist scholarship and to concentrate on criticizing the concept of reason as an integral part of masculinity.[30]

---

[26] NAGL-DOCEKAL 2000.
[27] NAGL-DOCEKAL 2000, 131.
[28] NAGL-DOCEKAL 2000, 151.
[29] NAGL-DOCEKAL 2000, 152.
[30] NAGL-DOCEKAL 2000, 177.

BEYOND FEMINIST OBJECTIVITY?

In my own account of feminist epistemology,[31] I question objectivity as a necessary concept for the legitimation of feminist knowledge. Instead, viewing scientific knowledge as materialized, historically constructed processes, makes it possible to overcome the problems of realism and relativism. Positioning oneself as a feminist while doing science evokes and represents political responsibility and solidarity with the feminist movement.[32] The sociohistorical character of scientific knowledge (as well as philosophical and all other knowledge) does not necessarily lead to epistemological relativism. One must proceed from the assumption that reality exists outside the scientific process of knowledge production, but that it is, nevertheless, constructed in a particular way through being described and explained as an object of knowledge.

It is crucial from which perspective one defines or describes how reality is structured and why. It is not sufficient to claim that knowledge is embodied and localized. It is absolutely necessary to know from which perspective and with which tools scholars point out what is real because there is no neutral standpoint, as Donna Haraway notes[33] – or as Herta Nagl-Docekal framed it, there is no value-freedom in science.[34] It is in this sense that political perspectives of feminist movements, developed in processes of collaborative consciousness in order to overcome injustice and to advocate for change of the experienced social reality of women's lives, shape or construct the scientific approaches of feminist inquiry. It is through involvement and concerns that scientific constructions of reality are motivated and produced. To acknowledge this reciprocal aspect of construction is crucial for being able to work for feminist change, and to explain the entanglement of the social and the scientific discursive material reality.

So, in my view, it is less a question of whether reality is constructed, but rather how it is constructed and what is envisioned. What is at

[31] ERNST 1999; 2016.

[32] For an emphasis on the importance of "doing science as a feminist" see also LONGINO 1990, 188.

[33] HARAWAY 1991.

[34] NAGL-DOCEKAL 2000, 131–151.

stake is less the true or objective description of reality, but instead the manifestations of realities that may overlap and expand, gain and lose influence. Important here is the investigation into the articulation and reception of feminist constructions of reality which are put forward in the name of science and through its claim to authority. This is not to deny the existence of knowledge or reality, or knowledge of reality. On the contrary, what I want to suggest is simply that it is possible to critically investigate how knowledge, reality, and knowledge about reality is socially constructed and manifest, in all of its performative dimensions. Challenging what is accepted as reality provides a powerful analytical tool, which feminist scholars employ constantly, in order to provide creative room for new knowledge, new realities, and new feminist knowledge about new feminist realities.

In concluding: For my own work in feminist philosophy, especially in feminist epistemology, I appropriated from Herta Nagl-Docekal the relevance of the research questions, which are always embedded in an individual and social context, which guide all scientific endeavors and knowledge projects, and which have to be justified. They reveal the interest in what is wanted to be known and why, the desire for a specific knowledge. They also reveal normative concerns and their embeddedness in issues of justice.

ཽ

REFERENCES

ERNST Waltraud, 1999, *Diskurspiratinnen. Wie feministische Erkenntnisprozesse die Wirklichkeit verändern*, Vienna: Milena

ERNST Waltraud, 2016, In Connection: Feminist Epistemology for the Twenty-First Century, *Transcultural Studies* 12, 267–287, https://doi.org/10.1163/23751606-01202006

HARAWAY Donna, 1991, *Simians, Cyborgs, and Women. The Reinvention of Nature*, London: Free Association Books

LONGINO Helen, 1990, *Science as Social Knowledge. Values and Objectivity in Scientific Inquiry*, Princeton, NJ: Princeton University Press

NAGL-DOCEKAL Herta, 1982, *Die Objektivität der Geschichtswissenschaft. Systematische Untersuchungen zum wissenschaftlichen Status der Historie*, Vienna – Munich: Oldenbourg (Überlieferung und Aufgabe 22)

NAGL-DOCEKAL Herta, 2000, *Feministische Philosophie. Ergebnisse, Probleme, Perspektiven*, Frankfurt/M.: Fischer

NAGL-DOCEKAL Herta, 2004, *Feminist Philosophy*, trans. Katharina Vester, Boulder, CO – Oxford, UK: Westview Press

NAGL-DOCEKAL Herta, 2012, Feministische Philosophie im post-feministischen Kontext, in: Hilge LANDWEER, Catherine NEWMARK, Christine KLEY & Simone MILLER (eds.), *Philosophie und die Potenziale der Gender Studies*, Bielefeld: transcript, 231–254

NAGL-DOCEKAL Herta, 2014, *Innere Freiheit. Grenzen der nachmetaphysischen Moralkonzeptionen*, Berlin – Boston, MA: De Gruyter (Deutsche Zeitschrift für Philosophie, Sonderband 36)

NAGL-DOCEKAL Herta, 2016, *Feministische Philosophie. Ergebnisse, Probleme, Perspektiven*, Frankfurt/M.: Fischer ([1]2000; [2]2001)

Cornelia Eşianu

CURRENT ARTISTIC FORMS FOR THE IMPLEMENTATION OF A FEMINIST AESTHETICS

In no profession are human beings
as far behind as in the practice of humanity.[1]
Friedrich Schlegel

INTRODUCTION

The domain I would like to investigate in this paper is the field of art and aesthetics, considered from the perspective of feminist philosophy. According to Herta Nagl-Docekal, feminist philosophy is not to be understood as a method, such as for example analytic language philosophy or phenomenology. Feminist philosophy is not a theory made by women, about women, and for women, but rather – as the author claims – "a philosophizing, guided by an interest in the liberation of women."[2] In my interpretation, the subject of her efforts, the decisive question, which focuses on the root of things, is how philosophy, understood as rational and critical thinking, can contribute to the elimination of gender asymmetries. As Fichte wrote in a letter to Friedrich Schiller dated December 2nd, 1800, "it is the task of philosophy, to help all other [sciences, C. E.] out of confusion."[3] It would be naive to think that this task has by now already been achieved.

In the history of the arts, it is known that the status of female artists was not considered equal to that of male artists. Many reasons could be adduced to explain this discrimination, which has been researched

[1] Schlegel 1988, 173 (English translation C. E.): "Menschen sind in keiner Profession noch so weit zurück als in der Humanität."
[2] Nagl-Docekal 2004, XIX; see also Nagl-Docekal 1994.
[3] Fichte 1962, 237 (English translation C. E.): "auf dem Gebiete der ersten Wissenschaft [...] allen andern aus der Verwirrung zu helfen."

in various papers, articles, and studies over time. Feminist criticism has the merit of highlighting a great many of these asymmetries in a variety of ways. However, in her book *Feminist Philosophy*,[4] Herta Nagl-Docekal raises some well-founded philosophical objections against a certain branch of this feminist critique, commonly referred to as difference feminism. In addition to general objections against Freud's psychoanalytic theory, which supports the thesis that women are lacking a sense of culture,[5] she points out the possible dangers of psychoanalytically informed theories which – by focusing on the text as a research method – tend to engage in excessive rhetoric and exaggerated demands (for example the death of the subject or the constructivist understanding of "the body" as also being part of the cultural concept of gender).[6] According to Nagl-Docekal, this makes them easy targets for discrediting feminist theory: "Rhetorically excessive theses have frequently been used as easy targets by those who wish to fight off the entire project of feminist philosophy."[7]

In the first part of my paper I will discuss Nagl-Docekal's account of a feminist aesthetics as developed in the second chapter of *Feminist Philosophy*, entitled "Art and Femininity."[8] As the title of my paper indicates – *Current Artistic Forms for the Implementation of a Feminist Aesthetics* – I will discuss in the second part of my text one current example of a woman artist who works in digital photography, and which, in my opinion, could serve to demonstrate what the implementation of a feminist aesthetics in a narrow sense might mean. What I have in mind is the aesthetic category of the grotesque, conceived as a subversive form. In this sense, I turn to the artistic work of the young Austrian artistic photographer Eva Kosinar which, although interesting, has not yet been internationally discovered. The aesthetics of the

---

[4] NAGL-DOCEKAL 2001; for the English translation see NAGL-DOCEKAL 2004.

[5] Cf. FREUD 2012, 162. In Freud's conception, the little girl is like a small man ("Wir müssen nun anerkennen, das kleine Mädchen sei ein kleiner Mann"). The clitoris is an equivalent of the penis. Describing the woman by what she lacks, comparing her to a man means using man as a paradigm.

[6] See here Nagl-Docekal's critical comments on the ideas of Hélène Cixous, Evelyn F. Keller, Luce Irigaray, or Judith Butler, NAGL-DOCEKAL 2004, 58–73.

[7] NAGL-DOCEKAL 2004, XXI.

[8] NAGL-DOCEKAL 2004, 41–85.

digital is still a new one, even though the aesthetics of photography has become, so to speak, a specific form of our reality.[9] In the third and last part, I come to a conclusion on feminist aesthetics.

WHAT THEN IS FEMINIST PHILOSOPHY?

Just to repeat it once again: Aesthetics is the science that investigates the laws of art and the categories of art, the relationship between art and reality, and the methods of artistic creation. The question that concerns aesthetics is, among other things, the problem of the beautiful, which was already addressed by the ancient Greeks. Plato and Aristotle (also much later, Plotinus) discussed this question, and treated it as part of philosophy, as a chapter of metaphysics, rather than an independent science. In Plato, the beautiful is a means that brings us closer to the eternal world.[10]

Herta Nagl-Docekal's considerations regarding feminist aesthetics highlight the necessity of updating elements of "classical" aesthetic concepts, for instance Kant's notion of beauty as "disinterested pleasure." What then is feminist aesthetics? The basic assumption, necessary in order to shape a feminist aesthetics project – *desideratum* of the 1960s and '70s – about which Nagl-Docekal speaks extensively in the second chapter, consists in the idea that art is gendered. Because the debate is much diversified at this point, she proposes a topology of discussion derived from a theoretical and scientific perspective, focusing on central themes, without the pretense of exhausting the subject. Within these considerations, she also discusses the concept of a feminist aesthetics in a narrower sense, stating that a philosophical definition of the concept is possible. What hides behind the attempt to define the concept of feminist aesthetics is the observation that considering art as a special domain is not the same as the idea that it has nothing to do with political purposes. As a philosopher, she investigates the premises of feminist aesthetics in its narrow sense.

---

[9] Cf. STIEGLER 2017.

[10] Concerning the relation between aesthetics and other fields interested in art, see WOLFF 1983.

It is necessary to highlight the differentiated perspective by which Nagl-Docekal approaches the basic texts of feminist aesthetics, including the book by Rita Felski, *Beyond Feminist Aesthetics. Feminist Literature and Social Change* (1989). In this text the author understands feminist aesthetics as "any theoretical position which argues a necessary or privileged relationship between female gender and a particular kind of literary structure, style, or form."[11] However, as Nagl-Docekal points out – in agreement with Felski –, it is not possible to establish a necessary relationship between feminist issues, on the one hand, and certain forms of artistic expression on the other hand. Why should critical thinking, Nagl-Docekal asks further, in the name of a specific political commitment – and that is what feminist theory is – bring with it specific forms of creativity or of aesthetic categories? "Such a claim cannot survive close scrutiny."[12] To avoid this type of misconception, she proposes a so-called "weak reading" of the categories of classical aesthetic positions in a feminist context. That is the context in which one should show the discrimination of female artists, and the derogatory treatment of women. A weak interpretation "is not so much interested in a precise account of the history of philosophy, but in the possibility that some differentiations of classical provenance can still be relevant."[13] To substantiate her view, Nagl-Docekal offers a reading of Kant's idea of the beautiful and the sublime that would reject gendered connotations.

To the extent that art leads us to adopt a new perspective, so Nagl-Docekal, it has the potential to change our thoughts on political realities. In this case, the political impulse is a consequence of the creative activity and not its normative condition.

Therefore, from a feminist perspective, one has to be interested in the implications that different forms of perception (initiated by art) have for the relationship between the genders. As Nagl-Docekal points out, this aspect must be addressed in two ways: First, it is a matter of

[11] FELSKI 1989, 19.

[12] NAGL-DOCEKAL 2004, 84.

[13] NAGL-DOCEKAL 2004, 82. It would be interesting to explore whether the same could be done with regard to romantic aesthetics, with categories such as "das Interessante," or "die Ironie" and "die Frechheit" (see here for instance Friedrich Schlegel's novel *Lucinde*).

raising objections if sexist forms of action can be deduced. To formulate these ideas, the author proposes, for instance, to read Kant's thoughts about the relationship between politics and morality, as developed in his work *Perpetual Peace*. She refers here in particular to the fact that, according to Kant, politics – as the "art" of the state – represents, quite rightly, a completely autonomous sphere, with morality serving as a "limiting condition."[14] By analogy, feminist perspectives could be the "limiting conditions" for art as an autonomous sphere. The second (stronger emphasized) aspect Nagl-Docekal considers is the extent to which political impulses, initiated by art, can contain a feminist potential. In order to address this issue, turning to Adorno might be helpful. Rita Felski rightly suggests – according to Nagl-Docekal – that Adorno's ideas about differences and the connection between art and politics could provide productive impulses for feminist theory.[15] In particular, the concept of a "negative aesthetics" might be helpful here since it shows that the autonomy of art forms a place of resistance to socially rooted conventions. Of course – and Felski shows this convincingly, as Nagl-Docekal remarks –, it is not possible to establish a necessary relationship between feminist issues on the one hand and forms of artistic expression on the other. Regarding our question about a "feminist aesthetics" in a narrow sense, Nagl-Docekal concludes that it would be wrong to understand this concept in the sense of a "feminist art" theory. Rather, the central goal is a theoretical construction, free of masculine patterns of thought, capable of opening up a space for art with feminist potential.[16]

[14] See KANT 2010, 37: "Politics may be regarded as saying, 'be wise (i.e. prudent) as serpents'; Morals adds as a limiting condition, 'and harmless (i.e. guileless) as doves.' If the two maxims cannot co-exist in one commandment, there is really an incongruity between Politics and Morals: but, if the two can be combined throughout, any idea of antagonism between them is absurd, and any question about harmonizing them, as if they were in conflict, need not be even raised."

[15] NAGL-DOCEKAL 2004, 85.

[16] NAGL-DOCEKAL 2004, 85.

CHALLENGING PROCEDURES

In the second part of my text, I will try to extend the thoughts of Herta Nagl-Docekal, wondering what art with a feminist potential might mean. In my view, the artistic work of the Austrian digital photographer Eva Kosinar might serve as a good example for artworks that convey feminist thought – something for which Kosinar received not only a positive reception. Some of her works are the direct result of her engagement with theological feminist literature. The texts she mentions as her influence include among others Uta Ranke Heinemann's *Nein und Amen. Anleitung zum Glaubenszweifel* (a sort of radical demythologization of the New Testament, understanding Christianity as a fairy-tale religion) and *Eunuchen für das Himmelreich*, or Elisabeth Gössmann's *Ob die Weiber Menschen seyn, oder nicht*? Kosinar considers herself an atheist.

In Kosinar's understanding of art, a digital copy still means the original, in which she has invested a lot of work and, above all, creativity. Her digital works are unique, so I will not show any pictures of her in my essay, but simply refer to her website, for which she has given me permission. However, by repeatedly referring to the artist's website on the internet, the audience can see and understand more of the work of this young artist at the same time. I think it's a new approach to digital art that might seem a bit strange at first glance but is nonetheless stimulating and above all arousing curiosity.

On Eva Kosinar's website[17] we can see on the web page "Last Exhibitions" some of her digitalized photos which were shown at a solo exhibition held in Vienna in 2015, entitled *La Femme Tragique?*[18] After the exhibition, the artist was curious to know what the critics were going to say about her pictures, so she addressed an international panel of six experts, three women and three men from Slovakia, Austria, The Netherlands, Germany, and Portugal, in order to hear their opinions. On the professional level these international experts were publishers, picture editors, critics, gallerists, and curators. One can book, for instance, five to ten single meetings of 20 minutes each. In conver-

[17] See https://www.evakosinar.at/, last accessed 9/17/2021.

[18] See https://www.evakosinar.at/last-exhibitions/, last accessed 9/17/2021.

sation with artists one hears again and again that such discussions are not very fruitful. However, Kosinar's digital image "The Mother"[19] received a positive response from some of the experts.

What exactly is a work of art with a feminist potential? Here we are dealing with Eva Kosinar's provocative image "The Mother,"[20] a photograph reminiscent of Hieronymus Bosch or the surrealists. But this figure is nothing like a human being, rather, a person with a dog head,[21] holding a plain slice of toast bread and instead of a chest we see a human butt. It is something that deviates from normality, something not part of the everyday experience. And although we might not encounter this figure in daily life, it refers to things that are done daily, and which are related to the physiology and the needs of the human body: eating, being undressed, relaxing. We could say that the acts envisaged concern the natural activities of human beings, which assures them their daily life, but also the realities of the character, which is the mother, as the title chosen by the artist indicates. Whereby the gender of the figure is not known – it could be a woman, a man, a transgender person, a fact highlighted by the rendering of the face, which is not human, but the mask of a dog under which hides a person, who may be anything – of a different nation, skin-color, religion, or gender.

The subversive form of art we observe here, and which I want to draw attention to, relies on the category of the grotesque, *das Groteske*, by mean of which the artist attempts to put a distance between the subject or subjects and the world inhabited by them. Under the label of the grotesque, the artist named the exhibition, which included two of the images discussed here, *La Femme Tragique?*[22] Generally, the grotesque comes to stand in for all those things, which do not fit into our existing philosophical and aesthetic categories: monsters, human-animal or human-plant hybrids, miniature or gigantic bodily forms, inappropriate intimacies between beings, or any other phenomena that

[19] See https://www.evakosinar.at/last-exhibitions/die-mutter, "Die Mutter," 2014, photomontage, 35 x 38 cm, last accessed 9/17/2021.

[20] See n. 19 above.

[21] See also https://www.evakosinar.at/people/es-war-einmal, "Es war einmal," 2009, photomontage, 69 x 50 cm, last accessed 9/17/2021.

[22] See n. 18 above.

estrange us from our familiar world. In the literature, this phenomenon of alienation is well known. Synonyms for the term "grotesque" are: *bizarre*, *absurd*, *comical*, *macabre*, *distorted*, *miraculous*, *ridiculous*, *silly*, *caricatured*, *weird*, *whimsical*, and *unnatural*. There are some other – so to say – distorted pictures, in fact revised photos, which challenge that tenacious inclination of her photographic characters to be different. As shown in her picture cycle "Deep Sea,"[23] it is possible to relate the distorted faces, which seem to replicate the behavior of fish in water, with the faces of the many refugees drowned in the Mediterranean, which the media don't show us.

The ambiguity of Kosinar's "characters" applies to women as well as men.[24] This could be considered as an attempt to evoke a feminist theory of aesthetics in a narrow sense, by provoking a discussion about the social status of people with another sexual orientation, or the performative aspect of gender.

What might be the social and political function of the grotesque, as it is represented for example in "The Mother" by Eva Kosinar? Kosinar's art has feminist potential, even if she does not consider herself a feminist artist. The fact that in the portrait "The Mother" the person's breasts, which are the source of food for a newborn baby, have been replaced with a butt and, instead of a human head, one can see a dog's head, might indicate gender neutrality, as the one who feeds does not have to be a female.[25] Just as well as a male can highlight this exact behavior of feeding a child. The slice of bread that "the mother" holds, is in fact, under these circumstances, the symbol of nourishment and care that any person, regardless of gender, can provide for a child. What Eva Kosinar calls into question, is precisely the traditional identification of women with the role of the mother – a situation that still is on the agenda, even in the most advanced societies, and especially now, during the coronavirus pandemic.

---

[23] See https://www.evakosinar.at/people/tiefsee-01 (-05), "Tiefsee I–V," 2009, last accessed 9/17/2021.

[24] See e.g. https://www.evakosinar.at/people/herr-mayer, "Herr Mayer," 2009, 20 x 30 cm, or https://www.evakosinar.at/art/zirkusant, "Zirkusant," 2008, 30 x 45 cm, both last accessed 9/17/2021.

[25] See above with n. 19.

I understand the aesthetic category of the grotesque in its alienating dimension as a challenging procedure in order to question philosophically, and at the same time politically, the role played by women as mothers. Confronting the public with an unfamiliar representation of the mother forces the viewers to rethink the concept of the mother, including the broad spectrum of activities a mother has to perform and the problems she has to solve. Kosinar's image "The Mother" (and many of her other works as well) clearly have the potential to raise questions of feminist concern.

The general sense in which this image challenges the masculine pattern of thinking (especially the bourgeois pattern) through the staging of the grotesque, is that a woman who is a mother does not have to stay outside of society and at home. She can pursue her own design of life by making sense of Kant's virtue of fulfilling one's own perfection. The mother is a human being and as such an acting being, a being with purposes. Perhaps Kosinar's picture "La Femme Tragique?" expresses this idea – it represents a woman, who – in spite of the many children around her – does not forget to look after herself, to take care of her own qualities.[26]

The grotesque, as employed by Kosinar, is supposed to alienate insofar, as it incites the minds of the observers to fundamental questions: What really is a mother? Eva Kosinar's use of the aesthetic category of the grotesque in her digital photography helps to deconstruct the traditional mode of thinking about mothers, which is encountered still today.

What I also want to emphasize here is that on a formal-legal-juridical level the status of mothers is well-defined, at least in Europe. But within actually lived relationships between the genders, men's expectations for women as mothers still seem to be rather traditional – in spite of the so-called *Papamonat* (daddy month), a one-month period of unpaid leave for the father to be with the newborn child. One cannot be a real father for one month. Who can therefore guarantee that these new initiatives do not later backfire against women, being reproached by the father/husband for having sacrificed his worktime and

---

[26] See https://www.evakosinar.at/last-exhibitions/la-femme-tragique, "La Femme Tragique?" 2015, photomontage, 30 x 50 cm, last accessed 9/17/2021.

his money for the family? One can only hope that this doesn't "verschlimmbessern"[27] the situation of the mother.[28]

CONCLUSION

I understand feminist aesthetics as a critical reflection on the aesthetical act, a reflection that confronts the artistic object – in our case "The Mother" by Eva Kosinar – as it employs certain aesthetic categories, such as the category of the grotesque, in order to question the reality of the genders. The grotesque is not seen here as a category, which has gender connotations; men could also be represented as grotesque creatures. This connotation is one that is applied to the artistic object. It may signal a Foucaultian way of reading the reality beyond what is seen at first glance.[29] The existence of a connection between the artistic object and the reality of genders can also be emphasized by the modality, in which the observer reads the artistic object. As Adorno stated in his *Aesthetic Theory*: "Aesthetic behavior is the ability to see more in things than they are. It is the gaze that transforms empirical being into imagery."[30]

From my point of view, a feminist aesthetic theory in a narrow sense, as developed by Herta Nagl-Docekal, assumes an overview: it implies not just the painting, the image or the picture itself, the artwork in one word, but all that is related to it and gives life, moreover, to the essential aspects of the artist who marked her career as a female artist. It involves a philosophy as an aesthetics about the whole human being,[31] seen as a dialectic between mind, sensibility, and action.

---

[27] This German verb denotes an action that is made with the intention of improving something, but in fact making it worse.

[28] With reference to the daddy month as a matter of pay, see ZAUNBAUER 2019.

[29] Cf. FOUCAULT 1970, 41: "The task of commentary can never, by definition, be completed. And yet commentary is directed entirely towards the enigmatic, murmured element of the language being commented on: it calls into being, below the existing discourse, another discourse that is more fundamental and, as it were, 'more primal', which it sets itself the task of restoring."

[30] ADORNO 1984, 453.

[31] Cf. EŞIANU 2004, 171–174.

REFERENCES

ADORNO Theodor W., 1984, *Aesthetic Theory*, trans. Christian Lenhardt, ed. by Gretel Adorno & Rolf Tiedemann, London – Boston – Melbourne – Henley: Routledge & Kegan Paul

EŞIANU Cornelia, 2004, *Hypostasen der Identität beim jungen Friedrich Schlegel. Eine Untersuchung von Leben und Werk aus identitätstheoretischer Sicht*, Bukarest: Paideia (GGR Beiträge zur Germanistik 13)

FELSKI Rita, 1989, *Beyond Feminist Aesthetics. Feminist Literature and Social Change*, Cambridge, MA: Harvard University Press

FICHTE Johann Gottlieb, 1962, *Briefe*, ed. by Manfred Buhr, Leipzig: Reclam

FOUCAULT Michel, 1970, *The Order of Things. An Archeology of the Human Sciences*, trans. Alan Sheridan, London – New York: Tavistock

FREUD Sigmund, 2012, *Neue Folge der Vorlesungen zur Einführung in die Psychoanalyse*, BoD – Books on Demand, https://books.google.at/books?id=bjoZyYpdVhQC&printsec=frontcover&hl=de#v=onepage&q&f=false (last accessed 9/9/2021)

KANT Immanuel, 2010, *Perpetual Peace*, Philadelphia, PA: Slought Foundation – Syracuse, NY: The Syracuse University Humanities Center, https://slought.org/media/files/perpetual_peace.pdf (last accessed 8/27/2021)

NAGL-DOCEKAL Herta (ed.), 1994, *Feministische Philosophie*. Mit einer Bibliographie zusammengestellt von Cornelia Klinger, 2nd ed., Vienna – Munich: Oldenburg

NAGL-DOCEKAL Herta, 2001, *Feministische Philosophie. Ergebnisse, Probleme, Perspektiven*, 2nd ed., Frankfurt/M.: Fischer

NAGL-DOCEKAL Herta, 2004, *Feminist Philosophy*, trans. by Katharina Vester, Boulder, CO – Oxford, UK: Westview Press

SCHLEGEL Friedrich, 1988, *Kritische Schriften und Fragmente*, vol. 2: *1798–1801*, ed. by Ernst Behler & Hans Eicher, Paderborn – Munich – Vienna – Zurich: Schöningh

STIEGLER Bernd, 2017, *Fotografie im digitalen Zeitalter (Einleitung)*, in: Bernd STIEGLER (ed.), *Texte zur Theorie der Fotografie*, 2nd ed., Stuttgart: Reclam, 339–343

WOLFF Janet, 1983, *Aesthetics and the Sociology of Art*, London: George Allen & Unwin

ZAUNBAUER Wolfgang, 2019, Wieso der Papamonat in Österreich kaum genutzt wird, *Kurier*, 02/05/2019, https://kurier.at/politik/inland/papamonat-eine-frage-der-bezahlung/400397723 (last accessed 8/27/2021)

BRIGITTE BUCHHAMMER

KANT'S "THE KNOWER OF THE HEART"[1] AS CONTRIBUTION TO A FEMINIST PHILOSOPHY OF RELIGION

INTRODUCTION

Feminist theological theories critically investigate Vatican doctrinal ordinances in which loyalty is demanded to the church tradition that God must be presented in male predicates; God is always to be imagined as man, as Father, Lord, King, Ruler, and that Jesus be called Son of Man (see e.g. the Vatican document *Liturgiam authenticam*). The salvific importance of God is bound to the biological-sex body. Feminist theological contributions juxtapose these male predicates with alternative views of God's image. Dorothee Sölle proposed to address God as a well-spring or as a breath of wind, i.e. worshippers could rather use images from the natural world. Mary Daly's feminist theological research mentions God as "Being."[2] Most feminist theological theories, however, bring forward the argument that God could be expressed through female imagery: sister, mother, Sophia, even Jesa Christa.[3] With regard to the predicates of God, Elisabeth Schüssler

---

[1] None of the translations seem completely convincing to me. The King James Version of the Holy Bible: Acts of the Apostles, 1, 24: "Thou, Lord, which knowest the hearts of all men." Act of the Apostles 15, 8: "And God, which knoweth the hearts." Allen Wood and George di Giovanni use the following translation: "God – the reader of hearts" (KANT 2018); J. W. Semple: "the searcher of hearts" (KANT 1886). In my view "the Knower of the Heart" is closest to Kant's original meaning. – All German citations from Herta Nagl-Docekal's and others' works in this text are translated into English by the author.

[2] See SÖLLE 1981; DALY 1978, VIII.

[3] See STRAHM-BERNET 1991.

Fiorenza, for example, indicates that it is well worth using female images of God, but always in the awareness of *via eminentiae*, so that an increase in images and symbols would be feasible.[4] Rosemary Radford Ruether, on the other hand, stresses that the appropriation of female traits for God would merely intensify the problem of gender asymmetry and inequality.[5]

With reference to current questions regarding gender justice in the shaping of religious communities, I would like to take up one example among many in the context of feminist theology, namely Elisabeth Schüssler Fiorenza's concept of an "*ekklesia* of wo/men" (*ekklesia* is always written in italics).[6] One of her key neologisms is the term "kyriarchy" instead of patriarchy. This neologism means the following: "Kyriarchy – a neologism coined by me – is best understood as a sociopolitical and cultural-religious system of domination that structures the identity slots open to members of society in terms of race, gender, nation, age, economy, and sexuality and configures them in terms of pyramidal relations of domination and submission, profit and exploitation. The Western kyriarchal system works simultaneously on four levels: first, on the sociopolitical level; second on the ethical-cultural level; third on the biological-natural level; and fourth, on the linguistic-symbolic level. [...] Kyriarchy (from the Greek *kyrios* for 'lord, master, father' and *archein* for 'to rule, dominate') is best theorized as a complex pyramidal system of intersecting multiplicative social and religious relations of superordination and subordination, of ruling and exploitation."[7]

In opposition to this kyriarchal system, she develops a "feminist the*logy" as a different "political the*logy of liberation."[8] What are the core components of an *ekklesia* of wo/men? "To give a political-the*logical name to such a critical alternative site to the discourse of kyriarchy, I have introduced the concept of the *ekklesia* of wo/men. *Ekklesia* is qualified by the genitive 'of wo/men', which points to the

[4] See SCHÜSSLER FIORENZA 2004a, 245–251.
[5] See RADFORD RUETHER 1981, 217–218.
[6] More nuanced and detailed see BUCHHAMMER 2011, 17–28.
[7] SCHÜSSLER FIORENZA 2011, 8–9.
[8] SCHÜSSLER FIORENZA 2011, 49.

non-citizens of modernity. The intention here is to bring to public awareness that is, the radical democratic assembly of responsible full citizens. Historically and politically the concept of *ekklesia* of wo/men is an oxymoron, that is, a combination of mutually contradictory concepts intended to articulate a feminist political 'other'. [...] The radical-democratic construct of the *ekklesia*, which is both unfulfilled vision and historical reality. [...] *Ekklesia* of wo/men constitutes itself wherever responsible people gather both to articulate, discuss, and celebrate their problems, visions, and goals and together decide on strategies and ways to political and religious self-determination. *Ekklesia* of wo/men emphasizes that wo/men are such responsible full citizens."[9] *Ekklesia* of wo/men implies a meaningful concept of action. "Its praxis and theory needs to create a feminist public space in which equality and full citizenship for wo/men can be pursued."[10] "Instead of a uniform discursive oppositional entity, the *ekklesia* of wo/men is best conceived as a coalition of overlapping feminist communities and quasi-independent realms that have a common interest in changing kyriarchal domination. As a feminist open space, the *ekklesia* or parliament/congress of wo/men is not to be seen as a unified monolithic block, but as a heterogeneous, multi-voiced forum of competing discourses, all of which have the goal of transforming kyriarchal structures of oppression."[11] She summarizes her concept of an *ekklesia* of wo/men more pointedly in another paragraph, as follows: "*Ekklesia* is best translated as 'democratic congress' of full decision-making citizens. Democratic equality, citizenship, and decision-making power are constitutive for the notion of *ekklesia*."[12] Who is included under the umbrella term wo/men? "So by writing 'wo/men' I want to convey to the reader that whenever I speak of 'wo/men' I am not only referring to all women but also to the situation of oppressed and marginalized men. 'Wo/men' must therefore be understood as an inclusive term rather than an exclusive, universal gender expression."[13] "I understand wo/men

---

[9] SCHÜSSLER FIORENZA 2011, 51.
[10] SCHÜSSLER FIORENZA 2011, 90.
[11] SCHÜSSLER FIORENZA 2011, 91.
[12] SCHÜSSLER FIORENZA 2011, 152.
[13] SCHÜSSLER FIORENZA 2004b, 319, n. 13.

in the inclusive sense as a word that means all subordinate and oppressed people."[14]

Main aspects of Elisabeth Schüssler Fiorenza's notion of an *ekklesia* of wo/men, as the democratic congress of citizens, for example, are confronted in my work with Kant's significant philosophical distinctions. In my mind, it is expedient to introduce differentiations into given conceptualizations – which is a genuine task of philosophy. Kant's distinguishing between citizen (rule of law) and human being (human rights), between political (national and international state relations) and ethical community, just to name a few, prove fruitful in this respect.

In the following I would like to confront the draft of an "*ekklesia* of wo/men" with Herta Nagl-Docekal's reflections on a non-exclusive community, in order to illustrate how insightful and differentiated this approach proves to be in relation to the concept of an "*ekklesia* of wo/men," taking into account both the phenomenon of religion and the complexity of the human condition. Significantly, this notion of "*ekklesia* of wo/men" is again a gendered idea. Is it helpful to subsume all the deprived and oppressed people in the world under the gendered umbrella term "wo/men"?

In this paper I would like to take up two aspects of Herta Nagl-Docekal's philosophy of religion: her interpretation of Kant's theory of the "Herzenskündiger"[15] and the conception of conscience, and Kant's reflections on an adequate theory of human community. The guiding question will be how these considerations can be made fruitful for feminist approaches to philosophy of religion.

---

[14] Schüssler Fiorenza 2004a, 1, n. 4.

[15] A more detailed explanation of Kant's Bible references see below on pp. 137–139.

WHERE IS THE SOURCE OF RELIGION WITHIN THE INNER LIFE OF HUMAN BEINGS?

Nagl-Docekal underlines a problem of great contemporary relevance: Whenever the current philosophical debate engages with the topic of "God," the question arises whether in the context of contemporary philosophy there is a place for a consistent conception of God at all. She emphasizes that, in her view, abandoning a philosophical theology, entails "the loss of differentiations that are indispensable for an adequate concept of action."[16]

For the most part, in contemporary philosophy the notion of God is discussed solely in the religious-philosophical context, ignoring the significance that Kant gave the idea of God in his moral-philosophical contexts. In her essay on the "Knower of the Heart," Nagl-Docekal scrutinizes the moral-philosophical relevance of the concept of God. "The focus will be on the fact that, within the scope of Kant's system, the responsibility of carefully and sincerely weighing-up our particular motives is rooted in the human relationship to God. In this context, the understanding of God as a 'Knower of the Heart' will be an important focus."[17]

Contrary to the current tendency of what Nagl-Docekal calls a "legal philosophical shortcoming" in recent debates on practical philosophy, she proposes to refer to Kant and to focus on the "inner dimension" of action, which for Kant constitutes the genuine source of morality. According to Kant, law and morality are clearly distinguished by the fact that law can ultimately merely refer to the empirically ascertainable dimension of action, but not to moral convictions, while the term "morality" is based on this "inner" aspect, i.e. on motivations not ascertainable from

[16] NAGL-DOCEKAL 2010, 319: "Sie suchen aufzuzeigen, inwiefern die Abkehr vom Projekt einer philosophischen Theologie den Verlust von Differenzierungen, die für einen angemessenen Begriff des Handelns unverzichtbar sind, nach sich zu ziehen droht."

[17] NAGL-DOCEKAL 2010, 319: "Der Blick wird darauf gerichtet sein, dass im Rahmen der Kant'schen Systematik die Aufgabe eines sorgfältigen und aufrichtigen Abwägens unserer jeweiligen Motive in der Beziehung des Menschen zu Gott zu verankern ist. In diesem Zusammenhang wird der Auffassung von Gott als 'Herzenskündiger' besonderes Augenmerk zu gelten haben."

the outside.[18] It is precisely for this reason that Kant discusses the topic of "morality" from the perspective of the first person: "What should I do?"[19]

Nagl-Docekal focuses on the following issues: What significance does religion – understood in Kant's sense as "pure moral religion" and not as a set of norms prior to morality – have for the motivation of individuals? She asks: "If we get involved in this faith founded in our reason – to what extent does it make a difference regarding to the morality of our actions? From this follows the subsequent question: If we do not get involved in this faith – does it inevitably lead to a deficiency in the cultivation of hearts?"[20]

PRACTICAL REASON AS BASIS OF RELIGION

In Kant's conception of philosophy, the task of philosophy is to develop a notion of human beings, which is a viable criterion in criticizing and refuting reductionist ideas of the human being. The practical reason in every human being implies the moral law that Kant elucidates in his concept of the categorical imperative. Our own practical reason, the categorical imperative, demands respecting every human's dignity (one's own human dignity and that of all other people) at all times, all over the world. We are not allowed to instrumentalize our fellow human beings and also ourselves. Every human being must be recognized as a reasonable person, with the competence of freedom of action. The categorical imperative comprises two facets: a command and a ban. According to the ban we are not allowed to instrumentalize any individual "merely as a means."[21] The command is a duty of wide ob-

[18] See NAGL-DOCEKAL 2010, 320.
[19] KANT 2019, 677.
[20] NAGL-DOCEKAL 2010, 320: "Wenn wir uns auf diesen in unserer Vernunft gegründeten Glauben einlassen – inwiefern macht das hinsichtlich der Moralität unseres Handelns einen Unterschied? Daran knüpft sich die weitere Frage: Wenn wir uns auf diesen Glauben nicht einlassen – kommt es dadurch unausweichlich zu einem Defizit an Herzensbildung?"
[21] See KANT 1911a, 428; 2008, 79.

ligation. It demands an active benevolence, an active practical beneficence that supports the welfare of others. This means the duty of making the ends of others my own end, insofar as these ends are not immoral. We are obligated to support others in a non-paternalistic manner and also to respect our own human dignity: "Become not the slaves of other men. Suffer not thy rights to be trampled underfoot by others with impunity."[22] The categorical imperative implies two social tasks – first, to found a political community, a state that is based on the rule of law, internally as well as in international relations: "A juridico-civil (political) state is the relation of human beings to each other inasmuch as they stand jointly under public juridical laws (which are all coercive laws); secondly, to establish an "ethico-civil state" in which people are "united under laws without being coerced, i.e. under laws of virtue alone."[23]

The utmost end of reason is morality. Consequently, the ultimate goal of the world is the existence of human beings, who are capable of being both, reasonable and moral, to maintain their lives under the claim of the moral law. Human beings are morally obligated to found a legal, judicially structured state (a juridico-civil political state), and in a cosmopolitan facet, to found a confederation of states. They need to enter into the "precinct" of a "civil union"[24] so that they are able to lead their lives as autonomous and self-legislative persons. Human rights are derived from the moral law. Our first duty at the source of the notion of right is to gather with other humans in a civil society, in a legally structured state that is based on a universal civil contract. The civil contract must be republican (*res publica*): I do not have to obey any other rules than those to which I give my consent. And since one state cannot be peaceful by itself, we need cohesive international law. Furthermore, to assure a permanent peace, which is the supreme political goal, we need voluntary entry into a League of Nations. A necessary supplement to public international law is the cosmopolitan right. The cosmopolitan right guarantees that every human being, all over the world, should be respected as an end in itself and treated under

[22] KANT 1886, 152.
[23] KANT 2018, 127.
[24] KANT 1923a, 22; 2014, 112.

human rights which are accorded to every human being as a human being. The violation of human rights in one place on the earth can be felt everywhere and by everyone.[25] But this merely highlights the legal-political issue. The state as legal system is merely able to regulate the external actions of humans. The only way out of moral derailment consists in the foundation of a moral union of all humans in an open, worldwide ethical community.

ETHICAL COMMUNITY

The second social consequence of the categorical imperative is the responsibility of establishing a worldwide moral community. In her current research work Herta Nagl-Docekal takes up the idea of community, for instance in her presentation "Towards a Global Non-Exclusive Community" which was presented at the XXIV World Congress of Philosophy in Beijing, in August 2018. Addressing Kant's view that we are obligated to found two types of community, she notes: "Examining the relation between these two types of community, he points out that the ethical state 'can exist in the midst of a political community and even be made up of all the members of the latter [...]. It has, however, a special unifying principle of its own (virtue)'."[26] Kant highlights that the command of the categorical imperative, to become a member of an "ethical community," concerns duty as such. "We are obligated to contribute to establishing a society 'in accordance with, and for the sake of, the laws of virtue – a society which reason makes it a task and a duty of the entire human race to establish in its full scope'."[27] All humans are included in this duty of virtue. "This inclusiveness means that the 'ethical community' clearly differs

[25] See KANT 1968, 216.

[26] NAGL-DOCEKAL 2018, 79, with reference to KANT 2018, 106. Nagl-Docekal clarifies some aspects of the German term "ethisches Gemeinwesen": "Since the German term Kant uses – 'ethisches Gemeinwesen' – has often been translated as 'ethical community', it is important to note that this term has a specific meaning in Kant that differs decisively from the way the term is employed with regard to communities based on a shared identity," NAGL-DOCEKAL 2018, 79.

[27] NAGL-DOCEKAL 2018, 79, with reference to KANT 2018, 106.

from any conventional community defined by particular shared identity. Moreover, since it abstains from the logic that draws a line between 'we' and 'they' the 'ethical community' implies the source of criticism with regard to practices of exclusion."[28]

We have to ensure conditions, which enable us to fulfill the duty of respecting each human being's dignity, i.e. the duty of respecting the autonomy and freedom of agency of each human being as much as possible. As Kant explains, our own practical reason demands that we establish and develop an ethical community, a "republic under laws of virtue."[29] Kant describes the ethical state as "a free, universal and enduring union of hearts."[30] It is our moral duty to strive for this community. "The idea of such a state has an entirely well-grounded, objective reality in human reason (in the duty to join such a state) [...]."[31]

It is at this point that the notion of church in Kant's thinking becomes relevant. In this context, Kant maintains that the ethical community can only be thought of as a church. "If, however, the community is to be an ethical one, the people, as a people, cannot itself be regarded as legislator. For in such a community all the laws are exclusively designed to promote the morality of actions (which is something internal, and hence cannot be subject to public human laws)."[32] This thesis presents itself as applicable to all religious communities.

How should this genuine church (*church invisible* – "the mere idea of the union of all upright human beings under direct yet moral divine world-governance, as serves for the archetype of any such governance to be found by human beings"[33]), this synthesis of idea (*church invisible*) and its realization (*church visible*) be organized? Kant describes this ethical community in the term of a *voluntary, universal and enduring, wholehearted and virtuous community*, i.e., in the manner of a friendship-based and trustworthy solidarity among human beings. He writes in his *Metaphysics of Ethics* about friendship: Friendship is "the intimate blending of love with respect." "Friendship, regarded in its perfection,

[28] NAGL-DOCEKAL 2018, 80, with reference to KANT 2018, 109.
[29] See KANT 1907, 100; 2018, 110.
[30] KANT 2018, 133.
[31] KANT 2018, 126–127.
[32] NAGL-DOCEKAL 2018, 80, with reference to KANT 2018, 109.
[33] KANT 2018, 132.

is the union of two persons by mutual equal love and reverence."[34] Friendship is a duty of virtue that aims at a union of persons who are united by their ethical goodwill.[35] It is our moral duty to unite with other humans all over the world in friendship and solidarity. Ultimately, the ethical community is conceived of as cosmopolitan union.

As Kant employs the concept of the ethical community in his reflections on "church," the question arises how this concept relates to the manifold historical communities of faith. Kant focuses in particular on communities that are based on so-called sacred scriptures. How must these writings be interpreted in the light of Kant's philosophy of religion? The sacred narrative's innermost core is the categorical imperative, the moral law, he argues. The innermost meaning of all sacred narratives is that they should encourage us to act well-intendedly and morally: to respect the inviolability of human dignity. The responsibility of the ethical community is to support humans in their development of moral autonomy and freedom of action, it is the place where humans are free to discuss and develop moral issues in autonomy. It is up to us to develop ourselves in morality, to scrutinize moral questions according to the criterion of the categorical imperative. We have to commit ourselves to improving the moral conditions of the world with a brave and fearless heart.

On the sound basis of the one and true "religion of reason" there can only be one religion (Vernunftreligion) and one God.[36] Regarding the historically developed faith communities there are, however, numerous regulations and norms decreed by church authorities which cannot be solely understood as derived from reason. Rather, all churches that have been established in history are deficient implementations of the church invisible, the idea of the true church. Kant describes it as the arrogance of a historically grown church to claim that it is the only true community required by God. In this way people are subjugated and deprived of freedom. The historical faith communities

---

[34] KANT 1886, 175.

[35] See KANT 1886, 175.

[36] See KANT 1907, 12; 2018, 40. Kant offers a much more detailed unfolding of this topic in the *Critique of Pure Reason* and in the *Prolegomena to any Future Metaphysic that Will be Able to Present Itself as a Science*. See also BUCHHAMMER 2011, 165–185.

may, however, serve as instruments, mediums and vehicles to promote morality. As Kant emphasizes, "there is only one (true) religion, but there can be several kinds of faith."[37] True worship consists of the effort of leading a virtuous way of life, Kant argues. With his concept of pure moral religion Kant seeks to illustrate "where faith has its seat in the human being at all; it is [...] about the condition of the possibility of any concrete church community. Kant thus says about any 'popular faith' that 'long before the latter the endowment to moral religion lay hidden in human reason'."[38] The true religion of reason can be found at the core of the various forms of faith. Nagl-Docekal reminds us here of the following: the multitude of faith communities "confronts us again with the problem of the state of nature."[39] Kant now proposes an intriguing solution. No "historical faith" can refer directly to God; each one is based on the task given to humans that we ourselves have to implement the idea of such a community based on reason. The "[...] 'so-called religious wars and conflicts, which have so often shaken the world and spattered it with blood, have never been anything but quarrels about historical faith'."[40]

Kant asserts that the idea of reason has always been conveyed to people in a particular cultural context. What Kant therefore demands is a critical examination of people's particular rules of their faith communities: these doctrines and rules have so often obscured and distorted the view of the common core (pure moral religion). Kant does not primarily recommend a dialogue between the religions, but encourages inner-church debates. "Precisely because the general idea

---

[37] KANT 2018, 153.

[38] NAGL-DOCEKAL 2006a, 103, with reference to KANT 1907, 111: "Mit dem Begriff der 'reinen moralischen Religion' sucht Kant zunächst zu zeigen, wo Gläubigkeit überhaupt ihren Sitz im Menschen hat; es geht, wie gesagt um die Bedingung der Möglichkeit jeder konkreten Kirchengemeinschaft. Kant sagt demgemäß über jedweden 'Volksglauben', dass 'lange vor diesem letzteren die Anlage zur moralischen Religion in der menschlichen Vernunft verborgen lag'."

[39] NAGL-DOCEKAL 2006a, 105: "Die gegebene Vielzahl von Glaubensgemeinschaften konfrontiert uns erneut mit dem Problem des Naturzustandes."

[40] See NAGL-DOCEKAL 2006a, 105, with reference to KANT 1907, 95: "Daher sind, wie Kant unterstreicht, 'die sogenannten Religionsstreitigkeiten, welche die Welt so oft erschüttert und mit Blut bespritzt haben, nie etwas anderes, als Zänkereien um den Kirchenglauben gewesen'."

is inherent in every church faith, careful interpretation can contribute to overcoming conflicting particular interests. [...] According to Kant, in a very long-term perspective a single, truly universal church can emerge from this kind of work of interpretation."[41]

THE SOURCE OF RELIGION

At this point I would like to turn to Kant's reflections on the source of religion. The first sentence in his *Religion within the Boundaries of Mere Reason* states: "So far as morality is based on the conception of the human being as one who is free but who also, just because of that, binds himself through his reason to unconditional laws, it is in need neither of the idea of another being above him in order for him to recognize his duty, nor for an incentive other than the law itself in order for him to observe it. [...] – Hence on its own behalf morality in no way needs religion (whether objectively, as regards willing, or subjectively, as regards capability)."[42] The entire issue of religion in Kant's view is summarized under the umbrella question: "What may I hope?"[43] We are free to be religious, nobody can force us to do so. The difference between religion and morality is crucial in Kant's concept of religion. What is required of humans in moral terms, we always know

---

[41] NAGL-DOCEKAL 2006a, 106, with reference to KANT 1907, 110: "Er macht vielmehr geltend, dass die 'Vernunftidee' den Menschen jeweils in einem bestimmten kulturellen Kontext vermittelt wurde. Mit dieser Differenzierung kommt ein Ausweg aus den Konflikten in Sicht: Kant fordert zu einer genauen philosophischen Interpretationsarbeit innerhalb aller Religionsgemeinschaften auf. Da die Weltreligionen auf ein und derselben Basis beruhen, könne eine vernünftige Deutung ihrer vielfältigen Glaubensinhalte den identischen Kern von ihnen frei legen. [...] Es fällt auf, dass Kant den Ausweg aus den 'Religionsstreitigkeiten' nicht primär in einem Dialog zwischen den verschiedenen Kirchen sieht, sondern in einer für alle Glaubensgemeinschafen notwendigen innerkirchlichen Auseinandersetzung um das, 'was das Wesentliche aller Religionen ausmacht'. Paradox formuliert: Gerade deshalb, weil in jedem Kirchenglauben der Gedanke der Allgemeinheit angelegt ist, kann eine sorgfältige Interpretation dazu dienen, eine Überwindung der konfligierenden Partikularitäten einzuleiten. [...] In sehr langfristiger Perspektive kann Kant zufolge aus einer derartigen Interpretationsarbeit eine einzige, wahrhaft allgemeine Kirche entstehen."

[42] KANT 2018, 39.

[43] KANT 2019, 677.

without any reference to religion, what we have to do, we know by means of the categorical imperative. But in the effort of leading a virtuous life we painfully experience how much bliss and virtue fall apart. Reason thinks with necessity of the idea of the highest good: that is the connection of virtue and bliss. Our practical reason has a need for a meaningful life on the whole, our practical reason urges that our moral effort should not be poiess or senseless. The source of religion is to be found in our insight that we are finite, mortal and vulnerable beings. The experience of moral fallibility on the one hand, and the painful experience, that moral action in terms of civil courage can lead to loss of bliss on the other hand, and the hope for an unconditional sense of our moral commitment – that is the source, on which reason reaches the postulates of God and immortality. These postulates are the core of the pure moral religion established in every human being. But practical reason can only postulate this, it does not come here to any theoretical proof. Kant characterizes faithlessness as the maxim of the independence of reason from its own need.

Under the question of how a meaningful speech of God is possible, I refer to Kant's theory of *symbolic anthropomorphism*. In the conceptual figure of analogy God's predicates (Gottesprädikate) are not attributed as attributes, but these predicates are only predicated on grounds of the relation of human to God. Through this figurative analogy,[44] we can express that God in and of himself is unknowable to our human reason. The highest being is merely thinkable in this form of analogy. Kant calls it a mistake in thinking when one transforms the sensualization of a pure idea of reason into a perception of an object of the senses. The only meaningful predicates of God are those which necessarily result from practical reason, they are all moral: sanctity, the justice of God as judge, and the benevolence of the "Knower of the Heart."[45]

---

[44] See KANT 1911b.

[45] Kant's translators Allen Wood and George di Giovanni use the three terms: "holiness, goodness and justice as judge" (KANT 2018, 21). I would like to use "sanctity and benevolence" instead of "holiness and goodness," because "goodness" seems superficial in the context of moral philosophy and the term "holiness" is inexact for these purposes (cf. *Oxford Online Etymology Dictionary*, s. v. above terms, https://www.etymonline.com/).

THE IDEA OF THE "HERZENSKÜNDIGER_IN"[46]

Nagl-Docekal indicates that Kant explains the subject of "morality" from two different perspectives: on the one hand with regard to the human being as *homo noumenon*, i.e. with regard to pure practical reason (the human as an autonomous person), on the other hand to the human as a "being of sensual reason" where the question of how it could be possible to act morally in the condition of mortality arises.[47]

Herta Nagl-Docekal highlights Kant's scrutiny of the crucial question: How can people develop an attitude, an awareness over time that guides them to act in accordance with the categorical imperative? The purpose of practical reason is to found a good and benevolent will. The moral attitude has a time index: we are obligated to decide to base our decisions on the moral law in every current and future circumstance. "When the pure practical reason, inherent in every human being, puts forward its 'you ought to do', the obligation founded in this manner has no punctual character – it concerns not merely an isolated decision situation, but also the further course of our life."[48] The foundation of a good, benevolent will is important, i.e. that I decide to become a good person. In this context Kant speaks of the "revolution in the disposition of the human being [...]":[49] as homo noumenon I am able to decide to radically change my moral attitude. But as mortal beings of sensual reason we can only endeavor to gradually come closer to the ideal of a well-meaning human being. From an intraworldly perspective, the phrase "human moral improvements" actually makes sense.

---

[46] A more detailed explanation of Kant's Bible references see below on pp. 137–139. I have decided to write the word *Herzenskündiger_in* in a gender-sensitive way, with underscore, in order to make visible and to sensitize to the fact that in the sociopolitical and especially in the religious and church context gender injustice and discrimination on the basis of gender still persist.

[47] See NAGL-DOCEKAL 2010, 320.

[48] NAGL-DOCEKAL 2010, 321: "Wenn die in jedem Menschen angelegte reine praktische Vernunft ihr 'du sollst' vorbringt, hat die darin begründete Verpflichtung keinen punktuellen Charakter – sie betrifft nicht nur eine jeweils aktuell vorliegende Entscheidungssituation, sondern auch den weiteren Verlauf unseres Lebens."

[49] KANT 2018, 78–79.

Kant is talking about "constant progress and rapprochement to the highest good (set as his aim)."[50] In this respect, he clarifies that the idea of "a morally good human being" is meant in the sense of moral completeness. This is where our pure practical reason opens up a relation to God, i.e., to God as the idea of moral completeness, God as the highest moral perfection. Our practical reason conceives of God as a moral "*ens perfectissimum*."[51] It is important to note that Kant describes the idea of God as a relationship, in the categoriality of relationality. "It is to be explained that Kant's more detailed specification of the 'idea of God' represents a relationship between humans and God – and between God and humans – which has profound consequences for the moral character of our everyday actions."[52] At this point, according to Nagl-Docekal, human reason considers itself compelled to establish a reference to God. Human reason requires in every recognition an idea of completeness as a yardstick for every knowledge of the same kind, as Kant explains. This likewise applies to practical reason, which imposes the unconditional practical law on us. There is a limit to this, however, because reason cannot make the absolute necessity of this law comprehensible. This is where human reason conceives of the idea of God: God as the supreme moral being. From the moral perspective, practical reason is able to specify God, as "ens perfectissimum," more closely; it can, as Kant explains, "make itself a precisely defined concept of God."[53] Kant now underscores: "The moral idea of God

---

[50] KANT 1923b, 335.

[51] See NAGL-DOCEKAL 2010, 322, with reference to KANT 1972a, 1235: "Dem entsprechend entwirft die praktische Vernunft 'die Idee von Gott' als 'ein Wesen der höchsten Moralität', und sie kann aus ihrer moralischen Perspektive dieses 'ens perfectissimum' näher bestimmen; genauer gesagt, kann sie sich aus diesem Blickwinkel 'einen ganz präcis bestimmten Begriff von Gott machen'. Kant hält fest: 'Der Moralbegriff von Gott besteht in den Begriffen der Heiligkeit, Gütigkeit und Gerechtigkeit.' [...] Diese Begriffstrias bildet auch die Grundlage für Kants Deutung der christlichen Trinitätskonzeption."

[52] NAGL-DOCEKAL 2010, 319: "Es soll erläutert werden, dass die von Kant entfaltete nähere Bestimmung der 'Idee von Gott' eine Beziehung des Menschen zu Gott – und Gottes zu den Menschen – zur Darstellung bringt, die weitreichende Konsequenzen für den moralischen Zuschnitt unserer alltäglichen Handlungen hat."

[53] NAGL-DOCEKAL 2010, 322.

consists in the notion of sanctity, benevolence and justice."[54] Nagl-Docekal underlines the significance of the succession of these terms. First of all, the importance of the moral legislator (law-giver) is in the center of attention by recognizing moral duties as divine commandments. The moral law is sacred, sacrosanct, it is inviolable. This means for the self-conception of the individual: "When I fulfill my moral responsibilities, I can understand this as 'conformity of my will with that of a holy and gracious world Creator'."[55]

Kant thus explains the connection between God as "moral legislator" and the moral law which is inherent in our reason: Our practical reason confronts us with an absolute duty, the absolute necessity of which, however, it cannot make comprehensible. With this, according to Nagl-Docekal, an essential question remains open: Why should we be motivated by a categorical norm when the reason for its binding nature is not obvious to us? "By now sketching the 'idea of God' as 'legislator' (law-giver), reason leads us to the 'knowledge of all our obligations as (instar) of divine commandments'."[56] In this case, however, the term "knowledge" is not to be understood as theoretical knowledge, but in the sense of recognition. "From this viewpoint 'God is the supreme ground of the system of all moral purposes, i.e. the highest good'."[57] Thus, the idea of God is founded on a subjective, yet true and unconditional necessity of reason. Kant explains this in his theory of "the postulates of pure practical reason." Pure practical reason establishes a pure faith in reason that is the foundation of all forms of historical faith. This pure reasonable faith has the character of an unshakable, unbreakable conviction, on the basis of which individuals are able to say: "I insist on it and will not let this faith be de-

---

[54] KANT 2018, 21.

[55] NAGL-DOCEKAL 2010, 322–323, with reference to KANT 1963a, 261. "Wenn ich meine moralischen Pflichten erfülle, kann ich dies als 'Übereinstimmung meines Willens mit dem eines heiligen und gütigen Welturhebers' verstehen."

[56] NAGL-DOCEKAL 2010, 323, with reference to KANT 1963a, 210: "Indem die Vernunft nun die 'Idee von Gott' als 'Gesetzgeber' entwirft, leitet sie uns an zur 'Erkenntnis aller unserer Pflichten als (instar) göttlicher Gebote'."

[57] NAGL-DOCEKAL 2010, 323, with reference to KANT 1972a, 1241: "Unter dieser Perspektive 'ist Gott der oberste Grund des Systems aller moralischen Zwecke, d. i. das höchste Gut'."

prived of me."[58] As Nagl-Docekal emphasizes, it is important to note this aspect as well as Kant's emphasis on the relational aspect of the idea of God as moral legislator.[59]

At the center of Kant's purely moral religion is the moral *relation* of humans to God with special importance placed on the dialogic aspect of morality. As stated already, on the one hand there is the I as noumenon, the morally legislative reason, on the other hand there is the I as a sensual being, the recipient of moral legislation. The I as rational sensuous being is being addressed by the I as noumenon, the law-giving authority in us, so that the revolution of the heart can be accomplished.[60] At that point, Kant's considerations about moral emotion attains relevance. "I, as a rational sensual being, see myself confronted with an 'idealistic person' and called by him to form and cultivate the attitude of sanctity in my inner life. More precisely, the reason achieves a translation: The practical reason is so concerned with the sensuousness of the recipient that it presents its idea of moral perfection in a visual vivid form – in a person – and in doing so, withdraws itself into the second row, as it were."[61] Though "Kant warns of

[58] See NAGL-DOCEKAL 2010, 324, with reference to KANT 1963a, 257: "Das bedeutet, dass die reine praktische Vernunft in uns einen – allen historisch kontingenten Bekenntnissen, i. e. allem 'Geschichtsglauben' voraus liegenden – 'reinen Vernunftglauben' begründet. Dieser hat den Charakter einer unerschütterlichen Überzeugung, aufgrund deren die Einzelnen sagen können: '[I]ch beharre darauf und lasse mir diesen Glauben nicht nehmen'."

[59] See NAGL-DOCEKAL 2010, 324, with reference to KANT 2005, 191: "Zu beachten ist nun, dass und wie Kant an der Idee von Gott als 'moralischem Gesetzgeber' bzw. als 'Oberhaupt' des Reiches der Sitten den relationalen Aspekt hervorhebt. Die reine moralische Religion bringt für die Einzelnen mit sich, dass sie ein Gegenüber haben; ihr Zentrum ist 'das moralische Verhältnis der Menschen zum höchsten Wesen'. Die Moralität erhält dadurch eine dialogische Komponente."

[60] See NAGL-DOCEKAL 2010, 325, with reference to KANT 1963b, 628: "Da bin zum einen ich als eine noumenale (übersinnliche) Instanz, insofern meine Vernunft moralisch gesetzgebend ist; zum anderen ich als ein vernünftiges Sinnenwesen, das Adressat der moralischen Gesetzgebung ist. […] 'Als Subjekt der moralischen […] Gesetzgebung', d. h. als '(homo noumenon), ist er als ein anderer als der mit Vernunft begabte Sinnenmensch (specie diversus) […] zu betrachten', wobei es an dem zweiten liegt, sich durch die Stimme der Moral so ansprechen zu lassen, dass die erläuterte 'Revolution' zustande kommt."

[61] NAGL-DOCEKAL 2010, 325: "Ich als vernünftiges Sinnenwesen sehe mich nun einer

the danger of a reductionist 'anthropomorphism' arising from the transforming of the 'schematism of analogy (for explanation), which we cannot do without [...], into a schematism of object determination (for the widening of our knowledge)'."[62]

Pure moral religion enables us to have a vis-à-vis, a companion; there is a moral relationship of human beings to the supreme being. Morality thus receives a dialogic component. In this personal relationship of humans to God, the emotional dimension has an important meaning. This is where Kant's conception of the virtue of friendship becomes relevant in that the relation of humans to God is represented in the categoriality of friendship. The relationship of humans to God implies complete confidence and trust. Nagl-Docekal points out to what extent Kant refers to the doctrine of God in his time, thus humans' relationship to God in two terms: "fear" and "love." Of particular interest is that Kant explains "fear of God" through the concept of respect (*Achtung*): "the relationship between respect and love, and the complementary of these two concepts, which for Kant contributes the fundamental principle of friendship, is thus evident as already signaled by the chapter title 'From the most intimate union of love with respect in friendship'."[63]

As we imagine God as our "most intimate present sacred being," this has crucial consequences for our own evaluation of our actions.

'idealischen Person' gegenübergestellt und von dieser aufgerufen, die Gesinnung der Heiligkeit in mir auszubilden und zu kultivieren. Genauer betrachtet, vollbringt die Vernunft eine Übersetzungsleistung: Sie lässt sich auf die sinnliche Ausrichtung ihres Adressaten so weit ein, dass sie ihre Idee moralischer Vollkommenheit in anschaulicher Form – in einer Person – präsentiert und dabei selbst gewissermaßen in die zweite Reihe zurück tritt."

[62] See NAGL-DOCEKAL 2010, 325, with reference to KANT 2005, 42: "Freilich warnt Kant vor der Gefahr eines verkürzenden 'Anthropomorphismus', der dadurch entsteht, dass der 'Schematismus der Analogie (zur Erläuterung), den wir nicht entbehren können [...] in einen Schematismus der Objektbestimmung (zur Erweiterung unseres Erkenntnisses)' verwandelt wird."

[63] NAGL-DOCEKAL 2010, 326, with reference to KANT 1963b, 608–613: "Aufhorchen lässt, dass Kant die 'Furcht Gottes' durch den Begriff der 'Achtung' erläutert: Damit tritt das Begriffspaar 'Achtung und Liebe' hervor, bzw. die Komplementarität dieser beiden Begriffe, die für Kant die Grundstruktur von Freundschaft ausmacht, wie bereits die Kapitelüberschrift 'Von der innigsten Vereinigung der Liebe mit der Achtung in der Freundschaft' signalisiert."

At this point the other moral characteristics of God become relevant: grace and justice, in addition to Kant's notion of conscience.

KANT'S THEORY OF CONSCIENCE

In this respect, it is important to respond to Kant's conception of conscience, where it refers to the image of various courtroom roles inherent in humans: accuser, prosecutor, judge. Conscience is a natural predisposition, a precondition of the heart for compulsory terms in general, "every human being has, as a moral being, a conscience. [...] Conscience is the human's practical reason, which does, in all circumstances, hold before him his law of duty, in order to absolve or to condemn him."[64] In this context, Kant describes the obligation upon people to cultivate their conscience: "To sharpen the attention to the voice of the inner judge and to use all resources (thus only indirect duty) to make him heard. The only duty there is here room for, is to cultivate one's conscience, and to quicken the attention due to the voice of a human's inward monitor, and to strain every exertion (i.e. indirectly duty) to produce obedience to what it says."[65] In this context, Kant mentions the connection of fear with respect in relation to this inner judge.[66]

Kant characterizes conscience as an internal court within the human being: "The consciousness of an internal tribunal in human, before which his thoughts accuse or excuse him, it what is called Conscience. Every human being has Conscience, and finds himself inspected by an inward censor [...]."[67] This inner judgment is inherently "incorporated" in its essence, "is interwoven with his substance."[68] "It follows him like his shadow, however he may try to flee from it. He may indeed deafen himself by pleasure or by business, or he may lull himself into a lethargy; but this is only for a while, and he must inevitably come

[64] KANT 1886, 131.
[65] KANT 1886, 132.
[66] See NAGL-DOCEKAL 2010, 327.
[67] KANT 1886, 153.
[68] KANT 1886, 153.

now and then to himself; nor can he hinder himself from ever and anon awakening, whereupon he hears his dreadful and appalling voice. In the last stage of reprobation human may indeed have ceased to heed him, but not to hear him, is impossible."[69]

Kant sketches the inner court as follows: there is the accuser, the accused, the defending instance and the judicial instance, which ultimately has to pronounce the sentence. All of these roles, however, I personally fulfill. The whole matter "is an affair of human with himself, he notwithstanding finds his reason constrained to carry on the suit, as if it were at the instigation of another person; for the procedure is the conduct of a case before a court. Now, that he who is the accused by his conscience should be figured to be just the same person as his judge, is an absurd representation of a tribunal; since in such an event the accuser would always lose his suit. Conscience must therefore always represent to itself someone other than itself as judge, unless it is to arrive at a contradiction with itself. This other may be either a real – or an ideal – person the product of reason."[70] Kant addresses the danger of an inconsistency here: if indeed only I myself exercise all these functions, it is very easy to exculpate myself, to avoid responsibility. So, the conscience of a human being in all its obligations will, accordingly, have to imagine someone other than herself (i.e., other than the human being as such) as the judge of her actions. This other person may now be a real or merely idealistic person who is created by reason for itself. Kant says: "Such an ideal person, authorized to sit as judge in the court of conscience, must be a searcher of the heart, for the tribunal is erected in the interior of human being. Further, this ideal person must hold all-obligatory power, i.e. be such a person, or at least be figured as if he were a person, in respect of whom all duty may be represented as his commandments, because conscience is judge over all free actions. Lastly, he must have all the power (in heaven and in earth) to absolve and to condemn, these properties being of the very essence of the functions of a judge: apart from his being endowed wherewith, he could give no effect to the law. But since he who *searches* the heart, and, having all-obligatory power, is

[69] KANT 1886, 153–154.
[70] KANT 1886, 154.

able to absolve and condemn, is called God, it follows that conscience must be regarded as a subjective principle implanted in the reason of human being, calling for an account of every action before God. Nay, this notion of responsibility is at all times involved, however darkly, in every act of moral self-consciousness."[71] Kant refers to the Acts of the Apostles 1, 24: "Lord, you know everyone's heart." And 15, 8: "God, who knows the heart […]." God is the *Knower of the Heart* (Luther's translation of the Latin phrase: *qui novit corda*).

The idea of the accused and the accuser on the one hand and the function of the judge on the other represent essentially Kant's differentiation between *homo noumenon* (judge) and *homo phaenomenon*. Through conscience, reason initiates the relationship with God.

Crucial to this concept of conscience as an internal court is the conception of the *Knower of the Heart*, where God is thought of as to know us well, to explore all our intentions and our emotions within our hearts. God as Knower of our Heart examines our attitudes, not our deeds, the attitudes that have determined our actions. From this perspective, our conscience scrutinizes in more detail what has been going on in our intentions and motivations before we commit the act in question. "[H]ere reason judges itself as to whether it has really taken over the judgment of actions with all caution (whether they are right or wrong), as a witness that this has happened or not."[72] Nagl-Docekal points out that Kant's word "caution" is decisive here: he has a process of careful self-evaluation in mind. In order to illustrate this caution, Kant explores an immanent tension between different actors. "Accordingly, we have the 'consciousness of an inner court in humans […]'. As the doer of my deed, I see myself confronted with a prosecutor and defended by a lawyer, after whose pleas (contra and pro) the judge makes his sentence. In view of this constellation, reason again 'compels' us to acquire the 'idea of God' at the level of imagination –

[71] KANT 1886, 154.

[72] KANT 1907, 186: "[…] hier richtet die Vernunft sich selbst, ob sie auch wirklich jene Beurteilung der Handlungen mit aller Behutsamkeit (ob sie recht oder unrecht sind) übernommen haben, und stellt den Menschen wider oder für sich selbst zum Zeugen auf, dass dieses geschehen oder nicht geschehen sei."

in this case, the idea of God as a perfectly righteous judge."[73] Conscience has to be thought of as a subjective principle of responsibility in the face of God. In this respect Kant puts the definition of God as Knower of the Heart in the foreground. Nagl-Docekal points out that this puts two common forms of moral judgment of people in their place: judgment by others, as well as by myself. Other people are merely able to judge my actions, but cannot perceive my innermost thoughts and attitudes. With regard to myself: even when exploring my attitudes, I am initially dependent on my actions in order to conclude from them my attitudes. In this respect, Kant emphasizes the need for sincerity of heart: a culture of sincerity. It is all too easy for us to evaluate our motives as being better than they are. According to Kant, it is not possible for human beings to look so profoundly into their own hearts that they could ever be completely sure of the purity of their own moral purpose and the integrity of their mindset.[74]

God as *Knower of the Heart* allows humans to hope that he or she will see through us completely and will also understands our good intentions. Just when we take ourselves morally seriously, it is consistent to develop in us the idea of an instance that knows us exactly and therefore cannot make a misjudgment because it is able to look into the deepest corners of our heart, which we ourselves are not able to fathom. The *Knower of the Heart* is so conceived that he or she will make no mistake, that we can trust on that. This gives us the assurance that we are not completely alone. This idea of God as *Knower of the Heart* is also an encouragement to carefully examine ourselves. By imagining that we are facing someone who knows us well and does not make any misjudgment, we are capable of self-critical examination of our minds as carefully as possible. With respect to the idea of the

[73] NAGL-DOCEKAL 2010, 328, with reference to KANT 1963b, 573: "Demnach haben wir das 'Bewusstsein eines inneren Gerichtshofes im Menschen (vor welchem sich seine Gedanken einander verklagen oder entschuldigen)'. Ich als Täter meiner Tat sehe mich mit einem Ankläger konfrontiert und von einem Advokaten verteidigt, nach deren Plädoyers (contra und pro) der Richter sein Urteil fällt. Im Blick auf diese Konstellation 'nötigt' uns nun die Vernunft erneut, uns die 'Idee von Gott' auf der Ebene der Vorstellung zu eigen zu machen – in diesem Fall die Idee von Gott als vollkommen gerechtem Richter."

[74] See NAGL-DOCEKAL 2010, 330–331.

Knower of the Heart Kant states the following: "'The eternal, for whom the condition of time is nothing, sees, in this – from our point of view – endless series of our decisions, the entirety of adequacy with the moral law in one single intellectual view, which is something human reason is never capable of.' That is," Nagl-Docekal concludes, "the 'Knower of the Heart' judges whether we have, indeed, made the 'change of heart' that the moral law requires, so that our deeds are still linked to 'immutable purposes'."[75]

Kant underlines that this kind of the relationality opens the hope for people that they will not be completely isolated and alone in their moral effort. Here Kant characterizes human's relationship to God in the categoriality of friendship.

In the background of this idea of relationship between human beings and God, Kant also ponders a philosophically reflected theory of service to God. Based on his thesis that all historically grown beliefs have at their very core moral attitude and guidance, Kant argues: "The true service of God is therefore [...] invisible, i.e. it is a service of the heart (in spirit and in truth) and can consist only in the disposition of obedience to all true duties as divine commands."[76] The rites, prayers and faith-practices are support instruments for the human imagination to encourage in people's hearts the will to lead a life well-pleasing to God,[77] and that can only mean affirming the motivation to be a good person in the sense of the categorical imperative.

---

[75] NAGL-DOCEKAL 2010, 332, with reference to KANT 1963a, 253–254: "'Der Unendliche, dem die Zeitbedingung nichts ist, sieht, in dieser für uns endlosen Reihe, das Ganze der Angemessenheit mit dem moralischen Gesetze, und die Heiligkeit, die sein Gebot unnachlaßlich fordert, [...] ist in einer einzigen intellektuellen Anschauung des Daseins vernünftiger Wesen ganz anzutreffen.' D. h., der 'Herzenskündiger' beurteilt, ob wir die von uns geforderte 'Änderung des Herzens' vollzogen haben, so dass unsere – unumgehbar zweideutigen – Taten dennoch mit einem 'unwandelbaren Vorsatze' verknüpft sind."

[76] NAGL-DOCEKAL 2010, 326–327, with reference to KANT 1907, 192: "Der 'wahre' Dienst Gottes ist demnach 'unsichtbar, d. i. ein Dienst der Herzen (im Geist und in der Wahrheit), und kann nur in der Gesinnung, der Beobachtung aller wahren Pflichten als göttlicher Gebote' bestehen."

[77] See NAGL-DOCEKAL 2014, 115.

BRIGITTE BUCHHAMMER

THE THEORY OF CONSCIOUSNESS, THE CONCEPT OF THE "KNOWER OF THE HEART," AND THE "ETHICAL COMMUNITY" FROM THE PERSPECTIVE OF PEOPLE IN THE AGE OF RELIGIOUS LOSS

Is it possible for Kant's theory of ethical community to be relevant for both believers and agnostics? For believers, the categorical imperative implies the obligation of renewal, of reform of their traditional teachings and practices in the sense of overcoming encrusted structures. To what extent are agnostics able to follow Kant's concept of the moral community? As Nagl-Docekal points out, many contemporary Kant scholars seem to agree that for agnostics Kant's conception of the ethical community is obsolete. But, Kant clearly states that historically evolved denominations are merely a vehicle for a united state of virtue. "However, in regard of current atomistic trends, it might prove inspiring, nevertheless, to re-consider his thesis that all human beings are called to commit themselves to forming a community under the 'banner of virtue'. Taking up this call in a secular context will require the development of innovative practices. In which way Kant questions views that define morality in terms of reciprocity is of relevance here. He introduces an important distinction: reciprocity, he argues, is a core element of an ideal moral community – something to hope for in the long run, but this does not justify the thesis that, from a moral point of view, we ought to make symmetry a precondition of our present actions. In general, the moral law rather imposes on us a unilateral duty: I am obliged to respect and treat others as persons, even when I have good reasons to doubt that they would behave likewise towards me. Poignantly phrased, Kant contends that the moral imperative appeals to the subject to make a beginning. Valuable guidelines may be drawn from Kant's reflections on the respect that we are obliged to show towards all other human beings, simply because they are humans."[78]

Kant's theory of the examination of conscience is imagined in that we are faced with someone who knows us well, whom we can trust completely. If this is omitted, "we have no hope of experiencing a wholly righteous judgment anywhere; we would regard ourselves as,

[78] NAGL-DOCEKAL 2018, 81.

in the end, lonely."[79] The result would be an attitude of being closed in oneself, which would affect how we perceive and shape our individual life's work.

How does Kant articulate the aporia of the agnostic human being? Those people "who reject the idea of the 'wise ruler of the governor' into a performative self-contradiction: what they theoretically deny, they are at the same time compelled (by the 'need' of their practical reason) to believe practically, because otherwise they would not have the strength to persevere with their moral intention."[80] Kant describes this in the following way: "'If we abandon this principle', we will either 'act against our conscience' or practically refute our theory – rake it 'ad absurdum practicum'."[81] Under current conditions, should the internal court in general be closed? But how can we philosophically explain what we are used to calling conscience in everyday language? In any case, such a closing of the internal court would have wide-ranging social consequences. "If we are reluctant to examine the moral quality of our actions as sincerely and 'cautiously' as possible, we would also lack vigilance, caution and carefulness towards others. That the moral legislative voice of our reason obligates us to respect the 'dignity' of those affected by our actions implies that we have to assess as precisely as possible – also in the medium of communication – the consequences of our actions on those affected. So, what would a consistent concept of moral action look like that renounces the conception of self-criticism?"[82]

---

[79] NAGL-DOCEKAL 2010, 334: "Wenn wir uns nicht vorstellen können, jemandem gegenüber gestellt zu sein, der uns genau durchschaut, hat unser Hang zur Unlauterkeit uns selbst gegenüber das letzte Wort. Wir haben dann keine Hoffnung, irgendwo eine ganz gerechte Beurteilung zu erfahren; auch müssen wir uns als im letzten einsam betrachten."

[80] NAGL-DOCEKAL 2010, 335: "Näherhin geht Kant davon aus, dass diejenigen, die die Idee des 'weisen Weltregierers' zurückweisen, in einen performativen Selbstwiderspruch geraten: Was sie theoretisch leugnen, sind sie zugleich (durch das 'Bedürfnis' ihrer praktischen Vernunft) genötigt, praktisch zu glauben, da sie sonst nicht die Kraft hätten, ihre moralische Intention handelnd durchzuhalten."

[81] NAGL-DOCEKAL 2010, 335, with reference to KANT 1972b, 1083: "'Wenn wir diesen Grundsatz aufheben', werden wir entweder 'wider [...] unser Gewissen handeln', oder unsere Theorie praktisch widerlegen – sie 'ad absurdum practicum' führen."

[82] NAGL-DOCEKAL 2010, 335–336: "Wenn wir nicht gesonnen sind, den moralischen

CONCLUSIONS FOR A FEMINIST PHILOSOPHY OF RELIGION

On grounds of the above explanations, it seems obvious to me that the complex conception of God as the *Knower of the Heart* takes the existential situation of human beings much more seriously than the debate about male or female predicates of God. It makes sense for feminist philosophy of religion to refer to this conception of the *Knower of the Heart*. This would open up a great chance to overcome some of the shortcomings within feminist theology.

If one follows Kant's explanation in his philosophy of religion, it can be demonstrated – as Nagl-Docekal evinces clearly and convincingly – in how much more a radical way human existence comes into view here. Kant differentiates between morality and religion, and he explains that people, in order to be able to act morally, do not need religion. But, he further explains, morality necessarily leads to religion, stemming from the need of human reason for a profound sense of moral action. We are familiar with our moral task through the moral law inherent in human's practical reason. But in order to endure over time in our efforts to be a good human being, to be morally committed, we need courage and the conviction that this actually makes sense. Nagl-Docekal, in her interpretation of Kant: "As soon as we engage ourselves in acting for a morally shaped co-existence, the meaning is already (practically necessary) presupposed – otherwise we would have no good reason to be active in this way. This means that, according to Kant, everyone is basically a believer – in the sense of 'pure moral religion'."[83]

Zuschnitt unseres Handelns so aufrichtig und 'behutsam' wie möglich zu erkunden, bedeutet dies, dass wir es auch anderen gegenüber an Achtsamkeit und Behutsamkeit ermangeln lassen. Dass die moralisch gesetzgebende Stimme unserer Vernunft uns dazu verpflichtet, die von unseren Handlungen Betroffenen in ihrer 'Würde' zu respektieren, schließt ja ein, dass wir so genau wie möglich – auch im Medium der Kommunikation – ermitteln müssen, welche Auswirkungen unsere Handlungsweisen auf die jeweils Betroffenen haben. Wie also sollte ein konsistenter Begriff moralischen Handelns aussehen, der auf die Konzeption der Selbstkritik verzichtet?"

[83] NAGL-DOCEKAL 2006a, 101: "Sobald wir uns handelnd für ein moralisch geprägtes Zusammenleben engagieren, ist das Sinnganze bereits (praktisch notwendig) vorausgesetzt – andernfalls hätten wir keinen guten Grund, in dieser Weise tätig zu sein. Das

Before arguing about God's predicates (male or female or any others), I consider it worthwhile to first take a look at the existential situation of human beings, where this need for a complete meaning breaks up in the human being. For Kant, the source of religion can be found in "our inevitable experiences of mortality. On the one hand we have to admit to ourselves that we always fail morally, we have to be conscious of our moral fallibility; on the other hand, we are confronted with the fact that our moral efforts are often counteracted by the actions of others, so that we suffer a disintegration of virtue and bliss. According to Kant, it is these inevitable experiences of failure that give rise to faith. Our pure practical reason thus arrives at the postulates of God and immortality, which constitute the 'pure moral religion' that is inherent in all human beings. [...] In Kant's point of view religion has its source in each and every one of us."[84] The shared origin of religion is founded in human experiences of fallibility, despair and death, but at the same time Kant addresses topics such as hope, salvation and grace as fundamental issues of the philosophy of religion.[85]

Reasonable predicates of God are purely moral predicates: Sanctity, benevolence, justice. The conception of God as the *Knower of the Heart* opens the perspective of dialogue and relationality. This perspective of hope, opened to us by our pure practical reason, constitutes a human attitude: filled with the vision (biblically speaking) and the idea of a righteous and solidary world (hope in the supreme good), belief in God, through whom the coincidence of virtue and bliss will hopefully be granted, we find ourselves in a dialogue with God, we have a counterpart, a source of encouragement, in order to engage ourselves with a cheerful

---

bedeutet, dass Kant zufolge jeder Mensch im Grunde gläubig ist im Sinne der 'reinen moralischen Religion'."

[84] NAGL-DOCEKAL 2006b, 262–263, with reference to KANT 1907, 103: "[...] Unsere reine praktische Vernunft gelangt so zu den Postulaten Gott und Unsterblichkeit, die Kant zufolge den Kern der in allen Menschen angelegten 'reinen moralischen Religion' ausmachen. [...] In dieser Form hat Religion also ihren Ort in jedem Einzelnen."

[85] See NAGL-DOCEKAL 2006b, 263: "In dieser Form hat Religion also ihren Ort in jedem Einzelnen. Die historisch-vielfältigen Konfessionen knüpfen an diese Verankerung an und haben insofern, ungeachtet ihrer Diversität, ein-und-denselben Bezugspunkt. Kennzeichnend ist, dass Kant diesen geteilten Ursprung von Religiosität in existentiellen Erfahrungen wie Schuld, Verzweiflung und Tod sieht und damit zugleich Themen wie Hoffnung, Gnade und Erlösung als Grundfragen der Religionsphilosophie exponiert."

heart for the proliferation of justice and benevolence in the world. For feminist philosophy of religion, the crucial question is the source of religion in the human being, and not the question of the gender of God or even the gender of religion. Human beings as mortal, vulnerable, assailable beings, burdened by suffering, are faced with the task of moral obligation and ask themselves what sense their moral commitment has, or may be hoped for. I think that this would be the starting point of a feminist philosophy of religion: to confront resignation with the vision of a just world and to be committed to it.

This raises the question of how people who are faced with the requirements of the moral law and whose reason necessarily demands the postulates of meaning can find the courage and strength for civil courage to lead a committed life. Here the theme of the ethical community becomes relevant. As the categorical imperative addresses its demand to us, how can we succeed in implementing this task in our own lives? This task can never be fully accomplished. As our self-education and mutual moral education is a permanent duty for all of us we have the obligation to encourage each other in morality.

The ethical community is a connection between people guided by the question: what can we do to foster morality, our own and that of our fellow human beings? How can we support each other in moral terms? In order to become morally developed human beings ourselves, we need other human beings and thus a public mutual understanding about morality. All morally relevant issues include questions relating to gender justice. Commitment to the world's best with a brave and cheerful heart includes commitment to the recognition of women's dignity, commitment to gender justice.

The virtue of friendship is important, as Kant demonstrates in the doctrine of virtue. Friendship among people is a duty of virtue, as is friendship practiced worldwide. There is an obligation of virtue not to isolate oneself, i.e. the moral imperative calls on us to cultivate a worldwide, cosmopolitan conviction, i.e. to be connected with people across the globe in a kind, virtuous attitude. It is important that those people who "need help or support can articulate their particular needs and concerns without fear and make themselves heard."[86] The maxim

[86] NAGL-DOCEKAL 2008, 137: "[...] dass diejenigen, die der Hilfe bzw. Unterstützung

of human love is an obligation of virtue: To love one's neighbor is the duty of all humans towards one another. This duty implies to make the ends of other people my own and to help other people in achieving their self-chosen goals in a non-paternalistic manner. With regard to gender relations, it is part of loving one another, to "take women seriously and fully as persons in all spheres of life."[87] More broadly, this means to engage in seeking a successful life for women and LGBTIQ-community members all over the world, and to stand up for all oppressed and disrespected people worldwide, and for overcoming those structures (intersectionally considered) that oppress people out of sexist, racist, ethnic, and other structural distortions. The ethical community could be the worldwide space where people are committed to make a contribution to the worldwide struggle for radical equality, justice and well-being in this global situation of exploitation, as Schüssler Fiorenza so courageously requests.[88] This is a starting point for feminist debates that could be made fruitful for a feminist philosophy of religion.

ꙮ

REFERENCES

BUCHHAMMER Brigitte, 2011, *Feministische Religionsphilosophie. Philosophisch-systematische Grundlagen*, Vienna – Berlin: LIT

DALY Mary, 1978, *Jenseits von Gottvater, Sohn & Co. Aufbruch zu einer Philosophie der Frauenbefreiung*, Munich: Frauenoffensive

KANT Immanuel, 1886, *The Metaphysics of Ethics*, trans. J. W. Semple, 3rd ed., Edinburgh: Clark

KANT Immanuel, 1907, *Die Religion innerhalb der Grenzen der bloßen Vernunft*, in: Immanuel KANT, *Gesammelte Schriften. Akademieausgabe*, VI: *Die Religion innerhalb der Grenzen der bloßen Vernunft; Die Metaphysik der Sitten*, Berlin: Reimer, 1–202

bedürfen, ihre jeweils besonderen Bedürfnisse und Anliegen angstfrei artikulieren und sich Gehör verschaffen können."

[87] NAGL-DOCEKAL 2008, 137: "In Sicht kommt nun, dass es zu den Verpflichtungen der Nächstenliebe gehört, Frauen in allen Lebensbereichen voll als Personen ernst zu nehmen."

[88] See SCHÜSSLER FIORENZA 2011, 54.

KANT Immanuel, 1911a, *Grundlegung zur Metaphysik der Sitten*, in: Immanuel KANT, *Gesammelte Schriften. Akademieausgabe*, IV: *Kritik der reinen Vernunft; Prolegomena; Grundlegung zur Metaphysik der Sitten; Metaphysische Anfangsgründe der Naturwissenschaft*, Berlin: Reimer, 385–463

KANT Immanuel, 1911b, *Prolegomena zu einer jeden künftigen Metaphysik*, in: Immanuel KANT, *Gesammelte Schriften. Akademieausgabe*, IV: *Kritik der reinen Vernunft; Prolegomena; Grundlegung zur Metaphysik der Sitten; Metaphysische Anfangsgründe der Naturwissenschaft*, Berlin: Reimer, 253–383

KANT Immanuel, 1923a, Idee zu einer allgemeinen Geschichte in weltbürgerlicher Absicht, in: Immanuel KANT, *Gesammelte Schriften. Akademieausgabe*, VIII: *Abhandlungen nach 1781*, Berlin: De Gruyter, 15–31

KANT Immanuel, 1923b, Das Ende aller Dinge, in: Immanuel KANT, *Gesammelte Schriften. Akademieausgabe*, VIII: *Abhandlungen nach 1781*, Berlin: De Gruyter, 325–339

KANT Immanuel, 1963a, *Kritik der praktischen Vernunft*, in: Immanuel KANT, *Werke in sechs Bänden*, IV: *Schriften zur Ethik und Religionsphilosophie*, ed. by Wilhelm Weischedel, Darmstadt: Wissenschaftliche Buchgesellschaft, 107–308

KANT Immanuel, 1963b, *Metaphysik der Sitten*, in: Immanuel KANT, *Werke in sechs Bänden*, IV: *Schriften zur Ethik und Religionsphilosophie*, ed. by Wilhelm Weischedel, Darmstadt: Wissenschaftliche Buchgesellschaft, 309–636

KANT Immanuel, 1968, *Zum ewigen Frieden. Ein philosophischer Entwurf*, in: Immanuel KANT, *Werkausgabe*, XI: *Schriften zur Anthropologie, Geschichtsphilosophie, Politik und Pädagogik*, 1, ed. by Wilhelm Weischedel, Frankfurt/M.: Suhrkamp, 195–251

KANT Immanuel, 1972a, Danziger Rationaltheologie nach Baumbach, in: Immanuel KANT, *Gesammelte Schriften. Akademieausgabe*, XXVIII: *Vorlesungen*, V: *Vorlesungen über Metaphysik und Rationaltheologie*, 2/2, Berlin: De Gruyter, 1231–1319

KANT Immanuel, 1972b, Philosophische Religionslehre nach Pölitz, in: Immanuel KANT, *Gesammelte Schriften. Akademieausgabe*, XXVIII: *Vorlesungen*, V: *Vorlesungen über Metaphysik und Rationaltheologie*, 2/2, Berlin: De Gruyter, 989–1126

KANT Immanuel, 2005, *Streit der Fakultäten*, ed. by Horst D. Brandt & Piero Giordanetti, Hamburg: Meiner

KANT Immanuel, 2008, Groundwork of The Metaphysics of Morals, in: Immanuel KANT, *Practical Philosophy*, trans. Mary Gregor & Allen B. Wood, 12th printing, Cambridge: Cambridge University Press, 37–108

KANT Immanuel, 2014, Idea for a universal history with a cosmopolitan aim, in: Günter ZÖLLER & Robert B. LOUDEN (eds.), *The Cambridge Edition of the Works of Immanuel Kant*, 7: *Anthropology, History and Education*, trans. Mary Gregor, Paul Guyer, Robert B. Louden, Holly Wilson, Günter Zöller & Arnulf Zweig, 4th printing, Cambridge: Cambridge University Press, 107–120

KANT Immanuel, 2018, *Religion within the Boundaries of Mere Reason and other Writings*, trans. Allen Wood & George di Giovanni, 2nd ed., Cambridge: Cambridge University Press

KANT Immanuel, 2019, *Critique of Pure Reason*, trans. Paul Guyer & Allen B. Wood, 6th printing, Cambridge: Cambridge University Press

NAGL-DOCEKAL Herta, 2006a, Religion unter säkularisierten Bedingungen? Habermas und Kant über Glaube und Moral in der Moderne, in: Christof GESTRICH & Thomas WABEL (eds.), *Gott in der Kultur. Moderne Transzendenzerfahrungen und die Theologie*, Berlin: Wichern, 87–110

NAGL-DOCEKAL Herta, 2006b, Religion in der Philosophie der Gegenwart, in: Dieter A. BINDER, Klaus LÜDECKE & Hans PAARHAMMER (eds.), *Kirche in einer säkularisierten Gesellschaft*, Innsbruck – Vienna – Bozen: Studienverlag, 257–273

NAGL-DOCEKAL Herta, 2008, Philosophische Reflexionen über Liebe und die Gefahr ihrer Unterbestimmung im zeitgenössischen Diskurs, in: Herta NAGL-DOCEKAL & Friedrich WOLFRAM (eds.), *Jenseits der Säkularisierung. Religionsphilosophische Studien*, Berlin: Parerga, 111–141

NAGL-DOCEKAL Herta, 2010, Ist die Konzeption des "Herzenskündigers" obsolet geworden?, in: *Philosophisches Jahrbuch* 117/2, Freiburg – Munich: Alber, 319–338

NAGL-DOCEKAL Herta, 2014, *Innere Freiheit. Grenzen der nachmetaphysischen Moralkonzeptionen*, Berlin: De Gruyter (Deutsche

Zeitschrift für Philosophie, Sonderband 36)

NAGL-DOCEKAL Herta, 2018, Towards a Global Non-Exclusive Community, in: *Learning to be Human. Congress Volume of the XXIV World Congress of Philosophy, August 13–20, 2018*, Beijing, 73–83

RADFORD RUETHER Rosemary, 1981, Das weibliche Wesen Gottes. Ein religiöses Problem von heute, *Concilium* 17 (3), 217–222

SCHÜSSLER FIORENZA Elisabeth, 2004a, *Grenzen überschreiten. Der theologische Anspruch feministischer Theologie. Ausgewählte Aufsätze*, Münster: LIT

SCHÜSSLER FIORENZA Elisabeth, 2004b, Feministische Theologie zwischen Moderne und Postmoderne, in: Klaus DETHLOFF, Rudolf LANGTHALER, Herta NAGL-DOCEKAL & Friedrich WOLFRAM (eds.), *Orte der Religion im philosophischen Diskurs der Gegenwart*, Berlin: Parerga, 315–339 (Schriften der Österreichischen Gesellschaft für Religionsphilosophie 5)

SCHÜSSLER FIORENZA Elisabeth, 2011, *Transforming Vision. Explorations in Feminist The*logy*, Minneapolis, MN: Fortress Press

SÖLLE Dorothee, 1981, Vater, Macht und Barbarei, *Concilium* 17 (3), 223–227

STRAHM-BERNET Silvia, 1991, Jesa Christa, in: Doris STRAHM & Regula STROBEL (eds.), *Vom Verlangen nach Heilwerden. Christologie in feministisch-theologischer Sicht*, Fribourg – Luzern: Ed. Exodus, 172–181

Herta Nagl-Docekal

CHALLENGING ISSUES AND MANY TASKS AHEAD: A RESPONSE

First, I would like to express my warmest thanks to Gertrude Postl for initiating the Close Encounter Panel at the 2019 APL conference in Klagenfurt, and to Brigitte Buchhammer for her perseverance and commitment to having the contributions to that panel published, in a considerably extended form, in the present book. I am also very grateful, indeed, to Waltraud Ernst, Cornelia Eşianu, and Bettina Zehetner, who took up the idea of responding to my work from the perspective of their individual concerns in such a magnificent way. Each panelist has implemented some of my thoughts in addressing her specific focus on theoretical issues as well as practical challenges that we face in the world we live in today, indicating that those thoughts have helped to shape individual trajectories. What I find most intriguing is the diversity of approaches: even where some essays refer to one and the same text, the aspects that are highlighted vary considerably. Through these diverse readings, I find myself confronted with some implications of my thoughts that I had not been clearly aware of. On the other hand, it is a pleasure for me to discover some overlapping between the reflections presented here, even though the authors do not cooperate on a daily basis.

While I was trying to find an adequate way of responding to such a rich constellation of thoughts, I concluded it might prove fruitful to take a look ahead – to discuss the individual essays in a way that highlights important topics that deserve to be taken up, and further elaborated, in future debates. Before addressing the contributions to the

Klagenfurt panel in this manner, I suggest turning to the two comprehensive introductions to the present volume.

TWO INTRODUCTIONS, TWO PERSPECTIVES

While both introductory texts provide well thought-out summaries of my research in feminist philosophy, it is interesting to observe the way in which each author's personal background shapes her perspective. It is perhaps also fair to say that each has a slightly different set of readers in mind. As the initiator of the Klagenfurt panel, *Gertrude Postl* addresses primarily the international group of members of the APL and, more generally, scholars in various fields of the humanities that may be attracted by the underlying aim of that Association. In a recent essay, she characterizes that aim with reference to the precursor of the APL, the *International Association for Philosophy and Literature* (IAPL), founded in 1976 by Hugh L. Silverman, philosophy professor at SUNY Stony Brook.[1] There, Postl maintains that this society has contributed significantly to the development of "continental postmodernisms in the USA and Canada." Explaining the initial concern of this innovative process, she cites the aim of challenging the dominance of analytic philosophy that had marked the Anglo-American philosophical discourse since World War II. The IAPL participated, she argues, in "promoting an opening of what it means to do philosophy by 'importing' European thinkers and theories into the mainstream academic discourse of North America." It is important to note, however, Postl adds, that "continental European philosophy underwent a transformation in the process of its transition from Europe to North America." Therefore, the term "continental philosophy" now commonly refers to "a distinctly US – and Canadian – enterprise." In this transformed version, "continental philosophy, a term rather unknown within the European philosophical scene," was finally "(re)introduced to Europe as a typically North American way of responding to and working with the European tradition."[2] Explaining

[1] POSTL 2021.
[2] POSTL 2021, 169–170.

one outstanding feature of the transformation that took place on American soil, Postl discusses the impact of French "postmodernist" approaches. She highlights the fact that "the term 'postmodernism' has never been limited to a strictly philosophical discourse," as authors such as Jacques Derrida, Michel Foucault, Jean-François Lyotard, Jean Baudrillard, Julia Kristeva, Luce Irigaray, and Hélène Cixous "situated traditional philosophical questions within the context of [...] literature, art, music, film, media, politics, or culture at large." American continental philosophy, Postl recounts, has embraced a mode of thinking that is based on interdisciplinary encounters ever since. Accordingly, "[o]ne of the founding premises of the IAPL was that literature is philosophical and that, vice versa, philosophy always has literary qualities."[3]

It is against the backdrop of this research program that Gertrude Postl evaluates my work in feminist philosophy. Thus she focuses in particular on my critical engagement with French feminism, post-structural feminism, and constructivism,[4] highlighting, for instance, my examination of Hélène Cixous's concept of an *écriture feminine*. She lucidly recounts my concern that the ideas of difference feminism might amount to a disguised revival of the traditional association of women with irrationality. In my view, it is important to consider the nuanced conclusion she reaches. While stressing that her "own research interest in French Feminism and issues of discourse, representation, and the signifying potential of the body, led at points to a philosophical parting" of her ways with mine, she suggests that some of my on-going concerns have "a certain affinity with aspects of those positions," contending, for instance, that my plea for a culture of listening "resonates with Cixous's and Irigaray's arguments in favor of – what they call – a feminine economy [...], an economy of the excess and of the gift." Similarly, she notes that my claim that "love is not sufficiently addressed in contemporary moral and social philosophy" is shared by authors such as Irigaray and Kristeva. As she points to such

[3] Postl 2021, 175. Postl refers here to Silverman's in-depth analysis of this development: Silverman 1994.

[4] For a detailed account of my critique see also Brigitte Buchhammer's introduction to the present volume.

deeply seated parallels, Postl – in my understanding – sketches a path forward that sounds promising. An in-depth investigation of key concerns which might be shared by the variety of languages shaping philosophical cultures that have evolved on either side of the Atlantic does indeed seem a worthwhile task. This task could perhaps eventually be taken up, in terms of an intellectual "joint venture," in the context of future events organized by the APL.

Brigitte Buchhammer approaches my work from the perspective of her continuing experience, as she has followed the development of my thoughts since the day when, as a philosophy student at the University of Vienna, she first participated in my courses. Since she gained her doctorate we have cooperated in many ways, sometimes within the framework of the SWIP Austria,[5] but also on many other occasions, of which only a few examples can be mentioned in this context. At an international symposium on Hegel that I co-organized at the Istituto Italiano per gli Studi Filosofici in Naples, Italy, in 2007, Brigitte Buchhammer read a paper on Religion and Homosexuality.[6] In the year 2016, we were among the Austrian hosts of the International Philosophical Seminar Riga-Vienna, which was arranged when a group of philosophy professors and graduate students from the Latvian Academy of Sciences visited the Austrian Academy of Sciences (ÖAW). In 2017 we co-organized "Learning to be Human in Global Times," an international symposium sponsored by the University of Vienna and the ÖAW. The papers presented at that event were published in a volume edited by Brigitte Buchhammer in Washington, DC;[7] among the authors is one of the contributors to the present volume, Cornelia Eşianu. Together we participated in the presentation of that research at the XXIV World Congress of Philosophy in Beijing, China, in 2018.

On the basis of her close knowledge of my work Buchhammer, in her introduction to the present volume, follows two guidelines that she manages to combine in a remarkable manner: On the one hand, she recounts the way in which my thoughts have evolved, as I examined

[5] Cf., for instance, NAGL-DOCEKAL 2021.
[6] BUCHHAMMER 2008.
[7] BUCHHAMMER 2018.

the different "schools" of gender theory that shaped successively, in the course of time, what was widely considered the "mainstream," reaching from early concepts of care ethics to feminist forms of post-humanism. Covering my work from 1990 to the present, this narrative deserves particular thanks for introducing an English-speaking readership to many thoughts and ideas that have been published exclusively in German. At the same time, Buchhammer provides a systematic assessment of my approach, in concise summaries of my thoughts in the fields of philosophical anthropology, aesthetics, the philosophical distinction between reason and rationality, ethics, and political philosophy. In the concluding section of her introduction, Buchhammer turns to one of my most recent forthcoming essays, in order to explain the way in which elements of Kant's concept of moral autonomy have always been instrumental in shaping my concept of feminist philosophy. It is in this context that Buchhammer specifies one of the concerns she considers most pressing, namely to challenge the oppression of people "on the grounds of being LGBTIQ." Thus she draws attention to many unresolved questions in public discourse that do, again, call for a "joint venture" in terms of careful philosophical differentiation in future research.

FOUR DISTINCT WAYS OF EMPLOYING MY THOUGHTS

1) In her essay "Feminist Philosophy Gets Practical" *Bettina Zehetner* introduces an ambitious mode of implementing some of my thoughts in dealing with contemporary challenges. It is certainly a most pressing social problem that she has shouldered in the context of "Frauen beraten Frauen" (Women Counseling Women), an association founded in 1980.[8] Thus it is of particular interest to me to learn how my book *Feminist Philosophy* might prove fruitful in the practice of feminist

[8] As Ebermann and Zehetner explain, that association founded the first autonomous institution dedicated to counseling women, into which both the Wiener Institut für frauenspezifische Psychotherapie and the Institut für frauenspezifische Sozialforschung were integrated. Cf. EBERMANN & ZEHETNER 2010; see also ZEHETNER 2017.

psychosocial counseling that focuses on women who experience violence inflicted by their partner. As she seeks to establish a sound theoretical basis of her counseling work, Zehetner discusses the "gender specific aspects of violence and vulnerability." First and foremost, she identifies the denial of one's own finiteness – that represents a key element of a widely shared ideal of masculinity – as one primary source of the propensity for acts of violence against women. Therefore she claims that the concept of "man as sovereign subject" needs to be confronted with "the foundation of human relatedness and interdependence, with our vulnerability." As she points out, vulnerability, while constituting an essential feature of the human existence in general, has been inscribed with gender specific connotations: "phantasmatic impenetrability and the power to hurt are symbolically assigned to masculinity," while "the openness to being hurt, the need for protection are symbolically ascribed to femininity. Women are symbolically conceived as passive objects of (at least potential) violation and fear, men as active subjects with full (aggressive) agency." To define this dyad of images, Zehetner introduces the terms "Verletzungsoffenheit" versus "Verletzungsmächtigkeit." Accordingly, she reports with regard to specific counseling processes that "no problem of women who seek counseling is just an individual problem." Rather, the painful experiences voiced are "always part of social, economic, and political relations and conditions." In my mind, the concept "Verletzungsmächtigkeit" (the power to injure others) is of eminent relevance today, as we face, across the globe, a popular culture that is increasingly shaped by images of masculine violence, for instance in blockbuster films, TV series, video games, including the corresponding franchise. From a feminist perspective, it is important to contend that the invention of female heroes that are also endowed with "Verletzungsmächtigkeit" does not represent a way out, since such images define human relations in terms of violence to an even larger extent. In a convincing manner, Zehetner claims that the ultimate task of counseling in the psychosocial field is to open up perspectives of shaping "gender relations in a new way." Of particular importance is the discursive method she advocates, as she describes an approach guided by a "reflected", or "differentiated partiality" which puts the counseling person in the position of "a serious and, if necessary, critical partner for a dialogue."

As to the specifically feminist element, she stresses the need "to support the counseling-seeking person in the widening of her own range of agency," which allows them "to develop new possibilities to think and speak about themselves," and to act in a way that leaves behind the traditional gender polarization. With regard to this specific topic, I would like to draw attention to Zehetner's study "Schreiben wirkt" (Writing is effective),[9] where she introduces the method of "counseling in the medium of writing."[10] As she explains, writing promotes the potential of self-reflection and agency, since it not only improves the clarity and structure of thinking but also helps to distance oneself from the urgent problem. This is, of course, a demanding project: Zehetner notes that counseling individuals need to train their competence of understanding nuances of expression and hidden meanings of the words used.[11] Raising this demand, she addresses the desideratum of an enhancement of future relations between feminist theory and practice. I do, indeed, share her hope that counseling competences might be enhanced by continued inter- and cross-disciplinary research involving, *inter alia*, philosophy of language, social psychology, political science as well as feminist legal theory.

2) An emancipatory commitment with regard to traditional views on women is also to be found in *Waltraud Ernst*'s research. One of her particular projects, as explained, for instance, in her essay "Emancipatory Interferences with Machines?,"[12] is to challenge the "persistent and widespread gender stereotype [...] that women in general – or by nature – lack technical competence. The flip side of this stereotype is that [...] men have been credited with technical omnipotence."[13] In contrast to this, her idea is to "reveal the fluidity of gender identities in social encounters."[14] Examining the roots of common gender clichés, Ernst contends that "scientific theories of the eighteenth and nineteenth centuries typically seek to solve complex issues of human social interaction, in particular issues of erotic relations, with reference

[9] ZEHETNER 2010.
[10] ZEHETNER 2010, 115.
[11] ZEHETNER 2010, 116.
[12] ERNST 2017.
[13] ERNST 2017, 179.
[14] ERNST 2017, 179.

to the external sphere of nature."[15] She presents Charles Darwin as a case in point, since he regards the sphere of the erotic as based upon the natural mechanisms of selection.[16]

As Waltraud Ernst has chosen feminist epistemology as her main field of research, she approaches my work from that perspective. It is with great interest that I read how she incorporates some of my thoughts in her analysis of "the sociohistorical character of scientific knowledge (as well as philosophical and all other knowledge)." As her essay in the present collection, "Norms – Reason – Justice: Herta Nagl-Docekal's Contribution to a Theory of Truth," provides a detailed account of my 1982 study on the possible meaning of the term "objectivity" in the context of the historical sciences, Ernst may well be the first author to introduce an English-speaking readership to the philosophical differentiation I elaborate in challenging the widely received ideal of a "value-free" science. She emphasizes my thesis "that truth about history can be achieved only if historical research is guided by concerns of justice," and that the principles of morality and justice guiding the historian "can be and therefore must be legitimized" in terms of philosophical argument. Raising the question of the extent to which this thesis might prove relevant in the contemporary discourse, she takes a nuanced standpoint. While consenting to the thesis that research questions "are always embedded in an individual and social context," she voices doubts whether "objectivity" is "a necessary concept for the legitimation of feminist knowledge." At this point she explains in the way in which her "own account of feminist epistemology" takes an alternative turn. Significantly, she suggests "viewing scientific knowledge as materialized, historically constructed processes." What is needed, she argues, is to focus on "the manifestations of realities that may overlap and expand, gain and lose influence."

It is important to note that, in the course of characterizing her point of view, Waltraud Ernst addresses issues that need further elaboration. From the perspective of the concept "truth" that the heading of her essay designates as a key concern, she draws attention to the problem of "epistemological relativism." As she argues that "[o]ne must

[15] Ernst 2015, 53.
[16] See Ernst 2015, 53.

proceed from the assumption that reality exists outside the scientific process of knowledge production, but that it is, nevertheless, constructed in a particular way through being described and explained as an object of knowledge," and as she adopts the term "scientific discursive material reality," she identifies precisely the two poles that call for future in-depth investigations.

3) In her essay "Current Artistic Forms for the Implementation of a Feminist Aesthetics" *Cornelia Eşianu* approaches my thoughts from the perspective of the sphere of art. I am impressed by the way in which she manages to inter-twine aesthetic theory, feminist connotations of exemplary works of art, and real life experience of gender bias. Exploring the implications of my concept of "art with a feminist potential," she argues that the artistic form of the "grotesque" proves significant in this regard: "In general," she notes, "the grotesque comes to stand in for all those things, which do not fit into our existing philosophical and aesthetic categories: monsters, human-animal or human-plant hybrids, miniature or gigantic bodily forms, inappropriate intimacies [...] phenomena that estrange us from our familiar world." Eşianu suggests seeing Eva Kosinar's works as a case in point, maintaining that it proves revealing to analyze these works by means of the "category of the grotesque." As she discusses in particular Kosinar's digitalized photo "Mother," Eşianu explains that the grotesque provides "a challenging procedure in order to question [...] the role played by women as mothers." It might prove relevant to compare this photo with Cindy Sherman's photo series in which the artist presents herself in a great variety of roles that have traditionally been allotted to women, and to raise the question of the way in which it matters that different generations of women artists are at work here. Against the backdrop of this comparison, we might be led to ponder whether the title "Mother" that Kosinar has chosen for this piece of art is itself part of the grotesque mode of expression. Would we have guessed this title just by looking at this photo? As Eşianu notes, it does not seem clear, in the first place, that the depicted figure is a woman – "the gender of the figure is not known [...], a fact highlighted by the rendering of the face, which is not human." One option for reading this piece of art seems to consist in relating it to the "post-gender-roles" situation of women. Does the title that Kosinar has chosen for the entire collection

of these photos – "La Femme Tragique?" – perhaps provide an important clue?

Generally speaking, Eşianu makes a plausible move in looking to art for one mode of pleading for a "non-reductionist concept of the human being"[17] – a concept that she has elaborated on in practically all her previous philosophical studies. In order to illustrate the need for feminist interventions today, she points out that in "the digital Eastern European media" traditional sexist views on women, i.e., claims of male superiority, have gained dominance.[18] Her focus on discrimination against women in the contemporary geopolitical context also characterizes her essay "Globalisierung und Identität. Philosophische Auseinandersetzung mit literarischen Texten über Rumänien" (Globalization and Identity. A Philosophical Examination of Literary Texts on Romania).[19] Here she analyzes, for instance, the deficits of the widely used expression "the identity of the woman." Challenging such traditional views, Eşianu suggests reconsidering Kant's and Schlegel's concepts of love that focus on the idea of "symmetry of the spirit";[20] she highlights the fact that both authors elaborate the demand for "respect for the individuality of the other."[21] "The woman in a globalized world," she argues, must be seen in terms of the "plurality of women in their uniqueness."[22] It would seem worthwhile to turn to aesthetics with regard to this comprehensive horizon once again. The question of which artistic forms might be employed, or reshaped, in elaborating a globalized feminist perspective could, to my mind, provide a demanding topic for a trans-disciplinary colloquium or a new book project for Cornelia Eşianu.

4) The commitment to defend a non-reductionist concept of the human being also constitutes the main motivation for *Brigitte Buchhammer*. The volume *Re-Learning to be Human in Global Times*[23] that she edited in Washington, DC, as cited above, clearly documents this concern.

---

[17] EŞIANU 2018, 185.
[18] EŞIANU 2018, 184.
[19] EŞIANU 2019.
[20] EŞIANU 2018, 193.
[21] EŞIANU 2018, 195.
[22] EŞIANU 2019, 350.
[23] BUCHHAMMER 2018.

The most remarkable feature of her research in feminist philosophy is her focus on religion – a field that the international discourse has neglected to a large extent. To take up this topic today requires being steadfast in challenging at least three forms of reservations: firstly, the view that issues of religion ought to be addressed in the context of theology and religious studies rather than that of philosophy; secondly, the widely shared mode of identifying the topic of religion *toto genere* with the gender hierarchies that have been established on the basis of traditional religious teachings and practices; thirdly, the thesis, accepted to a large extent in contemporary social theory and in public discourse, that believers of any kind of religious creed adhere to a pre-modern attitude that fails to grasp what the secular age is all about. Buchhammer's contribution to the present volume expresses her resolve to distinguish carefully between the all too legitimate and necessary feminist critique of the oppressive social structures defended and supported by church authorities, on the one hand, and the systematic question of what a feminist philosophy of religion ought to look like, on the other. Having been raised in a Roman Catholic context, Buchhammer refers in particular to the teachings and traditional practices of that church, as grounded, for instance, on Vatican doctrinal ordinances. She has voiced well-argued criticism in many of her writings, for instance in her essay "Römisch-katholische Kirche – 'Expertin der Menschlichkeit'?" (The Roman-Catholic Church – an "Expert in Humaneness"?)[24] I see the main thrust of her work in the following way: while the majority of committed feminists have regarded the persistence of the common oppressive attitudes as good reason for considering the entire field of religion as obsolete, she aims to defend religious faith, including her own – saving it, as it were, with philosophical means.

Elaborating her strictly philosophical approach, Buchhammer takes issue with a number of received theories in the field of feminist theology. She dismisses, for instance, the discourse on whether God is to be understood as male or female, or whether "alternative views of God's image" are needed – issues that have been a focus of feminist theology to this day. Citing, *inter alia*, Dorothee Sölle's suggestion that worshipers might use "images of the natural world," like a "well-spring," and Mary

---

[24] BUCHHAMMER 2017.

Daly's way of replacing the term "God" with "Being," Buchhammer insists on the relevance of "Kant's theory of *symbolic anthropomorphism*," which claims that moral predicates commonly attributed to God need to be understood in terms of figurative analogies – "[t]he highest being is merely thinkable in this form of analogy." She emphasizes that "Kant calls it a mistake in thinking when one transforms the sensualization of a pure idea of reason into a perception of an object of the senses." In her present essay, "Kant's 'The Knower of the Heart' as Contribution to a Feminist Philosophy of Religion," Buchhammer takes issue specifically with Elisabeth Schüssler Fiorenza's idea of an "*ekklesia* of wo/men." Her key concern is to confront this idea with my reflections on Kant's concept of the "ethical community."

In order to establish a sound foundation for her argument, Brigitte Buchhammer reconstructs in an amazingly precise manner my thoughts on Kant's thesis that the source of religion lies in the moral competence of every human being. She underscores that religion is deeply ingrained in our insight that we are "mortal, vulnerable, assailable beings, burdened by suffering," as this insight generates a longing ("Bedürfnis," in Kant's terms) for the absolute that even agnostics experience. In particular, she takes up my examination of Kant's understanding of conscience that highlights his reading of the biblical concept of God as "The Knower of the Heart."[25] Explaining what she considers the main feature of that concept, she writes: "By imagining that we are facing someone who knows us well and does not make any misjudgment, we are capable of self-critical examination of our minds as careful as possible." This assessment indicates that Buchhammer also has a more far-reaching perspective in mind. Her concern is not merely to charge received theses of feminist theology; she rather contends that Kant's concept of religion provides sophisticated insights into the complexity of the human heart that, unfortunately, mainstream contemporary theories of morality fail to address properly.

This broader perspective also guides her discussion of my reading of Kant's concept of the "ethical community." While Kant introduces this concept in defining his notion of "church," Buchhammer empha-

[25] Buchhammer has previously referred to my interpretation of Kant's reflections on the "Knower of the Heart" in her interview, see BUCHHAMMER 2011.

sizes the relevance it might have for all people "in the age of religious loss." Focusing on Kant's thought that we have the obligation to encourage one another in terms of morality, she argues: "Our self-education and mutual moral education is a permanent duty for all of us" as human beings. Against this systematic backdrop, she formulates an interpretation that is significant for her approach, as she maintains that "[a]ll morally relevant issues include questions relating to gender justice." Elaborating this view, she refers to the way in which Kant, in his doctrine of virtue, explains that the "maxim of human love is an obligation of virtue." As she applies this thought to gender relations, she emphasizes my view that it is part of loving one another to take women fully as persons in all spheres of life; she adds that this means engaging in promoting "a successful life for women and LGTBTIQ-community members all over the world." Proceeding in this manner, Buchhammer suggests, in the concluding section of her essay, employing Kant's concept of the "ethical community" as a philosophical basis in the "worldwide struggle for radical equality." It is important to note that, in the very last sentence of her essay, Buchhammer describes her investigation as a possible "starting point for feminist debates." To my mind, she may claim more than that: I think this complex research might represent a substantial part of her own new book.

Concluding my brief response to the essays in this book, I would like to emphasize once again that I am deeply impressed by the many different paths of thought and practical commitment that have been linked to my work. With my warmest thanks to all contributors for sharing these relations, I am looking forward, indeed, to learning what their future work may achieve.

ꟳ

REFERENCES

BUCHHAMMER Brigitte, 2008, Religion und Homosexualität. Eine Relektüre von Hegels Religionsphilosophie, in: Herta NAGL-DOCEKAL, Wolfgang KALTENBACHER & Ludwig NAGL (eds.), *Viele Religionen – eine Vernunft? Ein Disput zu Hegel*, Vienna – Berlin: Böhlau – Akademie Verlag, 211–233

BUCHHAMMER Brigitte, 2011, *Feministische Religionsphilosophie* [Interview], Philosophie im Gespräch, 51. Sendung, OKTO-TV: July 7, 2011, 20:00, DVD/VOB-Datei, 57 min., produced by I. C. Klammer, Vienna: Philosophische Werkstatt & Atelier Galerie

BUCHHAMMER Brigitte, 2017, Römisch-katholische Kirche – "Expertin der Menschlichkeit"?, in: Utta ISOP (ed.), *Gewalt im beruflichen Alltag. Wie Hierarchien, Einschlüsse und Ausschlüsse wirken*, Neu-Ulm: AG SPAK, 208–221

BUCHHAMMER Brigitte (ed.), 2018, *Re-Learning to be Human in Global Times. Challenges and Opportunities from the Perspectives of Contemporary Philosophy of Religion*, Washington, DC: The Council for Research in Values and Philosophy

EBERMANN Trude & ZEHETNER Bettina, 2010, Einleitung, in: FRAUEN BERATEN FRAUEN (eds.), *Anerkennung der Differenz. Feministische Beratung und Psychotherapie*, Giessen: Psychosozial-Verlag, 9–17

ERNST Waltraud, 2015, Intime Begegnungen: Narrative des Erotischen in naturwissenschaftlicher Forschung, in: Brigitte BUCHHAMMER (ed.), *Neuere Aspekte in der Philosophie. Aktuelle Projekte von Philosophinnen am Forschungsstandort Österreich*, Vienna: Axia Academic Publ., 38–57

ERNST Waltraud, 2017, Emancipatory Interferences with Machines?, *International Journal of Gender, Science and Technology* 9 (2), 178–196

EŞIANU Cornelia, 2018, The Conception of Love in Immanuel Kant and Friedrich Schlegel: Its Relevance for a Comprehensive Theory of the Human Being, in: Brigitte BUCHHAMMER (ed.), *Re-Learning to be Human in Global Times. Challenges and Opportunities from the Perspectives of Contemporary Philosophy of Religion*, Washington, DC: The Council for Research in Values and Philosophy, 183–196

EŞIANU Cornelia, 2019, Globalisierung und Identität. Philosophische Auseinandersetzung mit literarischen Texten über Rumänien, in: Brigitte BUCHAMMER (ed.), *Freiheit – Gerechtigkeit – Liebe, Freedom – Justice – Love. Festschrift zum 75. Geburtstag von Herta Nagl-Docekal. Celebratory Volume for Herta Nagl-Docekal's 75th Birthday*, Vienna: LIT, 335–355

NAGL-DOCEKAL Herta, 2021, Film as Moral Theory, or: Do we Have to Draw a Sharp Distinction between Ethical Common Sense and Supererogatory Deeds? in: Brigitte BUCHHAMMER (ed.), *The Future of Europe – an Urgent Challenge to Global Philosophy*, Vienna: LIT, 195–218 (Women* Philosophers at Work. A Series of SWIP Austria 4)

POSTL Gertrude, 2021, Continental Postmodernism in the USA and Canada: The Mediating Role of the International Association of Philosophy and Literature (IAPL), in: Waldemar ZACHARASIEWICZ & Herta NAGL-DOCEKAL (eds.), *Transatlantic Elective Affinities. Traveling Ideas and their Mediators*, Vienna: Austrian Academy of Sciences, 167–182

SILVERMAN Hugh L., 1994, Nachwort. Textualität der Philosophie – Philosophie und Literatur, in: Ludwig NAGL & Hugh L. SILVERMAN (eds.), *Textualität der Philosophie. Philosophie und Literatur*, Vienna: Oldenbourg, 246–257

ZEHETNER Bettina, 2010, Schreiben wirkt. Feministische Onlineberatung, in: FRAUEN BERATEN FRAUEN (eds.), *Anerkennung der Differenz. Feministische Beratung und Psychotherapie*, Giessen: Psychosozial-Verlag, 113–118

ZEHETNER Bettina, 2017, Berührbarkeit, Verletzlichkeit und Geschlecht. Gewalt in Paarbeziehungen, feministische Philosophie und psychosoziale Beratung, in: Brigitte BUCHHAMMER (ed.), *Lernen, Mensch zu sein. Beiträge des 2. Symposiums der SWIP Austria*, Vienna: LIT, 213–226 (Women Philosophers at Work. A Series of SWIP Austria 2)

BIOGRAPHICAL NOTE: HERTA NAGL-DOCEKAL

Herta Nagl-Docekal was born in Wels, Austria. University Professor in Retirement of the Department of Philosophy at the University of Vienna, Austria.

1967 doctoral examination sub auspiciis praesidentis rei publicae in the discipline of history (about Ernst von Lasaulx); 1968–1985 University Assistant at the Department of Philosophy, University of Vienna; 1981 habilitation not only for a subdiscipline but for the entire discipline of Philosophy ("Gesamtfach Philosophie") at the Department of Philosophy, University of Vienna (habilitation thesis: "Die Objektivität in der Geschichtswissenschaft"); 1985–2009 University Professor at the Department of Philosophy, University of Vienna, since 2009 in Retirement at the Department of Philosophy, University of Vienna.

Visiting professor at the Universities of Utrecht (Netherlands), Frankfurt/M., Konstanz, Innsbruck, Free University of Berlin and University of St. Petersburg. She gave lectures in Austria, Belgium, Bosnia-Herzegovina, Brazil, Bulgaria, Canada, China, Croatia, Czech Republic, Finland, Germany, Greece, Great Britain, Hungary, Ireland, Italy, Japan, Korea, Latvia, Mexico, Poland, Slovakia, Sweden, Switzerland, Thailand, and USA.

Functions and (Co-)Organization (Selection): From the large number of significant functions and activities I would like to list only a small selection here. More detailed descriptions can be found under the links below.

Full Member of the Austrian Academy of Sciences; Vice President of Fédération Internationale des Sociétés des Philosophie (FISP) (2008–2013); Member of the FISP "Committee on Gender Issues"; Membre Titulaire, Institut International de Philosophie (I.I.P.), Paris (Member of the Administrative Committee of I.I.P. 2014–2017). 1998–2013 Member of Steering Committee of FISP; since 2012 Member of the Committee of the Philosophical-Historical Section of the Austrian Academy of Sciences "The North Atlantic Triangle: Social and Cultural Exchange between Europe, the USA and Canada."

Since 2005 Conception and moderation of the annual "Leibniz-Lectures" at the Austrian Academy of Sciences. The Leibniz-Lecture 2013 took place under the patronage of UNESCO at the "World Day of Philosophy"; Co-Organization: November 3–4, 2016 Austrian Academy of Sciences, Vienna: "Leibniz heute lesen: Wissenschaft, Geschichte, Religion. International Symposium on the occasion of the 300th anniversary of the death of Leibniz" (organized by Herta Nagl-Docekal, Austrian Academy of Sciences, and Wenchao Li, University of Hannover/Leibniz-Edition Potsdam BBAW). With lecturers from the four Academies of Sciences, which go back to drafts of Leibniz: Berlin-Brandenburg Academy of Sciences (BBAW), Saxon Academy of Sciences (SAW), Russian Academy of Sciences (RAS, Moscow, originally St. Petersburg), Austrian Academy of Sciences. December 2–4, 2016, Austrian Academy of Sciences, Vienna: Co-Organization of the Conference "Ideas Crossing the Atlantic: Theories, Normative Conceptions and Cultural Images" (hosted by the organization "The North Atlantic Triangle").

Herta Nagl-Docekal organizes a lot of innovative and important congresses. She has frequently participated in international conferences (American Philosophical Association, the Canadian Philosophical Association, International Association of Philosophy and Literature). She has presented guest lectures at Harvard University, Lehigh University, at the Canadian Royal Society, and at the Universities of Calgary and Edmonton.

Since the 1980s she has endeavoured to establish international contacts in feminist philosophy. It is important to her that research on feminist philosophy is adequately represented within the framework of general philosophy congresses and symposia of the General Society of

Philosophy in Germany, the Austrian Society of Philosophy and especially at the FISP World Congress of Philosophy. As co-editor of the *Deutsche Zeitschrift für Philosophie*, she was committed to publish volumes with specific main emphases and articles with the main topics on current feminist issues. A further focus is on contacts with female philosophers in Central and Eastern European countries.[1]

Awards: Gabriele Possanner-Würdigungspreis 2015 for scientific achievement in the field of feminist and gender research, warded by the Austrian Federal Ministry of Science, Research and Economics on December 11, 2015.[2]

1967: Doctoral examination sub auspiciis praesidentis rei publicae;
1983: Förderpreis der Stadt Wien;
1997: Käthe Leichter Preis – Österreichischer Staatspreis;
2009: Preis für Geistes- und Sozialwissenschaften der Stadt Wien.

WIKIPEDIA entry Herta Nagl-Docekal:
http://de.wikipedia.org/wiki/Herta_Nagl-Docekal

See also, for Herta Nagl-Docekal's bio-bibliography:
Phaidra (Permanent Hosting, Archiving and Indexing of Digital Resources and Assets) at http://phaidra.univie.ac.at/o:925435

See also:

BUCHHAMMER Brigitte, 2018, s. v. Nagl-Docekal, Herta, in: Ilse KOROTIN & Nastasja STUPNICKI (eds.), *Biographien bedeutender österreichischer Wissenschafterinnen. "Die Neugier treibt mich, Fragen zu stellen"*, Vienna – Cologne – Weimar: Böhlau, 635–645, https://austria-forum.org/web-books/biografienosterreich00de2018isds/000633

Brigitte Buchhammer

---

[1] For more detailed account see: https://www.oeaw.ac.at/en/members/commissions/commission-the-north-atlantic-triangle

[2] See https://www.oeaw.ac.at/detail/news/herta-nagl-docekal-fuer-lebenswerk-gewuerdigt

HERTA NAGL-DOCEKAL'S LIST OF PUBLICATIONS*

AUTHORED BOOKS

– *Filozofie feministă. Rezultate, probleme, perspective* [Romanian edition of: *Feministische Philosophie. Ergebnisse, Probleme, Perspektiven*], trans. Cornelia Eşianu (forthcoming)

2016 *Hegelis par milestibu [Hegel on Love]. Philosophical lectures in Riga*, Riga, Latvia: FSI

2014 *Innere Freiheit. Grenzen der nachmetaphysischen Moralkonzeptionen*, Berlin: De Gruyter (Deutsche Zeitschrift für Philosophie, Sonderband 36)

2012 *Kas ir feministiskā filosofija? [What is feminist philosophy?]*, *Philosophical lectures in Riga*, Riga, Latvia: FSI

2007 *Feministická filozofie. Výsledky, problémy, perspektivy* [Czech edition of: *Feministische Philosophie. Ergebnisse, Probleme, Perspektiven*], trans. Hana Havelková, Prague: SLON [with a new foreword]

2006 *Feminista filozófia* [Hungarian edition of: *Feministische Philosophie. Ergebnisse, Probleme, Perspektiven*], trans. Judit Hell, Budapest: Áron Kiadó [with a new foreword]

2006 [Japanese edition of: *Feministische Philosophie. Ergebnisse,*

* Adapted and updated by the 10/20/2021 from Herta Nagl-Docekal's homepage, see https://homepage.univie.ac.at/herta.nagl/; an earlier version was published as "Schriftenverzeichnis Herta Nagl-Docekal," in: Brigitte BUCHHAMMER (ed.), *Freiheit – Gerechtigkeit – Liebe, Freedom – Justice – Love. Festschrift zum 75. Geburtstag von Herta Nagl-Docekal. Celebratory Volume for Herta Nagl-Docekal's 75th Birthday*, Vienna: LIT, 41–64.

Probleme, Perspektiven], trans. Eichi Hirano, Tokyo: The SAKAI Agency [with a new foreword]

2004 *Feminist Philosophy* [American edition of: *Feministische Philosophie. Ergebnisse, Probleme, Perspektiven*], trans. Katharina Vester, Boulder, CO – Oxford, UK: Westview Press

2000 *Feministische Philosophie. Ergebnisse, Probleme, Perspektiven*, Frankfurt/M.: Fischer (^{2}2001, Reprint 2016)

1982 *Die Objektivität der Geschichtswissenschaft. Systematische Untersuchungen zum wissenschaftlichen Status der Historie*, Vienna – Munich: Oldenbourg (Überlieferung und Aufgabe 22)

1970 *Ernst von Lasaulx. Ein Beitrag zur Kritik des organischen Geschichtsbegriffs*, Münster: Aschendorff

EDITED BOOKS

2022 *Artificial Intelligence and Human Enhancement. Affirmative and Critical Approaches in the Humanities*, ed. by Herta NAGL-DOCEKAL & Waldemar ZACHARASIEWICZ, Berlin – Boston: De Gruyter (forthcoming)

2021 *Transatlantic Elective Affinities. Traveling Ideas and their Mediators*, ed. by Waldemar ZACHARASIEWICZ & Herta NAGL-DOCEKAL, Vienna: Austrian Academy of Sciences

2018 *Leibniz heute lesen. Wissenschaft, Geschichte, Religion*, ed. by Herta NAGL-DOCEKAL, Berlin: De Gruyter (Wiener Reihe 20)

2017 *La religione dopo la critica alla religione. Un dibattito filosofico*, ed. by Herta NAGL-DOCEKAL, Wolfgang KALTEN-BACHER & Claudia MELICA, Napoli: La scuola di Pitagora editrice

2013 *Hegels Ästhetik als Theorie der Moderne*, ed. by Annemarie GETHMANN-SIEFERT, Herta NAGL-DOCEKAL, Ersébet RÓZSA, Elisabeth WEISSER-LOHMANN, Berlin: Akademie Vlg. (Wiener Reihe 17)

2008 *Jenseits der Säkularisierung. Religionsphilosophische Studien*, ed. by Herta NAGL-DOCEKAL & Friedrich WOLFRAM, Berlin: Parerga

2008 *Viele Religionen – eine Vernunft? Ein Disput zu Hegel*, ed. by Herta NAGL-DOCEKAL, Wolfgang KALTENBACHER & Ludwig NAGL, Vienna: Böhlau – Berlin: Akademie Vlg. (Wiener Reihe 14)

2007 *Glauben und Wissen. Ein Symposium mit Jürgen Habermas*, ed. by Rudolf LANGTHALER & Herta NAGL-DOCEKAL, Vienna – Munich: Oldenbourg – Berlin: Akademie (Wiener Reihe 13)

2004 *Recht – Geschichte – Religion. Die Bedeutung Kants für die Gegenwart*, ed. by Herta NAGL-DOCEKAL & Rudolf LANGTHALER, Berlin: Akademie Vlg.

2004 *Orte der Religion im philosophischen Diskurs der Gegenwart*, ed. by Klaus DETHLOFF, Rudolf LANGTHALER, Herta NAGL-DOCEKAL & Friedrich WOLFRAM, Berlin: Parerga

2003 *Geschichtsphilosophie und Kulturkritik. Historische und systematische Studien*, ed. by Johannes ROHBECK & Herta NAGL-DOCEKAL, Darmstadt: Wissenschaftliche Buchgesellschaft

2002 *Freiheit, Gleichheit und Autonomie*, ed. by Herlinde PAUER-STUDER & Herta NAGL-DOCEKAL, Vienna – Munich: Oldenbourg – Berlin: Akademie Vlg. (Wiener Reihe 11)

2000 *Continental Philosophy in Feminist Perspective. Re-Reading the Canon in German*, ed. by Herta NAGL-DOCEKAL & Cornelia KLINGER, University Park, PA: The Pennsylvania State University Press

1996 *Politische Theorie: Differenz und Lebensqualität. Beiträge zur feministischen politischen Philosophie*, ed. by Herta NAGL-DOCEKAL & Herlinde PAUER-STUDER, Frankfurt/M.: Suhrkamp

1996 *Der Sinn des Historischen. Geschichtsphilosophische Debatten*, ed. by Herta NAGL-DOCEKAL, Frankfurt/M.: Fischer

1993 *Jenseits der Geschlechtermoral. Beiträge zur feministischen Ethik*, ed. by Herta NAGL-DOCEKAL & Herlinde PAUER-STUDER, Frankfurt/M.: Fischer

1992 *Postkoloniales Philosophieren: Afrika*, ed. by Herta NAGL-DOCEKAL & Franz M. WIMMER, Vienna – Munich: Oldenbourg (Wiener Reihe 6)

1990 *Denken der Geschlechterdifferenz*, ed. by Herta NAGL-DOCEKAL & Herlinde PAUER-STUDER, Vienna: Wiener Frauenverlag

1990 *Feministische Philosophie*, ed. by Herta NAGL-DOCEKAL, Vienna – Munich: Oldenbourg (Wiener Reihe 4) ([2]1994)

1989 *Ludwig Wittgenstein und die Philosophie des 20. Jahrhunderts*, ed. by Herta NAGL-DOCEKAL, Vienna: Verein "Freunde des Hauses Wittgenstein" (Miscellanea Bulgarica 6)

1987 *Tod des Subjekts?*, ed. by Herta NAGL-DOCEKAL & Helmuth VETTER, Vienna – Munich: Oldenbourg (Wiener Reihe 2)

1984 *Neue Ansätze in der Geschichtswissenschaft. Dokumentation der philosophisch-historischen Tagung vom 30.9. bis 2.10.1983 in Wien*, ed. by Herta NAGL-DOCEKAL & Franz WIMMER, Vienna: Verband der wissenschaftlichen Gesellschaften Österreichs (Conceptus-Studien 1)

1982 *Überlieferung und Aufgabe. Festschrift für Erich Heintel zum siebzigsten Geburtstag*, I–II, ed. by Herta NAGL-DOCEKAL, Vienna: Braumüller

ARTICLES AND CONTRIBUTIONS

2022 Feminist Perspectives on Kant's Conception of Autonomy: On the Need to Distinguish between Self-determination and Self-legislation, in: Susanne LETTOW & Tuija PULKKINEN (eds.), *Palgrave Handbook on German Idealism and Feminist Philosophy*, Basingstoke: Palgrave Macmillan (forthcoming)

2022 "Heiligkeit des Willens ist eine praktische Idee, welche notwendig zum Urbilde dienen muss." Über den von Kant skizzierten Ausweg aus dem Bösen, in: Michael KÜHNLEIN (ed.), *Religionsphilosophie nach Kant*, Stuttgart: Metzler (forthcoming)

2022 Zwischen Nähe und Differenz: Tu Weimings Konzeption des "Geistigen Humanismus" aus dem Blickwinkel von Kants Moralphilosophie betrachtet, in: Kai MARCHAL (ed.), *Tu Weiming: Wie man Menschlichkeit lernt*, Berlin: Mathes & Seitz (forthcoming)

2021 Film as Moral Theory, or: Do we Have to Draw a Sharp Distinction between Ethical Common Sense and Supererogatory Deeds?, in: Brigitte BUCHHAMMER (ed.), *The Future of Europe – an Urgent Challenge to Global Philosophy*, Vienna: LIT, 195–218 (Women* Philosophers at Work. A Series of SWIP Austria 4)

2021 (with Waldemar Zacharasiewicz) Introduction, in: Waldemar ZACHARASIEWICZ & Herta NAGL-DOCEKAL (eds.), *Transatlantic Elective Affinities. Traveling Ideas and their Mediators*, Vienna: Austrian Academy of Sciences, 9–22

2020 Joint Explorations and Probing Discussions, in: William SWEET & HU Yeping (eds.), *George F. McLean. Reminiscences and Reflections*, Washington, D.C.: The Council for Research in Values and Philosophy, 133–140, http://crvp.org/publications/Series-I/I-49.pdf

2020 Immanuel Kant's Concept of Reasonable Hope, in: Miloš LICHNER (ed.), *Hope. Where Does our Hope Lie? International Congress of the European Society for Catholic Theology (August 2019, Bratislava, Slovakia)*, Vienna: LIT, 177–192

2020 Nach einer erneuten Lektüre: Max Horkheimer, "Die Sehnsucht nach dem ganz Anderen," *Deutsche Zeitschrift für Philosophie* 68 (5), 659–88, https://doi.org/10.1515/dzph-2020-0046

2020 Antizipationen alternativer Lebensformen. Eine philosophische Skizze, in: Elisabeth SCHÄFER & Brigitte BUCHHAMMER (eds.), *Erinnerung und Gedächtnis. Festschrift für Ingvild Birkhan zum 80. Geburtstag*, Vienna: LIT, 33–54 (Women Philosophers at Work. A Series of SWIP Austria, Special Volume)

2020 Wie ist feministische Politik zu denken? Judith Butler in Diskussion mit feministischen Forscherinnen in Wien (1995), in: Ingrid BAUER, Christa HÄMMERLE & Claudia SPITZ-BELAKHAL (eds.), *Politik – Theorie – Erfahrung. 30 Jahre feministische Geschichtswissenschaft im Gespräch*, Göttingen: Vandenhoeck & Ruprecht, 222–224

2020 (with Ludwig Nagl) Nachruf Elisabeth List (1945–2019), *Zeitschrift für Didaktik der Philosophie und Ethik* 2/2020, 119

2020 Between Berlin and Königsberg: Toward a Global Community of Well-Disposed Human Beings, in: Ruth ABBEY (ed.), *Cosmopolitan Civility. Global-Local Reflections with Fred Dallmayer*, New York: SUNY Press, 83–96

2020 "Lived Concreteness": Reading Tu Weiming from the Perspective of the Enlightenment's Cosmopolitanism, in: *The Second Spiritual Humanism Symposium (On the Occasion of Professor Tu Weiming's 80th Birthday*, Beijing, China: Institute for Advanced Humanistic Studies at Peking University, vol. 1, 19–38

2019 Feministická filozofie v postfeministickém kontextu (= Czech translation of: "Feministische Philosophie im post-feministischen Kontext"), in: Věra SOKOLOVÁ & L'ubica KOBOVÁ (eds.), *Odvaha nesouhlasit. Feministické myšlení Hany Havelkové a jeho reflexe*, Prague: Univerzita Karlova, Fakulta humanitních studií, 318–344

2018 Vers une communauté mondiale non exclusive, *Diogène* 263–264, 153–167, https://doi.org/10.3917/dio.263.0153

2018 Towards a Global Non-Exclusive Community, in: *Learning to be Human. Congress volume of The XXIV World Congress of Philosophy, August 13–20, 2018*, Beijing, 73–83

2018 Respecting Difference: A Moral Commitment with Universalist Implications, in: *Proceedings, Songshan Forum 2018: Multicultural Coexistence, Harmonious Symbiosis, Sharing Future, Dengfeng, China*, co-organized by the Institute for Advanced Humanistic Studies at Peking University, Beijing China, 55–68

2018 Olympe de Gouges, in: *Calender of Women Philosophers 2019*, ed. by FISP Committee on Gender Issues, World Congress of Philosophy Beijing, China [without page numbers]

2018 Geschichte, Geschichtsphilosophie, in: *Staatslexikon Recht – Wirtschaft – Gesellschaft*, II, Freiburg – Basel – Vienna: Herder, col. 1187–1196

2018 Educating Humanity. A Core Concern of Kant's Philosophy of History, in: Brigitte BUCHHAMMER (ed.), *Re-Learning to be Human in Global Times: Challenges and Opportunities from the Perspective of Contemporary Philosophy of Religion*, Washington, DC: Council for Research in Values and Philosophy, 183–196

2018 Why Ethics Needs Politics: A Cosmopolitan Perspective (With a Little Help from Kant), in: Kuisma KORHONEN, Arto HAAPALA, Sara HEINÄMAA, Kristian KLOCKARS & Pajari RÄSÄNEN (eds.), *Chiasmatic Encounters. Art, Ethics, Politics*, Lanham, MD: Lexington Books, 149–166

2018 Leibniz heute lesen. Eine Einführung, in: Herta NAGL-DOCEKAL (ed.), *Leibniz heute lesen. Wissenschaft, Geschichte, Religion*, Berlin: De Gruyter, 1–23 (Wiener Reihe 20)

2017 (with Waltraud Heindl) "… aber ein stolzer Bettler." Friedrich Engel-Janosi (1893–1978): Emigration und Rückkehr aus der Perspektive seiner Autobiographie, in: Waldemar ZACHARASIEWICZ & Manfred PRISCHING (eds.), *Return from Exile – Rückkehr aus dem Exil. Exiles, Returnees and their Impact in the Humanities and Social Sciences in Austria and Central Europe*,

Vienna: Austrian Academy of Sciences, 271–286

2017 Geschlechtlichkeit und Normativität. Die katholische Kontroverse zu Gender aus philosophischer Perspektive, in: Katharina KLÖCKER, Thomas LAUBACH & Jochen SAUTERMEISTER (eds.), *Gender – Herausforderung für die christliche Ethik*, Freiburg – Basel – Vienna: Herder, 37–67 (Jahrbuch für Moraltheologie 1)

2017 Learning to be Human: Das Thema des XXIV. Weltkongresses für Philosophie, in: Brigitte BUCHHAMMER (ed.), *Lernen, Mensch zu sein. Beiträge des 2. Symposiums der SWIP Austria*, Vienna: LIT, 11–19 (Women Philosophers at Work. A Series of SWIP Austria 2)

2017 Religion unter Bedingungen der Moderne, in: *Jahrbuch der Österreich-Bibliothek in St. Petersburg*, 2015/2016, vol. 12, St. Petersburg, Russia: PETERBURG XXI VEK Publ., 182–195

2017 Religion in the Context of Modernity: John Rawls and Jürgen Habermas, in: Herta NAGL-DOCEKAL, Wolfgang KALTENBACHER & Claudia MELICA (eds.), *La religione dopo la critica alla religione. Un dibattito filosofico*, Napoli: La scuola di Pitagora editrice, 35–57

2017 Introduzione. Recenti discorsi filosofici sulla religione nella modernità, in: Herta NAGL-DOCEKAL, Wolfgang KALTENBACHER & Claudia MELICA (eds.), *La religione dopo la critica alla religione. Un dibattito filosofico*, Napoli: La scuola di Pitagora editrice, 9–17

2016 Leibniz heute lesen, in: *Die Furche*, November 3, 2016, 22

2016 Towards Just Gender Relations: How the Public Debate Could Benefit from a Philosophical Approach, in: Suwanna SATHA-ANAND, Kanit SIRICHAN & Lowell SKAR (eds.), *Proceedings of the International Symposium "Philosophies in Dialogue: Bridging the Great Philosophical Divides," 26–28 March 2015, Department of Philosophy, Faculty of Arts, Chulalongkorn University, in cooperation with the International Federation of Philosophical Societies*, Bangkok, Thailand, 149–161

2016 (rev.) Der Ort der Moral im aufgeklärten Liberalismus. Otfried Höffe, Kritik der Freiheit. Das Grundproblem der Moderne (2015), *Deutsche Zeitschrift für Philosophie* 64 (2), 313–319, https://doi.org/10.1515/dzph-2016-0024

2016 Film als Tugendlehre? Eine Diskussionsbemerkung zu Robert Pippins Deutung von *Le Fils*, in: Ludwig NAGL & Waldemar ZACHARASIEWICZ (eds.), *Ein Filmphilosophie-Symposium mit Robert B. Pippin. Western, Film Noir und das Kino der Brüder Dardenne*, Berlin: De Gruyter, 205–215

2016 Virtue and Bliss. Rousseau's Reflections on an Un-Alienated Mode of Life, *Diotima. Revue de recherche philosophique* 44, Athens, 64–81

2015 Love in "Our Time": Why Hegel's Reflections on Gender Relations Might Prove Relevant Today, in: *Filosofiya v Peterburge: vchera, segodnya, zavtgra. Dni filosofii v Sankt-Peterburge 2014* [Philosophy in St. Petersburg: Yesterday, Today, Tomorrow. Days of Philosophy in St. Petersburg 2014], Sankt Petersburg: Nauka Publ., 100–117 (Russian translation, ibid. 83–100)

2015 (with Ludwig Nagl) Glaube und Vernunft. Im Gedenken an Friedrich Wolfram, den Religionsphilosophen, *Quart. Zeitschrift des Forums Kunst-Wissenschaft-Medien* 4, 25–26

2015 Recht, Geschichte, Religion – Ein Bericht über zwei internationale Kant-Symposien in Wien 2004 und 2005, in: Violetta L. WAIBEL (ed.), with the collaboration of Max BRINNICH, Sophie GERBER & Philipp SCHALLER, *Umwege. Annäherungen an Immanuel Kant in Wien, in Österreich und in Osteuropa*, Göttingen: Vienna University Press / V&R unipress, 102–108 (English edition: Right, History, Religion. A Report on two International Kant Symposia in Vienna, 2004 and 2005, *Detours. Approaches to Immanuel Kant in Vienna, in Austria, and in Eastern Europe*, Göttingen: Vienna University Press, 102–108)

2015 How Kant's Conception of the "Ethical Commonwealth" Might Prove Relevant for the Current Debate on a Life Focused on a Truly Human Community, in: *Conference Papers, Songshan Forum 2015: Spiritual Humanism and the Living Community of Humankind, Dengfeng, China*, co-organized by the Institute of Advanced Humanistic Studies, Peking University, Beijing, China, 189–198

2015 Geschlechtergerechtigkeit: Wie könnte eine philosophische Perspektive für die theologische Debatte von Relevanz sein?, *Theologische Quartalschrift Tübingen* 1/2015, 75–94

2015 Ein Wiener Philosophieprojekt in internationalem Kontext, in: Hubert Christian EHALT & Oliver RATHKOLB (eds.), *Wissens- und Universitätsstadt Wien. Eine Entwicklungsgeschichte seit 1945*, Vienna: Vienna University Press, 243–250

2014 Equality and the Uniqueness of the Individual. Towards Just Gender Relations, *Pro-fil. An Internet Journal of Philosophy* 15 (2), Masaryk University Brno, Czech Republic, https://doi.org/10.5817/pf15-2-1031

2014 Some Aspects of the Current Debate on Religion in the Context of Western Modernity: John Rawls and Jürgen Habermas, in: *Songshan Forum On Chinese and World Civilizations 2014, Academic Forum Collected Papers*, Institute for Advanced Humanistic Studies at Peking University, Beijing, China, 148–163

2014 Learning to Listen or Why Morality Calls for Liberal Politics, in: Guttorm FLØISTAD (ed.), *Ethics or Moral Philosophy*, Dordrecht – Heidelberg – New York – London: Springer, 109–130 (Contemporary Philosophy. A New Survey 11)

2014 Wo steht die feministische Theorie heute? Philosophische Perspektiven, in: Barbara RENDTORFF, Birgit RIEGRAF & Claudia MAHS (eds.), *40 Jahre Feministische Debatten. Resümee und Ausblick*, Weinheim – Basel: Beltz Juventa, 134–149

2013 Justice, Morality, Love. Re-Reading Rousseau from the Perspective of Feminist Philosophy, in: Andrea JAVORSKÁ, Michal CHABADA & Silvia GÁLIKOVÁ (eds.), *L'udská prirodzenosť: rozum, vôl'a, cit (k 300. Výročiu narodenia J.-J. Rousseaua)*, Filozofická Fakulta Univerzity Konštantina Filozofa v Nitre, Slovenské filozofické združenie pri Slovenskej akadémii vied, Nitra, Slovakia, 8–20

2013 Simposi virtuali: 17 volumi della collana "Wiener Reihe. Themen der Philosophie": Presentatione del volume *Hegels Ästhetik als Theorie der Moderne* (a cura di Annemarie Gethmann-Siefert, Erzsébet Rózsa, Herta Nagl-Docekal, Elisabeth Weisser-Lohmann, Akademie Vlg., Berlin 2013), Istituto Italiano per gli Studi Filosofici, Napoli, 30 Settembre 2013. Internet publication of the Italian translation of the text read at the book presentation (trans. Wolfgang Kaltenbacher) http://www.iisf.it

2013 Ein säkularer Trost? Sterblichkeit als Thema des nachmetaphysischen Denkens, in: Michael HOFER, Christopher MEILLER, Hans SCHELKSHORN & Kurt APPEL (eds.), *Der Endzweck der Schöpfung. Zu den Schlussparagraphen (§§ 84–91) in Kants Kritik der Urteilskraft (Festschrift für Rudolf Langthaler zu seinem 60. Geburtstag)*, Freiburg – Munich: Alber, 254–281

2013 Liebe in "unserer Zeit." Unabgegoltene Elemente der Hegelschen Ästhetik, in: Annemarie GETHMANN-SIEFERT, Herta NAGL-DOCEKAL, Erzsébet RÓZSA, Elisabeth WEISSER-LOHMANN (eds.), *Hegels Ästhetik als Theorie der Moderne*, Berlin: Akademie Vlg., 197–220

2013 (with Elisabeth Weisser-Lohmann) Einleitung: Hegels Ästhetik als Theorie der Moderne, in: Annemarie GETHMANN-SIEFERT, Herta NAGL-DOCEKAL, Erzsébet RÓZSA, Elisabeth WEISSER-LOHMANN (Hrsg.), *Hegels Ästhetik als Theorie der Moderne*, Berlin: Akademie Vlg., 7–13

2012 Feministische Philosophie im post-feministischen Kontext, in: Hilge LANDWEER, Catherine NEWMARK, Christine KLEY & Simone MILLER (eds.), *Philosophie und die Potenziale der Gender Studies*, Bielefeld: transcript, 231–254

2012 Issues of Gender in Catholicism: How the Current Debate Could Benefit from a Philosophical Approach, in: Charles TAYLOR, José CASANOVA & George F. MCLEAN (eds.), *Church and People: Disjunctions in a Secular Age*, Washington, DC: The Council for Research in Values and Philosophy, 155–186 (Series VIII, Christian Philosophical Studies 1)

2012 Feministische Philosophie, *Information Philosophie*, October 2012, no. 3/4 (200th issue: "Rückblick auf 40 Jahre Philosophie"), 95–100

2012 Zukunft in der Gegenwart. Geschichtsphilosophie bei Danto, Arendt und Kant, in: Philipp SCHMIDT & Anja WEIBERG (eds.), *Einheit und Vielfalt in der Gegenwartsphilosophie*, Frankfurt/M. et al.: Peter Lang, 133–152

2012 Religiöse Vielfalt im modernen Rechtsstaat. Ungeklärte Fragen in einer philosophischen Diskussion der Gegenwart, in: Kurt APPEL, Johann Baptist METZ & Jan-Heiner TÜCK (eds.), *Dem Leiden ein Gedächtnis geben*, Göttingen: Vienna University Press / V&R unipress, 429–448 (Wiener Forum für Theologie und

Religionswissenschaft 4)

2011 Liebe, die Gerechtigkeit fordert. Eine universalistische Konzeption, in: Mechtild M. JANSEN & Ingeborg NORDMANN (eds.), *Gerechtigkeit, von Philosophinnen gesehen*, Frankfurt/M.: Hessische Landeszentrale für politische Bildung, 31–47 (Polis 53)

2011 Denken der Gegenwart. Ein geschichtsphilosophisches Projekt, *Information Philosophie*, Electronic Publication, www.information-philosophie.de

2010 Was wird die Zukunft bringen? Geschichts- und religionsphilosophische Perspektiven, in: Ulrike BECHMANN & Christian FRIEDL (eds.), *Zeit. Beiträge von Vortragenden der Montagsakademie 2009/10*, Graz: Universitätsverlag, 129–150

2010 Über Selbstgesetzgebung und das Glück. Autonomie bei Kant, in: Elisabeth LIST & Harald STELZER (eds.), *Grenzen der Autonomie*, Weilerswist: Velbrück Wissenschaft, 33–53

2010 Ist die Konzeption des "Herzenskündigers" obsolet geworden?, in: *Philosophisches Jahrbuch* 117/2, Freiburg – Munich: Alber, 319–338

2010 Feministische Philosophie: Wie Philosophie zur Etablierung geschlechtergerechter Bedingungen beitragen kann, in: Ruth BECKER & Beate KORTENDIEK (eds.), with the collaboration of Barbara Budrich, Ilse Lenz, Sigrid Metz-Göckel, Ursula Müller & Sabine Schäfer), *Handbuch Frauen- und Geschlechterforschung. Theorien, Methoden, Empirie*, 3rd ed., Wiesbaden: VS Verlag für Sozialwissenschaften, 302–311

2010 (rev.) "Einführung in die Ästhetik" von Evelin Klein, in: Evelin KLEIN, *Wege der Theorie – Hodos Theorias*, Frankfurt/M.: Peter Lang, 10–11

2010 "Many Forms of Nonpublic Reason"? Religious Diversity in Liberal Democracies, in: Stefan TOLKSDORF & Holms TETENS (eds.), *In Sprachspiele verstrickt, oder: Wie man der Fliege den Ausweg zeigt: Verflechtungen von Wissen und Können. Festschrift für Hans Julius Schneider*, Berlin – New York: De Gruyter, 363–377

2010 Zur Aktualität dieses Buches, in: Maria Isabel Peña AGUADO & Bettina SCHMITZ (eds.), *Klassikerinnen des modernen Feminismus*, Aachen: ein-FACH-verlag, 112–117

2010 Was ist Feministische Philosophie?, in: Maria Isabel Peña AGUADO & Bettina SCHMITZ (eds.), *Klassikerinnen des modernen Feminismus*, Aachen: ein-FACH-verlag, 117–149

2010 Feministische Ethik oder eine Theorie weiblicher Moral?, in: Maria Isabel Peña AGUADO & Bettina SCHMITZ (eds.), *Klassikerinnen des modernen Feminismus*, Aachen: ein-FACH-verlag, 149–181

2009 "Viele Formen nicht-öffentlicher Vernunft"? Religiöse Diversität in liberalen Demokratien [in Russian], in: *Voprosi filosofii* 9/2009, Moscow, 12–21

2009 "Many Forms of Nonpublic Reason"? Religious Diversity in Liberal Democracies, in: Hans LENK (ed.), *Comparative and Intercultural Philosophy, Proceedings of the IIP Conference Seoul 2008*, Berlin – Münster: LIT, 79–92

2009 "Angewandte Forschung" – an wen ist sie gerichtet?, in: *Wissenschaftsbericht der Stadt Wien 2008*, ed. by Geschäftsgruppe Kultur und Wissenschaft der Stadt Wien, Vienna: Magistrat, 30–31

2009 Eine "entgleisende Modernisierung." Aufklärung und Religion bei Habermas und Hegel [in Czech], *Filosofický Časopis* 57 (1), Prague, 69–86

2009 Interview with Dr. Wolfgang Kaltenbacher: "FilosofIschia. Pensatori a convegno sull'Isola verde in vista del congresso mondiale," *Corriere della Sera*, April 2, 2009, Milano, 19

2008 Interview with Etela Farkašová a Zuzana Kiczková: "Problémy a perspektívy feministického výskumu. Rozhovor s Hertou Nagl-Docekal," in: *Filozofia* 63 (6), Bratislava, 529–534

2008 Moral und Religion aus der Optik der heutigen rechtsphilosophischen Debatte, *Deutsche Zeitschrift für Philosophie* 6/2008, 843–855

2008 Feministická filozofia: Ako môže filozofia prispiet' k etablovaniu rodovo spravodlivých podmienok [Feminist Philosophy: How Philosophy Can Contribute to the Establishment of Gender-Equitable Conditions], *Filozofia* (Bratislava, Slovakia), 2008, č. 6, 469–479

2008 Feminismus, in: Stefan GOSEPATH, Wilfried HINSCH & Beate RÖSSLER (eds.), *Handbuch der Politischen Philosophie und Sozialphilosophie*, Berlin: De Gruyter, 315–321

2008 Philosophische Reflexionen über Liebe und die Gefahr ihrer Unterbestimmung im zeitgenössischen Diskurs, in: Herta NAGL-DOCEKAL & Friedrich WOLFRAM (eds.), *Jenseits der Säkularisierung. Religionsphilosophische Studien*, Berlin: Parerga, 111–141

2008 (with Friedrich Wolfram) Einleitung, in: Herta NAGL-DOCEKAL & Friedrich WOLFRAM (eds.), *Jenseits der Säkularisierung. Religionsphilosophische Studien*, Berlin: Parerga, 11–32

2008 25 Jahre "Stichwort." Grußadresse, in: *Stichwort. Newsletter* 28/2008, Vienna: Archiv der Frauen- und Lesbenbewegung, 4

2008 Feministische Philosophie: Wie Philosophie zur Etablierung geschlechtergerechter Bedingungen beitragen kann, in: Ruth BECKER & Beate KORTENDIEK (eds.), with the collaboration of Barbara Budrich, Ilse Lenz, Sigrid Metz-Göckel, Ursula Müller & Sabine Schäfer, *Handbuch Frauen- und Geschlechterforschung. Theorien, Methoden, Empirie*, 2nd ed., Wiesbaden: VS Verlag für Sozialwissenschaften, 295–304

2008 Eine "entgleisende Modernisierung." Aufklärung und Religion bei Habermas und Hegel, in: Herta NAGL-DOCEKAL, Wolfgang KALTENBACHER & Ludwig NAGL (eds.), *Viele Religionen – eine Vernunft? Ein Disput zu Hegel*, Vienna: Böhlau – Berlin: Akademie Vlg., 154–175 (Wiener Reihe 14)

2008 (with Wolfgang Kaltenbacher & Ludwig Nagl) Einleitung: Viele Religionen – eine Vernunft, in: Herta NAGL-DOCEKAL, Wolfgang KALTENBACHER & Ludwig NAGL (eds.), *Viele Religionen – eine Vernunft? Ein Disput zu Hegel*, Vienna: Böhlau – Berlin: Akademie Vlg., 9–32 (Wiener Reihe 14)

2007 Eine rettende Übersetzung? Jürgen Habermas interpretiert Kants Religionsphilosophie, in: Rudolf LANGTHALER & Herta NAGL-DOCEKAL (eds.), *Glauben und Wissen. Ein Symposium mit Jürgen Habermas*, Vienna – Munich: Oldenbourg – Berlin: Akademie Vlg., 93–119 (Wiener Reihe 13)

2007 (with Rudolf Langthaler) Vorwort, in: Rudolf LANGTHALER & Herta NAGL-DOCEKAL (eds.), *Glauben und Wissen. Ein Symposium mit Jürgen Habermas*, Vienna – Munich: Oldenbourg – Berlin: Akademie Vlg., 7–8 (Wiener Reihe 13)

2006 Konac moderne? Filozofijsko-povijesna razmišljanja [Has Modernism Come to an End? Historico-philosophical Considerations,

Croatian trans. by Ante Periša, Ante Sesar & Jure Zovko], in: Klaus DETHLOFF, Ludwig NAGL & Friedrich WOLFRAM (eds.), *Religija, Moderna, Postmoderna. Filozofsko-teološka razmatranja* [Religion, Modernism, Postmodernism. Philosophical-Theological Explorations. Croatian trans. by Ante Periša, Ante Sesar & Jure Zovko], Zadar/Croatia, 105–122

2006 Religion in der Philosophie der Gegenwart, in: Dieter A. BINDER, Klaus LÜDECKE & Hans PAARHAMMER (eds.), *Kirche in einer säkularisierten Gesellschaft*, Innsbruck – Vienna – Bozen: Studienverlag, 257–273

2006 "Zukunft" als Schlüsselkategorie der Geschichtsphilosophie, in: Friedrich STADLER & Michael STÖLTZNER (eds.), *Time and History. Proceedings of the 28 International Ludwig Wittgenstein Symposium*, Frankfurt/M. – Lancaster, UK: Ontos, 509–524

2006 Beitrag zur Podiumsdiskussion "Der Gott des Christentums und der Gott der Religionen?" in: Christof GESTRICH & Thomas WABEL (eds.), *Gott in der Kultur. Moderne Transzendenzerfahrungen und die Theologie*, Berlin: Wichern, 111–124

2006 Religion unter säkularisierten Bedingungen? Habermas und Kant über Glaube und Moral in der Moderne, in: Christof GESTRICH & Thomas WABEL (eds.), *Gott in der Kultur. Moderne Transzendenzerfahrungen und die Theologie*, Berlin: Wichern, 87–110

2005 Feminista kutatás a filozófiában: Kísérlet egy ideiglenes mérleg megvonására három évtized után [Feminist Research in Philosophy: Attempt of a Provisional Appraisal after Three Decades], *Magyar Filozófiai Szemle* 4/2005, Budapest, 699–717

2005 Liebe als Widerstand: Eine philosophische Konzeption, in: Ingrid BAUER, Christa HÄMMERLE & Gabriella HAUCH (eds.), *Liebe und Widerstand. Ambivalenzen historischer Geschlechterbeziehungen*, Vienna – Cologne – Weimar: Böhlau, 69–78 (L'Homme Schriften 10)

2005 Kosmopolitismus – Einleitung zum Heftschwerpunkt, *Deutsche Zeitschrift für Philosophie* 53 (1), 46–48, https://doi.org/10.1524/dzph.2005.53.1.46

2005 Feminist Philosophy in German: A Historical Perspective, *Hypatia. A Journal of Feminist Philosophy* 20 (2), 1–6, https://doi.org/10.1111/j.1527-2001.2005.tb00464.x

2005 Why Kant's Reflections on History Still Have Relevance, in: Peter KOSLOWSKI (ed.), *The Discovery of Historicity in German Idealism and Historism*, Berlin – Heidelberg – New York: Springer, 172–186

2004 (with Rudolf Langthaler) Vorwort, in: Herta NAGL-DOCEKAL & Rudolf LANGTHALER (eds.), *Recht – Geschichte – Religion. Die Bedeutung Kants für die Gegenwart*, Berlin: Akademie Vlg., 7–9

2004 (with Klaus Dethloff, Rudolf Langthaler & Friedrich Wolfram) Einleitung: Orte der Religion im philosophischen Diskurs der Gegenwart, in: Klaus DETHLOFF, Rudolf LANGTHALER, Herta NAGL-DOCEKAL & Friedrich WOLFRAM (eds.), *Orte der Religion im philosophischen Diskurs der Gegenwart*, Berlin: Parerga, 11–26

2004 Feministische Philosophie – aktuelle Perspektiven, in: Brigitte DOETSCH (ed.), *Philosophinnen im dritten Jahrtausend. Ein Einblick in aktuelle Forschungsfelder*, Bielefeld: Kleine Verlag, 53–68

2004 Geschlechterasymmetrien aus der Perspektive der zeitgenössischen Rechtsphilosophie, in: *Publicationes Universitatis Miskolcinensis, Sectio Philosophica* IX (2), Miskolc, Ungarn, 7–27

2004 Entgrenzungsmuster in der Geschichtsphilosophie. Einleitung, in: Wolfram HOGREBE (ed.), *Grenzen und Grenzüberschreitungen, XIX. Deutscher Kongress für Philosophie, Bonn, 23–27. September 2002, Vorträge und Kolloquien*, Berlin: Akademie Vlg., 589–591

2003 Neoliberale Globalisierung aus feministischer Perspektive. Einleitung zum Heftschwerpunkt, *Deutsche Zeitschrift für Philosophie* 51 (4), 582–584, https://doi.org/10.1524/dzph.2003.51.4.582

2003 Die Demokratisierung der Ausnahme bei Hannah Arendt, in: Claus DIERKSMEIER (ed.), *Die Ausnahme denken. Festschrift zum 60. Geburtstag von Klaus-Maria Kodalle*, I, Würzburg: Königshausen & Neumann, 143–151

2003 (with Ludwig Nagl) Augustinuslektüren im Kontext der Gegenwartsphilosophie, in: Bert van den BRINK, Marcus DÜWELL, Hermann van DOORN & Wolfgang ESSBACH (eds.), *Geschichte – Politik – Philosophie. Festschrift für Willem van Reijen zum 65. Geburtstag*, Munich: Fink, 24–38

2003 Hoffen auf künftige Freiheit. Führt Hannah Arendts Konzeption des Politischen die Geschichtsphilosophie Kants weiter?, in: Johannes ROHBECK & Herta NAGL-DOCEKAL (eds.), *Geschichtsphilosophie und Kulturkritik. Historische und systematische Studien*, Darmstadt: Wissenschaftliche Buchgesellschaft, 231–263

2003 (with Johannes Rohbeck) Geschichtsphilosophie und Kulturkritik. Eine Einleitung, in: Johannes ROHBECK & Herta NAGL-DOCEKAL (eds.), *Geschichtsphilosophie und Kulturkritik. Historische und systematische Studien*, Darmstadt: Wissenschaftliche Buchgesellschaft, 7–20

2003 Es aun posible hoy en dia la filosofia de la historia?, in: Gustavo LEYVA (ed.), *Politica, identitad y narracion*, Mexico, DF: Universidad autonoma metropolitana, 517–534 (Biblioteca de signos 26)

2003 Ist Geschichtsphilosophie heute noch möglich?, in: Milan ZNOY (ed.), *Hegelovskou stopou: k poctě profesora Milana Sobotky*, Prague: Univerzita Karlova v Praze, 219–228 (Studia Philosophica XIV)

2002 Die Kunst und das Weibliche [in Czech], *Aspekt. Feministische Kulturzeitschrift* 1/2002, Bratislava, 88–106

2002 Anthropologie (Kulturanthropologie), in: Renate KROLL (ed.), *Metzler Lexikon Gender Studies / Geschlechterforschung*, Stuttgart – Weimar: Metzler, 15–17

2002 Ästhetik, weibliche (feministische), in: Renate KROLL (ed.), *Metzler Lexikon Gender Studies / Geschlechterforschung*, Stuttgart – Weimar: Metzler, 24–25

2002 Fraser, Nancy, in: Renate KROLL (ed.), *Metzler Lexikon Gender Studies / Geschlechterforschung*, Stuttgart – Weimar: Metzler, 115–116

2002 Philosophie, in: Renate KROLL (ed.), *Metzler Lexikon Gender Studies / Geschlechterforschung*, Stuttgart – Weimar: Metzler, 306–308

2002 Autonomie zwischen Selbstbestimmung und Selbstgesetzgebung oder Warum es sich lohnen könnte, dem Verhältnis von Moral und Recht bei Kant erneut nachzugehen, in: Herlinde PAUER-STUDER & Herta NAGL-DOCEKAL (eds.), *Freiheit, Gleichheit und Autonomie*, Vienna – Munich: Oldenbourg – Berlin: Akademie Vlg., 296–326 (Wiener Reihe 11)

2002 (with Herlinde Pauer-Studer) Einleitung: Freiheit, Gleichheit und Autonomie als Schlüsselbegriffe zeitgenössischer Gerechtigkeitstheorien, in: Herlinde PAUER-STUDER & Herta NAGL-DOCEKAL (eds.), *Freiheit, Gleichheit und Autonomie*, Vienna – Munich: Oldenbourg – Berlin: Akademie Vlg., 7–20 (Wiener Reihe 11)

2002 Einsamkeit. Einleitung zum Heftschwerpunkt, *Deutsche Zeitschrift für Philosophie* 50 (5), 712–714, https://doi.org/10.1524/dzph.2002.50.5.712

2002 Doing Philosophy as a Feminist. Ergebnisse und Perspektiven der internationalen Debatte, in: Birgit CHRISTENSEN (ed.), *Wissen / Macht / Geschlecht. Philosophie und die Zukunft der "condition féminine,"* Zürich: Chronos, 175–183

2002 Ist die Moderne zu Ende? Geschichtsphilosophische Überlegungen, in: Klaus DETHLOFF, Ludwig NAGL & Friedrich WOLFRAM (eds.), *Religion, Moderne, Postmoderne. Philosophisch-theologische Erkundungen*, Berlin: Parerga, 203–218

2002 Dualismus, philosophisch, in: Elisabeth GOESSMANN, Helga KUHLMANN, Elisabeth MOLTMANN-WENDEL et al. (eds.), *Wörterbuch der Feministischen Theologie*, 2nd ed., Gütersloh: Gütersloher Verlagshaus, 98–99

2002 Feministische Philosophie – Frauenforschung – Gender Studies. Ein Interview [Herta Nagl-Docekal in a conversation with Yvanka B. Raynova], in: Yvanka B. RAYNOVA (ed.), *Rethinking Modernity: Philosophy, Values, Gender*, Vienna: Institut für axiologische Forschung, 111–121

2000 (with Cornelia Klinger) Introduction: Feminist Philosophy in German, in: Herta NAGL-DOCEKAL & Cornelia KLINGER (eds.), *Continental Philosophy in Feminist Perspective. Re-Reading the Canon in German*, University Park, PA: The Pennsylvania State University Press, 1–30

2000 Philosophy of History as a Theory of Gender Difference: The Case of Rousseau, in: Herta NAGL-DOCEKAL & Cornelia KLINGER (eds.), *Continental Philosophy in Feminist Perspective. Re-Reading the Canon in German*, University Park, PA: The Pennsylvania State University Press, 77–100

2000 Egalität und Differenz in der philosophischen Perspektive, in:

Anne JENSEN & Maximilian LIEBMANN (eds.), *Was verändert Feministische Theologie?*, Münster – Hamburg – London: LIT, 37–46

2000 Feministische Ästhetik: Versuch einer Zwischenbilanz, in: Jörg HUBER (ed.), *Darstellung. Korrespondenz*, Zürich: Edition Voldemeer – Vienna – New York: Springer, 75–98

2000 Gleichheit und Differenz: Neue Debatten in der feministischen Rechtsphilosophie und politischen Theorie, in: Sigrid BERKA, Susanne MOSER & Yvanka RAYNOVA (eds.), *Die Feministische Philosophie: Perspektiven und Debatten*, Sofia: OSI & Nauka i izkoustvo, 140–148 (Bulgarian translation, ibid. 33–43)

2000 Ist eine Rehabilitierung von Geschichtsphilosophie möglich? [Editorial zum Heftschwerpunkt], *Deutsche Zeitschrift für Philosophie* 48 (1), 49–50, https://doi.org/10.1524/dzph.2000.48.1.49

2000 Anerkennung von Differenz: Die heutige Debatte zur feministischen politischen Theorie, in: MÜNSTERANER ARBEITSKREIS FÜR GENDER STUDIES (ed.), *Kultur, Geschlecht, Körper*, Münster: agenda, 20–39

1999 (with Gudrun Wolfgruber) Glück, *L'Homme. Zeitschrift für Feministische Geschichtswissenschaft* 10 (2), 169–172

1999 Unabgegoltene Motive der Geschichtsphilosophie Kants, in: Jürgen MITTELSTRASS (ed.), *Die Zukunft des Wissens. XVIII. Deutscher Kongreß für Philosophie, Konstanz 1999*, Konstanz: Universitätsverlag, 1157–1164

1999 Philosophie, feministische [rev. ed.], in: Peter PRECHTL & Franz-Peter BURKARD (eds.), *Metzlers Philosophie-Lexikon*, 2nd ed., Stuttgart: Metzler, 441–442

1999 Feministische Politische Theorie: Ergebnisse und aktuelle Probleme, in: Birgit CHRISTENSEN (ed.), *Demokratie und Geschlecht. Interdisziplinäres Symposium zum 150 jährigen Jubiläum des Schweizerischen Bundesstaates*, Zürich: Chronos, 15–31

1999 The Feminist Critique of Reason Revisited, *Hypatia. A Journal of Feminist Philosophy* 14 (1), 49–76, https://doi.org/10.1111/j.1527-2001.1999.tb01039.x

1998 Anerkennung von Differenz. Fragen der Gerechtigkeit in der heutigen feministischen Theorie, in: Brigitta KEINTZEL (ed.), *Be-*

wegliche Ziele. Positionen zur Philosophie der Gefühle, Vienna: Turia + Kant, 195–205

1998 Feministische Theorie – Zwischenbilanzen [Einleitung zum Heftschwerpunkt], *Deutsche Zeitschrift für Philosophie* 46 (5), 780–782, https://doi.org/10.1524/dzph.1998.46.5.780

1998 Nach der Gleichstellung. Fragen der Gerechtigkeit in der heutigen feministischen Theorie, in: Marion HEINZ & Friederike KUSTER (eds.), *Geschlechtertheorie / Geschlechterforschung – ein interdisziplinäres Kolloquium*, Bielefeld: Kleine, 105–116

1998 Eine Wiederkehr des Nebenwiderspruchs? (Kommentar zu Amartya Sen), in: Julian NIDA-RÜMELIN & Wolfgang THIERSE (eds.), *Philosophie und Politik II. Soziale Gerechtigkeit und ökonomische Differenz*, Essen: Klartext, 85–89 & 123

1998 Modern Moral and Political Philosophy, in: Alison M. JAGGAR & Iris M. YOUNG (eds.), *A Companion to Feminist Philosophy*, Oxford: Blackwell, 58–74

1998 Ein Postscriptum zum Begriff "Gerechtigkeitsethik," in: Detlef HORSTER (ed.), *Weibliche Moral – ein Mythos?*, Frankfurt/M.: Suhrkamp, 142–153

1998 Feministische Ethik oder eine Theorie weiblicher Moral?, in: Detlef HORSTER (ed.), *Weibliche Moral – ein Mythos?*, Frankfurt/M.: Suhrkamp, 42–72

1997 Feministische Vernunftkritik: Eine Zwischenbilanz, *L'Homme. Zeitschrift für Feministische Geschichtswissenschaft* 8 (1), 21–29

1997 Feministische Politische Theorie: Ergebnisse und aktuelle Probleme, in: Peter KOLLER & Klaus PUHL (eds.), *Current Issues in Political Philosophy: Justice in Society and World Order*, Vienna: Hölder-Pichler-Tempsky, 236–252

1997 Seyla Benhabib und die radikale Zukunft der Aufklärung, *Deutsche Zeitschrift für Philosophie* 45 (6), 943–956, https://doi.org/10.1524/dzph.1997.45.6.943

1997 Seyla Benhabib and the Radical Future of the Enlightenment, *Philosophy and Social Criticism* 23 (5), 63–78, https://doi.org/10.1177%2F019145379702300503

1997 Feminist Ethics: How It Could Benefit from Kant's Moral Philosophy, in: Robin May SCHOTT (ed.), *Feminist Interpretations of Immanuel Kant*, University Park, PA: The Pennsylvania State

University Press, 101–124

1997 Untiefen der Essentialismuskritik [Einleitung zum Heftschwerpunkt], *Deutsche Zeitschrift für Philosophie* 45 (1), 20–22, https://doi.org/10.1524/dzph.1997.45.1.20

1997 Towards a New Theory of the Historical Sciences: The Relevance of Truth and Method, in: Lewis Edwin HAHN (ed.), *The Philosophy of Hans-Georg Gadamer*, Chicago – La Salle, IL: Open Court, 193–204 (The Library of Living Philosophers 24)

1996 Moralphilosophie und politische Theorie unter feministischer Perspektive, in: Helmuth VETTER, Konrad Paul LIESSMANN & Ulrike ANGSÜSSER (eds.), *Philosophia practica universalis. Festgabe für Johann Mader zum 70. Geburtstag*, Frankfurt/M.: Peter Lang, 215–228

1996 Ist Geschichtsphilosophie heute noch möglich? Einleitung, in: Herta NAGL-DOCEKAL (ed.), *Der Sinn des Historischen. Geschichtsphilosophische Debatten*, Frankfurt/M.: Fischer, 9–63

1996 Gleichbehandlung und Anerkennung von Differenz: Kontroversielle Themen feministischer politischer Philosophie, in: Herta NAGL-DOCEKAL & Herlinde PAUER-STUDER (eds.), *Politische Theorie: Differenz und Lebensqualität. Beiträge zur feministischen politischen Philosophie*, Frankfurt/M.: Suhrkamp, 9–53

1996 Feministische Vernunftkritik, in: Karl-Otto APEL & Matthias KETTNER (eds.), *Die eine Vernunft und die vielen Rationalitäten*, Frankfurt/M.: Suhrkamp, 166–205

1995 Existuje morálna diferenciácia rodov?, *Aspekt* 2-3/1995, Bratislava, Slovakia, 24–29

1995 Die Philosophie der Familie bei Rousseau, Kant und Hegel. Ein Schlüssel zum Verständnis heutiger Lebensformen [in German and Czech], in: Hana HAVELKOVÁ (ed.), *Gibt es ein mitteleuropäisches Ehe- und Familienmodell?*, Prague: Arts and Theatre Institute, 9–18

1995 Feministische Philosophie, in: Peter PRECHTL & Franz-Peter BURKARD (eds.), *Metzler Philosophie-Lexikon*, Stuttgart: Metzler, 454–457

1995 Schwerpunkt: Familie und Gerechtigkeit, *Deutsche Zeitschrift für Philosophie* 43 (6), 964–966, https://doi.org/10.1524/dzph.1995.43.6.964

1995 Die Kunst der Grenzziehung und die Familie. Eine feministische Kritik der Gerechtigkeitskonzeption von Michael Walzer, in: Christoph DEMMERLING & Thomas RENTSCH (eds.), *Die Gegenwart der Gerechtigkeit. Diskurse zwischen Recht, praktischer Philosophie und Politik*, Berlin: Akademie Vlg., 261–176 (repr.)

1995 Feministische Ethik. Ein Bericht, *Information Philosophie* 2/1995, 24–31

1995 Frauengeschichte, Geschlechtergeschichte, feministische Philosophie. Ein Gespräch zwischen Herta Nagl-Docekal, Edith Saurer, Ulrike Döcker und Gabriella Hauch, *Österreichische Zeitschrift für Geschichtswissenschaften* 6 (2), 273–284, https://doi.org/10.25365/oezg-1995-6-2-7

1995 Wie ist feministische Politik zu denken? (Eine kritische Frage an Judith Butler), *L'Homme. Zeitschrift für Feministische Geschichtswissenschaft* 6 (1), 95–96

1995 Feministische Ethik: Die philosophische Debatte, *AUF. Eine Frauenzeitschrift* 88, 6–14

1995 Gender Parody as a Form of Resistance?, in: Agnes HELLER & Sonja PUNTSCHER RIEKMANN (eds.), *Biopolitics. The Politics of the Body, Race and Nature*, Aldershot: Avebury, 143–156

1994 Ist Fürsorglichkeit mit Gleichbehandlung unvereinbar?, *Deutsche Zeitschrift für Philosophie* 42 (6), 1045–1050, https://doi.org/10.1524/dzph.1994.42.6.1045

1994 Geschlechterparodie als Widerstandsform? [revised version], in: Sigrid HAASE (ed.), *Musen und Mythen III. Frauenjahrbuch der Hochschule der Künste Berlin*, Berlin: Hochschule der Künste, 159–169

1994 Rozhovar Aspektu (Wie kann man Demokrat und dabei nicht feministisch sein?), *Aspekt* 2/1994, Bratislava, Slovakia, 66–67

1994 Zenská Estetika alebo "Utópia zvlástneho"? [Female Aesthetics or "Utopia of the Special"?], in: Herta NAGL-DOCEKALOVA, Brigitte WEISSHAUPTOVA, Evelyn FOX-KELLEROVA & Lorraine CODEROVA, *Styri Pohl'ady do Feministickej Filozofie*, Bratislava: Archa, 25–41

1994 Gibt es eine moralische Differenz der Geschlechter? Zum Problem einer feministischen Ethik, in: Sabine DOYÉ, Marion HEINZ & Friederike KUSTER (eds.), *Perspektiven Feministischer Philoso-*

phie, Wuppertal: Bergische Universität Gesamthochschule Wuppertal, 125–152

1994 Geschichtsphilosophie als Theorie der Geschlechterdifferenz. Das Beispiel Rousseaus, *Deutsche Zeitschrift für Philosophie* 42 (4), 571–589, https://doi.org/10.1524/dzph.1994.42.4.571

1994 Feminism and the Post-Modern, in: Jeff BERNARD & Katalin NEUMER (eds.), *Zeichen, Sprache, Bewußtsein. Österreichisch-Ungarische Dokumente zur Semiotik und Philosophie* 2, Vienna – Budapest: ÖGS/ISSS, 225–246 (repr.)

1993 Das Institut für Philosophie der Universität Wien. Der Status quo und seine Genese, in: Kurt R. FISCHER & Franz M. WIMMER (eds.), *Der geistige Anschluß. Philosophie und Politik an der Universität Wien 1930–1950*, Vienna: Wiener Universitätsverlag, 206–220

1993 Utopie des Besonderen [shortened version], *Art Fan* 9, 3–5

1993 Die Kunst der Grenzziehung und die Familie. Ein Kommentar zu Michael Walzer: Sphären der Gerechtigkeit. Ein Plädoyer für Pluralität und Gleichheit, *Deutsche Zeitschrift für Philosophie* 41 (6), 1021–1033, https://doi.org/10.1524/dzph.1993.41.6.1021

1993 (with Axel Honneth, Hans-Peter Krüger & Hans Julius Schneider) Editorial, *Deutsche Zeitschrift für Philosophie* 41 (2), 187–188, https://doi.org/10.1524/dzph.1993.41.2.187

1993 Jenseits der Geschlechtermoral. Eine Einführung, in: Herta NAGL-DOCEKAL & Herlinde PAUER-STUDER (eds.), *Jenseits der Geschlechtermoral. Beiträge zur feministischen Ethik*, Frankfurt/M.: Fischer, 7–32

1993 Läßt sich Geschichtsphilosophie tropologisch fundieren? Kritische Anmerkungen zu Hayden White, *Österreichische Zeitschrift für Geschichtswissenschaften* 4 (3), 466–478, https://doi.org/10.25365/oezg-1993-4-3-8 (repr.)

1993 (rev.) Judith Butler, Das Unbehagen der Geschlechter, *L'Homme. Zeitschrift für Feministische Geschichtswissenschaft* 4 (1), 141–147

1993 Geschlechterparodie als Widerstandsform? Judith Butlers Kritik an der feministischen Politik beruht auf einem Trugschluß, *Frankfurter Rundschau*, June 29, 1993, 12

1993 Philosophinnen in Europa 1992. Zukunft ohne Diskriminierung?

Bericht über das Amsterdamer Symposium der Internationalen Assoziation von Philosophinnen, *Information Philosophie* 1/1993, 103–105

1993 Towards a Feminist Transformation of Philosophy, in: Harry KUNNEMAN & Hent de VRIES (eds.), *Enlightenments. Encounters between Critical Theory and Contemporary French Thought*, Kampen: Kok Pharos, 305–318

1993 Kritische und feministische Theorie. Ein Bericht, in: Theodor SCHNEIDER & Helen SCHÜNGEL-STRAUMANN (eds.), *Theologie zwischen Zeiten und Kontinenten. Festschrift für Elisabeth Gössmann*, Freiburg – Basel – Vienna: Herder, 224–238

1993 Für eine geschlechtergeschichtliche Perspektivierung der Historiographiegeschichte, in: Wolfgang KÜTTLER, Jörn RÜSEN & Ernst SCHULIN (eds.), *Geschichtsdiskurs*, 1: *Grundlagen und Methoden der Historiographiegeschichte*, Frankfurt/M.: S. Fischer, 233–256

1992 Feminism and the Post-Modern, *Transactions of the Royal Society of Canada* 3, Ottawa, 147–162

1992 Philosophie 5: Feministische Philosophie, in: Erwin FAHLBUSCH, Jan Milic LOCHMAN, John MBITI et al. (eds.), *Evangelisches Kirchenlexikon*, 3: *L–R*, Göttingen: Vandenhoeck & Ruprecht, 1202–1205

1992 Anknüpfungen und Einsprüche. Ein Versuch, auf sehr unterschiedliche Kommentare zur Feministischen Philosophie zu antworten, *Ethik und Sozialwissenschaften. Streitforum für Erwägungskultur* 3 (4), 577–592

1992 Von der feministischen Transformation der Philosophie, *Ethik und Sozialwissenschaften. Streitforum für Erwägungskultur* 3 (4), 523–531

1992 Co je feministická filozofie? [What is Feminist Philosophy?], *Filosofický Časopis 5, Ročník* 40, Filosofický USTAV CSAV, 742–756

1992 Feminist Ethics: The Controversy Between Contextualism and Universalism Revisited, in: Maja PELLIKAAN-ENGEL (ed.), *Against Patriarchal Thinking. A Future without Discrimination? Proceedings of the VIth Symposium of IAPh*, Amsterdam: VU Press, 163–172

1992 Kann die postmoderne Fortschrittskritik zur Erneuerung der Sozialdemokratie beitragen?, in: Peter MUHR, Paul FEYERABEND & Cornelia WEGELER (eds.), *Philosophie, Psychoanalyse, Emigration. Festschrift für Kurt Rudolf Fischer zum 70. Geburtstag*, Vienna: Universitätsverlag, 237–250

1992 Postkoloniales Philosophieren: Afrika. Eine Einleitung, in: Herta NAGL-DOCEKAL & Franz M. WIMMER (eds.), *Postkoloniales Philosophieren: Afrika*, Vienna – Munich: Oldenbourg, 7–14

1992 Weibliche Ästhetik oder "Utopie des Besonderen"? [extended version], *Die Philosophin* 5/1992, 30–44

1992 Dualismus, in: Elisabeth GOESSMANN, Helga KUHLMANN, Elisabeth MOLTMANN-WENDEL et al. (eds.), *Wörterbuch der Feministischen Theologie*, Gütersloh: Gerd Mohn, 64–67

1991 Geschlecht – Macht – Geschichte: Zur Theorie der Feministischen Geschichtswissenschaft, *Filozofski Vestnik* 12 (2), Ljubljana, 49–67

1991 Kritische en feministische theorie, in: Lieteke van VUCHT TIJSSEN & Willem van REIJEN (eds.), *Kennis en Werkelijkheid benaderingen*, Muiderberg, 219–231

1991 Modernität der Historie. Jörn Rüsen zu neuen Ansätzen einer Geschichte der Historiographie (Interview), *Österreichische Zeitschrift für Geschichtswissenschaften* 2 (3), 90–95, https://doi.org/10.25365/oezg-1991-2-3-6

1990 (with Klaus Ammon, Gerhard Botz et al.) Struktur, Sprache und Ideologie im "Kärntner Grenzland-Jahrbuch 1989," in: Gero FISCHER & Peter GSTETTNER (eds.), *"Am Kärntner Wesen könnte diese Republik genesen." An den rechten Rand Europas: Jörg Haiders "Erneuerungspolitik,"* Klagenfurt: Drava, 108–127

1990 Ist der Fortschrittsbegriff der Aufklärung durch die Kritik der Gegenwart obsolet geworden?, in: *Annalen der internationalen Gesellschaft für dialektische Philosophie – Societas Hegeliana* VI, 1989: *Die Französische Revolution: Philosophie und Wissenschaften*, Bd. 1, ed. by Hans Heinz Holz et al., Milano: Guerini, 41–45

1990 Feministische Philosophie – ein Randproblem? Mit den amerikanischen Philosophinnen Seyla Benhabib und Alison Jaggar sprachen Herta Nagl-Docekal und Herlinde Pauer-Studer, *Falter* 27, 8–9

1990 Rückkehr des Subjekts?, in: Adolf VUKOVICH, Ulrich BAR-TOSCH,

Guido POLLAK & Hans-Joachim REINECKE (eds.), *Natur-Selbst-Bildung. Festschrift für Joachim Christian Horn*, Regensburg: Bosse, 112–119

1990 Ist die Geschichtsphilosophie obsolet geworden?, in: Rudolf WOHLGENANNT & Rainer BORN (eds.), *Reflexion und Wirklichkeit. Akten des Ersten Österreichischen Kongresses für Philosophie*, Vienna: Verband der wissenschaftlichen Gesellschaften Österreichs, 45–56 (Conceptus-Studien 6)

1990 Zwischen Institutionalisierung und Ausgrenzung: Feministische Philosophie an der Universität Wien, *Die Philosophin. Forum für feministische Theorie und Philosophie* 1 (1), 7–17

1990 Feministische Geschichtswissenschaft – ein unverzichtbares Projekt, *L'Homme. Zeitschrift für Feministische Geschichtswissenschaft* 1 (1), 7–18

1990 Weibliche Ästhetik oder "Utopie des Besonderen"?, in: AKADEMIE DER BILDENDEN KÜNSTE (ed.), *Über die Wahrheit in der Malerei*, Vienna: Verlag der Akademie der Bildenden Künste, 41–48

1990 Paradoxien der Evolutionären Erkenntnistheorie, in: August FENK (ed.), *Evolution und Selbstbezug des Erkennens*, Vienna – Cologne: Böhlau, 69–82

1990 Was ist Feministische Philosophie?, in: Herta NAGL-DOCEKAL (ed.), *Feministische Philosophie*, Vienna – Munich: Oldenbourg, 7–39 (Wiener Reihe 4)

1989 1789/1989 – Die Revolution hat nicht stattgefunden: Bericht über die Berliner Tagung der Internationalen Assoziation von Philosophinnen, *Information Philosophie* 4/1989, 80–84

1989 Feministische Philosophie: Versuch einer Begriffsbestimmung, in: Astrid DEUBER-MANKOWSKY, Ulrike RAMMING & E. Walesca TIELSCH (eds.), *1789/1989 – Die Revolution hat nicht stattgefunden. Dokumentation des V. Symposions der Internationalen Assoziation von Philosophinnen*, Tübingen: edition discord, 13–18

1989 Wittgensteinrezeption im Neostrukturalismus: Jean-François Lyotard, in: Herta NAGL-DOCEKAL (ed.), *Ludwig Wittgenstein und die Philosophie des 20. Jahrhunderts*, Vienna: Verein "Freunde des Hauses Wittgenstein," 97–100 (Miscellanea Bulgarica 6)

1988 (rev.) Helmuth Vetter, Günther Pöltner, Peter Kampits (Hrsg.),

Verantwortung. Beiträge zur praktischen Philosophie, *Wiener Jahrbuch für Philosophie* XX, 248–251

1988 (rev.) Susanne Heine, Frauen der frühen Christenheit; dies., Wiederbelebung der Göttinnen?, *Wiener Jahrbuch für Philosophie* XX, 247–248

1988 (rev.) Walter Reese-Schäfer, Lyotard zur Einführung, *Wiener Jahrbuch für Philosophie* XX, 251–252

1988 Evolutionäre Erkenntnistheorie?, in: Manfred HORVAT (ed.), *Das Phänomen Evolution*, Vienna: literas, 141–153 (repr.)

1988 Was bleibt vom Fortschrittsbegriff? Die "Dialektik der Aufklärung" als Geschichtsphilosophie, *Doxa* 14/1988 = *Semiotische Berichte* 1 (2), 85–112

1988 Das heimliche Subjekt Lyotards, in: Manfred FRANK, Gérard RAULET & Willem van REIJEN (eds.), *Die Frage nach dem Subjekt*, Frankfurt/M.: Suhrkamp, 230–246

1988 Kulturwissenschaft und Utopie, in: Venant CAUCHY (ed.), *Philosophy and Culture: Proceedings of the XVII World Congress of Philosophy, Montreal, 1983*, 112–116

1988 Geschichtsphilosophie, in: Erwin FAHLBUSCH, Jan MILIC LOCHMAN, John MBITI et al. (eds.), *Evangelisches Kirchenlexikon*, 2: *G–K*, 3rd ed., Göttingen: Vandenhoeck & Ruprecht, col. 115–117

1987 Tod des Subjekts? Die Thematik dieses Bandes, in: Herta NAGL-DOCEKAL & Helmuth VETTER (eds.), *Tod des Subjekts?*, Vienna – Munich: Oldenbourg, 7–21 (Wiener Reihe 2)

1986 Die Gefahr einer halbierten Institutionalisierung historischer Frauenforschung, *Mitteilungen des Instituts für Wissenschaft und Kunst, Wien* 41 (4), 127–128

1986 Kommentar zu den Beiträgen von W. Küttler, G. Lozek und H.-U. Wehler, in: Jürgen KOCKA (ed.), *Max Weber. Der Historiker*, Göttingen: Vandenhoeck & Ruprecht, 204–208

1986 (rev.) Josef Meran, Theorien in der Geschichtswissenschaft. Die Diskussion über die Wissenschaftlichkeit der Geschichte, *Wiener Jahrbuch für Philosophie* XVIII, 256–257

1985 Läßt sich die Geschichtsphilosophie tropologisch fundieren? Kritische Bemerkungen zur Annäherung der Analytischen Philosophie an den Strukturalismus, in: Wolfdietrich SCHMIED-KOWARZIK (ed.), *Objektivationen des Geistigen. Beiträge zur*

Kulturphilosophie, Berlin: Reimer, 201–214

1985 Evolutionäre Erkenntnistheorie?, in: Hubert Ch. EHALT (ed.), *Zwischen Natur und Kultur. Zur Kritik biologistischer Ansätze*, Vienna: Böhlau, 247–263

1984 (rev.) Kurt Röttgers, Der kommunikative Text und die Zeitstruktur von Geschichten, *Wiener Jahrbuch für Philosophie* XVI, 265–268

1984 Frauengeschichte als Perspektive und Teilbereich der Geschichtswissenschaft, in: Herta NAGL-DOCEKAL & Franz WIMMER (eds.), *Neue Ansätze in der Geschichtswissenschaft*, Vienna: Verband der wissenschaftlichen Gesellschaften Österreichs, 128–132 (Conceptus-Studien 1)

1984 Von der Notwendigkeit einer transzendentalphilosophischen Transformation der Diskurstheorie, in: Willem van REIJEN & Karl-Otto APEL (eds.), *Rationales Handeln und Gesellschaftstheorie*, Bochum: Germinal, 219–226

1984 Immanuel Kants Philosophie des Friedens und was die Friedensbewegung der Gegenwart daraus gewinnen könnte, in: Gernot HEISS & Heinrich LUTZ (eds.), *Friedensbewegungen: Bedingungen und Wirkungen*, Vienna: Verlag für Geschichte und Politik, 55–74

1979 (rev.) Kurt Röttgers & Hans Saner (Hrsg.), Gewalt, *Wiener Jahrbuch für Philosophie* XII, 342–345

1979 "Für einen Kammerdiener gibt es keinen Helden." Hegels Kritik an der moralischen Beurteilung "welthistorischer Individuen," in: Grete KLINGENSTEIN, Heinrich LUTZ & Gerald STOURZH (eds.), *Biographie und Geschichtswissenschaft*, Vienna: Verlag für Geschichte und Politik, 68–80

1978 (with Edith Saurer) Friedrich Engel-Janosi (1893–1978) (Nachruf), *Zeitgeschichte* 5 (9/10), 396–399

1977 Philosophische Überlegungen zur Legitimationsfähigkeit oppositioneller Gewalt, in: Friedrich ENGEL-JANOSI, Grete KLINGENSTEIN & Heinrich LUTZ (eds.), *Gewalt und Gewaltlosigkeit*, Vienna: Verlag für Geschichte und Politik, 15–40

1976 (rev.) Herbert Schnädelbach, Geschichtsphilosophie nach Hegel, *Wiener Jahrbuch für Philosophie* IX, 326–330

1976 Die Bedeutung Max Webers für die gegenwärtige Auseinandersetzung um die sogenannten Geisteswissenschaften, *Wiener Jahrbuch für Philosophie* IX, 114–138

1975 Geschichtsphilosophie ohne Geschichte. Reflexionen zu zwei Neuerscheinungen über analytische Geschichtsphilosophie, *Wiener Jahrbuch für Philosophie* VIII, 378–391

1974 Zum Problem des Relativismus in der neueren amerikanischen Geschichtstheorie, in: Friedrich ENGEL-JANOSI, Grete KLINGENSTEIN & Heinrich LUTZ (eds.), *Denken über Geschichte*, Vienna: Verlag für Geschichte und Politik, 128–141

1972 (rev.) Fritz-Joachim v. Rintelen, Der Aufstieg im Geiste, *Wiener Jahrbuch für Philosophie* V, 378–380

1972 (rev.) Fritz-Joachim v. Rintelen, Contemporary German Philosophy and its Background, *Wiener Jahrbuch für Philosophie* V, 376–378

1970 Gab es schon zur Zeit Hegels ein "Wiener Jahrbuch für Philosophie"?, *Wiener Jahrbuch für Philosophie* III, 360

CONTRIBUTORS

BRIGITTE BUCHHAMMER, Dr. Mag., Philosopher, teaching at universities in Austria and abroad, lectures in Berlin, Paderborn, Stuttgart, Athens, Washington, Linz, ETH Zürich, Erfurt.
brigitte.buchhammer@a1.net / ☎ +43-650-7040706
https://brigittebuchhammer.wordpress.com/
http://regiowiki.at/wiki/Brigitte_Buchhammer

WALTRAUD ERNST, Dr., M.A., Philosopher, Senior Researcher, Institute for Women's and Gender Studies, Johannes Kepler University Linz, Austria.
waltraud.ernst@jku.at / ☎ +43-732-24683731
https://www.jku.at/institut-fuer-frauen-und-geschlechterforschung/ueber-uns/team/ernst/

CORNELIA EŞIANU, DDr., Lecturer at the Vienna Adult Education Centers (Politics, Society, and Culture); *Teaching and research*: German language and literature, philosophy with main interests in: aesthetics, political philosophy, philosophy for children, and ethics. *Publications*: Monographs: *"Und so führt die Philosophie zur Poesie" – Systematische Forschungen zu Friedrich Schlegel,* Vienna: LIT, 2016; *Hypostasen der Identität beim jungen Friedrich Schlegel. Eine Untersuchung von Leben und Werk aus identitätstheoretischer Sicht*, Bukarest: Paideia, 2004; Article to be published in 2022: Thomas Bernhard, Kant und der Papagei, in: *Kronstädter Beiträge zur germanistischen*

Forschung, vol. 22. Translation completed for publication in Romanian of Herta Nagl-Docekal's book *Feministische Philosophie. Ergebnisse, Probleme, Perspektiven.*
cornelia.esianu@gmx.at / ☎ +43-676-5174736

GERTRUDE POSTL, Dr. Mag., Prof., Department of Philosophy, Women's and Gender Studies Program, Suffolk County Community College, Selden, NY, USA. Research focus: feminist philosophy, especially the intersection between body, language, and representation (Luce Irigaray, Julia Kristeva, Hélène Cixous), and issues of reading/writing, author, and text (Roland Barthes and Jacques Derrida).
postlg@sunysuffolk.edu / www.gertrudepostl.com

BETTINA ZEHETNER, Dr. Mag., psychosocial counsellor at "Frauen* beraten Frauen*. Institute for women*specific social studies", trainer for gender competence in counseling and the alliance of feminist theory and practice, lecturer at the Department of Philosophy at the University of Vienna.
bettina.zehetner@univie.ac.at
http://homepage.univie.ac.at/bettina.zehetner/

Brigitte Buchhammer (Ed.)
The Future of Europe – an Urgent Challenge to Global Philosophy
Die Zukunft Europas – eine drängende Herausforderung für die globale Philosophie
This current volume of the series *Women* Philosophers at Work. A Series of SWIP Austria* reflects the wide spectrum of the philosophers' research work. Eleven essays highlight the subject of the publication from different points of view.
The targets and duties of the *Society for Women* in Philosophy* are as follows: the Society is a non-profit organization to support women* and LGBTIQ-people working in and committed to the study of philosophy in Austria. Its purpose is to advance equal treatment and gender justice for everyone in philosophy, both students and professionals, philosophers at all levels of academia, colleagues in other institutions and also in our society as a whole.
Bd. 4, 2021, 244 S., 34,90 €, br., ISBN 978-3-643-51034-1

Brigitte Buchhammer (Hg.)
Philosophie in einer Welt der Ökonomisierung
Theorie und Praxis
Der vorliegende Band versammelt die Beiträge des 3. Symposiums der SWIP Austria, der das breite Spektrum der Forschungsarbeiten der Philosoph_innen widerspiegelt. Die SWIP Austria sieht eines ihrer wesentlichen Ziele darin, die philosophische Arbeit von Frauen* in allen Teilbereichen der Philosophie sichtbar zu machen.
SWIP Austria Society for Women* in Philosophy Austria: Förderung wissenschaftlich arbeitender Frauen* in der Philosophie.
Bd. 3, 2020, 224 S., 34,90 €, br., ISBN 978-3-643-50978-9

Brigitte Buchhammer (Hg.)
Lernen, Mensch zu sein
Beiträge des 2. Symposiums der SWIP Austria, Linz, Johannes-Kepler-Universität, 10. – 11. Dezember 2015
Bd. 2, 2017, 332 S., 39,90 €, br., ISBN 978-3-643-50801-0

Elisabeth Schäfer; Brigitte Buchhammer (Hg.)
Erinnerung und Gedächtnis
Kunst – Philosophie – Feminismus. Festschrift für Ingvild Birkhan zum 80. Geburtstag
Bd. Sonderband 2, 2020, 244 S., 34,90 €, br., ISBN 978-3-643-51007-5

Brigitte Buchhammer (Hg.)
Freiheit – Gerechtigkeit – Liebe. Freedom – Justice – Love
Festschrift zum 75. Geburtstag von Herta Nagl-Docekal. Celebratory Volume for Herta Nagl-Docekal's 75th Birthday
Bd. Sonderband 1, 2019, 360 S., 39,90 €, br., ISBN 978-3-643-50926-0